# ENGAG.. ..
## —— *the* ——
# CIVIL WAR

*Chris Mackowski and Brian Matthew Jordan, Series Editors*

A Public-History Initiative of Emerging Civil War
and Southern Illinois University Press

# WHERE VALOR PROUDLY SLEEPS

## A HISTORY OF FREDERICKSBURG NATIONAL CEMETERY, 1866–1933

Donald C. Pfanz

Southern Illinois University Press
*Carbondale*

Southern Illinois University Press
www.siupress.com

21  20  19  18    4  3  2  1

*Cover illustration*: (*foreground*) headstone for Sergeant Edward L. Townsend
of the Twenty-Fifth New Jersey Volunteers, one of just two stones in
Fredericksburg National Cemetery erected at private expense for a soldier
who died during the war. The other, an obelisk marking the grave of
Colonel Joseph A. Moesch of the Eighty-Third New York Volunteers,
appears in the background. *Photo by author.*

Library of Congress Cataloging-in-Publication Data
Names: Pfanz, Donald, author.
Title: Where valor proudly sleeps : a history of Fredericksburg National
    Cemetery, 1866–1933 / Donald C Pfanz.
Description: Carbondale : Southern Illinois University Press, 2018.
    | Series: Engaging the civil war | Includes bibliographical references
    and index.
Identifiers: LCCN 2017027465 | ISBN 9780809336456 (paperback)
    | ISBN 9780809336463 (ebook)
Subjects: LCSH: Fredericksburg National Cemetery (Fredericksburg,
    Va.)—History. | Fredericksburg and Spotsylvania National Military
    Park (Va.)—History. | BISAC: HISTORY / United States / Civil War
    Period (1850–1877). | HISTORY / United States / 19th Century.
    | SOCIAL SCIENCE / Death & Dying.
Classification: LCC E474.85 .P43 2018 | DDC 975.5/366—dc23 LC
    record available at https://lccn.loc.gov/2017027465

*To American soldiers who have fought and died for this country*
*and to the loved ones they left behind*

Rest on, embalmed and sainted dead!
Dear as the blood ye gave,
No impious footsteps here shall tread
The herbage of your grave;
Nor shall your story be forgot,
While Fame her record keeps,
Or Honor points the hallowed spot
Where Valor proudly sleeps.

—Theodore O'Hara,
"The Bivouac of the Dead"

# Contents

# Illustrations

# Preface

Less than a mile from downtown Fredericksburg, Virginia, Lafayette Boulevard turns sharply left before making a dangerous hairpin turn back to the right. Residents long ago nicknamed the second turn "Deadman's Curve," presumably because of motorists who have lost their lives there. It is an appropriate name for another reason, however, for on the hill overlooking the road stands the town's most recognizable feature, Fredericksburg National Cemetery, a twelve-acre parcel of land whose steep green terraces cascade like a series of waterfalls toward the town. Thousands of people drive past it every day, yet only a few ever stop to visit.

At the entrance to the cemetery stands a two-story stone lodge once occupied by cemetery superintendents and their families but now used by the National Park Service as an employee residence. As a newly christened park historian, I was privileged to live there from 1981 to 1985. At first, I found it a bit intimidating. Living alone in a drafty old house surrounded by the graves of 15,300 men—most of whom had met a violent end—is enough to put anyone on edge, and I was no exception. I felt uneasy about venturing outside at night among the graves. To overcome my fears, I started taking walks up into the cemetery at sunset. I would start when it was still light and not return until darkness had fully set in.

After a couple of weeks, I no longer felt anxious about living in the cemetery; instead, I came to feel at ease there. Although more than thirty years have passed, I still feel that way. My apprehensions have long since given way to curiosity. Who are the individuals buried there? Why do they have different types of headstones? Who lived in the cemetery lodge before me? When were the monuments erected? Who built the terraces and why? Such questions set me on a quest to learn more about the cemetery and the people interred there. This book is the result of that quest.

# Acknowledgments

The help and expertise of several individuals contributed to this book. Ginny Cook of Overland Park, Kansas, spent hundreds, perhaps thousands, of hours identifying soldiers buried at Fredericksburg National Cemetery and helped me to conduct a statistical survey of the cemetery headstones. Her work on the cemetery truly was a labor of love. The National Park Service and future generations of genealogists stand greatly in her debt.

Historian Kati Singel put the Fredericksburg National Cemetery roster in its final form, painstakingly reviewing each entry for accuracy and making any necessary corrections. Joe Rokus of Fredericksburg uncovered information on Edith Rose Tench, Annie Florence Lockhart, Jerome Peirce, and Jack Butler—four soldiers buried in the cemetery. The thoroughness of Joe's genealogical research evokes my highest admiration.

During his life, Jerry Brent collected hundreds of images and other documents pertaining to Fredericksburg's history, which he has generously and unstintingly shared with me and others. Several of the earliest and most important images of Fredericksburg National Cemetery that appear in this book belonged to Jerry, and I am indebted to him and his wife, Lou, for their use. I also owe a great deal of gratitude to others who kindly permitted me to use photographs under their care, including Robert K. Krick, Mrs. Robert Hileman, Brad Butler, Roy S. Stevens, Bill Sielski, John Kuhl, Patricia M. Mason, Sarah L. Thayer, Joseph G. Bilby, George Combs of the Alexandria Library, and Sean Maroney and Emily Schricker of Historic Fredericksburg Foundation, Inc.

Many others have helped me in the course of this project. Elizabeth Dinger-Glisan of Petersburg National Battlefield sent me a copy of the quartermaster general's annual report for 1865 and other documents; Sara Amy Leach of the National Cemetery Administration pointed me to the mother lode of cemetery documents at the National Archives and sent me an early photograph of the lodge; Dr. Luther Hanson and curator Jimmy Blankenship of Fort Lee, Virginia, provided me with copies of Edward Steere's articles; Trevor Plante scanned a photograph for me, thus saving me a trip to the National Archives; Jack Bales and Carolyn Parsons assisted me in tracking down articles at the University of Mary Washington's Simpson Library; Jake Wynn of the National Museum of Civil War Medicine uncovered the fascinating story of the Workman brothers that appears in chapter 11; and Historic Fredericksburg Foundation, Inc., kindly granted me permission to publish several images in its collection.

Several colleagues at Fredericksburg and Spotsylvania National Military Park also assisted me. John Hennessy permitted me to make several trips to the National Archives to examine national cemetery documents, while Daniel Davis tracked down a photograph there, thus saving me another trip to that invaluable but bewildering place. Janice Frye and Luisa Dispenzirie answered several inquiries I had about cemetery registers and other artifacts in the park's curatorial collection, Eric Mink assisted me in finding and identifying old cemetery photographs, Rebecca Capobianco identified A. J. Grant as a probable Confederate soldier, Craig Johnson helped me look up land records, and Noel Harrison used his expert knowledge of the Fredericksburg area to help me in more ways than I can recall. Finally, I am grateful for Dr. Chris Mackowski, Kris White, and the staff of Southern Illinois University Press for piloting this book through the publication process. I am particularly indebted to copy editor Julie Bush, whose meticulous review of the manuscript elicits my highest gratitude and praise.

My thanks go to you all.

ENGAGING
—*the*—
CIVIL WAR

For additional content that will let you engage this material further, look for unique QR codes at the end of each chapter. Scanning them will take you to exclusive online material, additional photos and images, links to online resources, and related blog posts at www.emergingcivilwar.com.

A QR scanner app is readily available for download through the app store on your smartphone.

# Where Valor Proudly Sleeps

Dead Confederate soldier on Spotsylvania Court House Battlefield. *Library of Congress.*

# ✻ Introduction:
## The National Cemetery System

The Civil War was the bloodiest conflict in American history, resulting in the deaths of an estimated 750,000 Americans.[1] In response to this tremendous loss of life, the U.S. government between 1862 and 1870 created a system of national cemeteries in which to bury the Northern dead. Fredericksburg National Cemetery ranks among the largest of those cemeteries.

The War Department took the first step toward burying the Union dead on September 11, 1861, when, in General Orders No. 75, it directed the Quartermaster Department to provide general and post hospitals and to use ledger books and forms to record burials. Special Orders No. 75, of the same date, assigned commanders of corps and departments responsibility for burying officers and soldiers who died within their jurisdictions. The orders charged them with carrying out the regulations provided by the quartermaster general for this purpose.[2] The War Department clarified its intent in General Orders No. 33, issued on April 3, 1862. Those orders required commanding generals to set aside ground near every battlefield for the interment of Union dead. Each grave was to have a headboard containing the plot number and the soldier's name, if known. The orders instructed generals to keep a register for each cemetery, listing the names of the soldiers buried there and the plots in which they were interred.[3]

Congress involved itself in the matter on July 17, 1862, with passage of Public Law 165, "An Act to Define the Pay and Emoluments of Certain Officers of the Army, and for Other Purposes." Prior to that time, the War Department had authorized commanding officers to seize land for burial grounds. The act gave the president authority to purchase parcels of land for national cemeteries and to erect enclosures around them. In doing so, it made clear its intention that every soldier who died in defense of the Union should receive a decent plot in a government-administered cemetery.[4]

The Quartermaster Department assumed responsibility for burying the dead, but it could do little as long as the fighting was in progress. In a survey ordered by Quartermaster General Montgomery C. Meigs on July 3, 1865, department officials reported that just 98,827 Union soldiers had been properly buried—fewer than 30 percent of the estimated 341,670 deaths sustained by the North during the war. Most of those had died at general hospitals in the North or on Northern battlefields. A far greater number of deceased soldiers—those who had died fighting in the South—either occupied temporary graves or had not been buried at all.[5] Obviously, the Quartermaster Department had a lot of work ahead of it.

To get some idea as to the magnitude of the task confronting him, Meigs, on October 30, 1865, issued General Orders No. 65, directing Quartermaster Department officers to report on "the location and condition of Cemeteries known to them, with recommendations of the means necessary to provide for the preservation of the remains interred therein from desecration." Specifically, the officers were to give the precise location of the cemeteries; state whether they had enclosures and headboards and whether remains in them could be identified; determine the existence and condition of any burial records associated with the cemeteries; and provide recommendations as to whether the government should maintain the cemeteries or transfer the remains to some other location.[6]

Meigs's investigation confirmed an obvious fact: the remains of approximately one-quarter of a million Union soldiers remained scattered throughout the South awaiting proper burial. A grieving nation demanded that the government take action. Congress responded on April 13, 1866, issuing a joint resolution that directed Secretary of War Edwin M. Stanton to protect the graves of Union dead from desecration, to establish cemeteries for permanent burial of the dead, and to construct enclosures around the cemeteries.[7] However, the resolution left several questions unanswered. How was cemetery land to be purchased? How were graves to be marked? Who would take care of the cemeteries once they were established? And, most important, who would provide the money necessary to create and maintain the cemeteries?

The National Cemetery Act, passed on February 22, 1867, addressed many of those questions. The bill authorized the secretary of war to acquire land for national cemeteries, enclose those areas with stone or iron fences, and construct caretaker lodges. In addition, it charged the secretary with maintaining burial registers for each cemetery and marking each grave with a headstone containing the number of the grave and the name, rank, company, regiment, and date of death of the soldier buried there. Superintendents, selected from enlisted men disabled during the Civil War, would administer the cemeteries and provide information to visitors, while officers in the Quartermaster

Corps would inspect the cemeteries annually, reporting to Congress on their condition and the amount of money necessary to maintain them. Congress appropriated $750,000 to begin the work.[8]

The Quartermaster Department implemented the provisions of the act quickly and efficiently. By 1870, it had collected the remains of 315,555 Union soldiers, interring them in seventy-three national cemeteries scattered throughout the country, prompting Brevet Brigadier General Judson D. Bingham to announce that "the work of collecting and reinterring the remains of the deceased Union soldiers is virtually completed." Identifying the remains proved more difficult than burying them, however. Even as late as 1874, the Quartermaster Department was able to ascertain the names of fewer than 50 percent of those it had interred.[9]

The National Cemetery System was hardly in place before Union veterans began clamoring for Congress to expand it. The Grand Army of the Republic wanted the government to allow surviving veterans the privilege of being buried in national cemeteries beside their fallen comrades, a proposal that would increase the annual cemetery budget considerably. Caught between the veterans and fiscal reality, Congress compromised, agreeing on June 1, 1872, to extend the burial privileges, but only to those veterans who died in poverty. Its decision pleased no one. Enraged veterans denounced the act as an effort to transform the cemeteries into potter's fields. They demanded that politicians open the national cemeteries to all veterans, regardless of their financial status. Congress relented. On March 3, 1873, it amended the legislation, permitting any honorably discharged veteran to be buried in a national cemetery. In subsequent years, it broadened the scope of the National Cemetery System still further to include the wives, unmarried daughters, and minor children of Civil War veterans. In time, veterans of later wars and their dependents likewise became eligible for burial.[10]

More burials meant more national cemeteries. By 1883, the Quartermaster Department had added six new sites to the system, increasing the total number of national cemeteries to seventy-nine. Fredericksburg, with 15,257 interments, was the fourth largest cemetery after Vicksburg, Mississippi (16,600); Nashville, Tennessee (16,526); and Arlington, Virginia (16,264). With 12,770 unknown interments, Fredericksburg had the largest number of unidentified dead of any national cemetery in the country, followed closely by Vicksburg (12,704) and Salisbury, North Carolina (12,032).[11]

The War Department (later the Department of the Army) maintained exclusive control over the country's national cemeteries and its smaller post cemeteries for sixty years. However, in 1933, President Franklin D. Roosevelt transferred eleven cemeteries to the National Park Service to be components of national military parks. Since then, one cemetery has reverted to the army's administration and four others have been added to the National Park Service, bringing the total number of national cemeteries administered by that agency to fourteen.

The Department of the Army continued to administer the remaining cemeteries until 1973. In that year, Congress passed the National Cemeteries Act (Public Law 93-43), transferring eighty-two cemeteries from the Department of the Army to the Veterans Administration. That left the army in control of just Arlington National Cemetery in Virginia, the U.S. Soldiers' and Airmen's Home (formerly the Old Soldiers' Home) Cemetery in Washington, D.C., and twenty-eight post cemeteries. The Department of Memorial Affairs administered the national cemeteries assigned to the Veterans Administration. In 1989, President George H. W. Bush elevated the secretary of the Veterans Administration to a cabinet-level post and renamed the agency the Department of Veterans Affairs. At the same time, the Department of Memorial Affairs became the National Cemetery System. Ten years later, the National Cemetery System changed names yet again, becoming the National Cemetery Administration. Currently, this organization manages 135 national cemeteries encompassing more than twenty thousand acres, plus affiliated government and soldiers' lots.[12]

With the expansion of the National Cemetery program have come advances in the identification of soldier remains. The U.S. Army began issuing dog tags to service members on the eve of World War I and today backs them up with dental records, fingerprints, and DNA.[13] Consequently, the concept of the "unknown soldier" has become virtually obsolete. But that was not always so. Little more than a century and half ago, American soldiers went into battle without any official means of identification whatsoever. To Union soldiers fighting in the South, death meant not only burial in a land far from home but also, in all probability, an anonymous grave. Nowhere was this more true than on the battlefields near Fredericksburg.

# 1. ✦ Wartime Burials

**B**uried within the walls of Fredericksburg National Cemetery are the remains of Union soldiers who died in six different Civil War battles: Fredericksburg, Chancellorsville, Mine Run, Wilderness, Spotsylvania Court House, and North Anna. Lying beside them are hundreds of others who perished while encamped in Stafford County, Virginia, in the winter of 1862–63. The treatment accorded the dead depended in large measure on where the soldier died and the military situation at that time. If a soldier died in camp or if he died within his own lines at a time when the army was not in motion, his comrades most likely would have given him a decent burial and placed a crude headboard over his grave. On the other hand, if he died between the lines or while the army was on the march, he might not be buried at all. In short, efforts to bury the dead were haphazard and wholly dependent on circumstance.

## Fredericksburg

The Battle of Fredericksburg was the exclamation point in a year crowned by Confederate success in Virginia. After a series of victories that started in the Shenandoah Valley and concluded on the rolling fields of Manassas, General Robert E. Lee led the Army of Northern Virginia across the Potomac River into Maryland only to be stopped by Major General George B. McClellan at Antietam Creek. The Confederate commander fell back into Virginia cautiously pursued by McClellan, whose obvious reluctance to engage Lee in battle led to his replacement on November 9, 1862, by Major General Ambrose E. Burnside.

Burnside displayed the energy McClellan had lacked. Upon taking command, he marched the Union Army of the Potomac to Fredericksburg, crossed the Rappahannock River, and attacked Lee's army on the heights beyond. The result was one of the most lopsided Confederate victories of the war. Lee's men, fighting a defensive battle on advantageous ground, repulsed Union attacks with slaughter both at Prospect Hill, south of Fredericksburg, and at Marye's

5

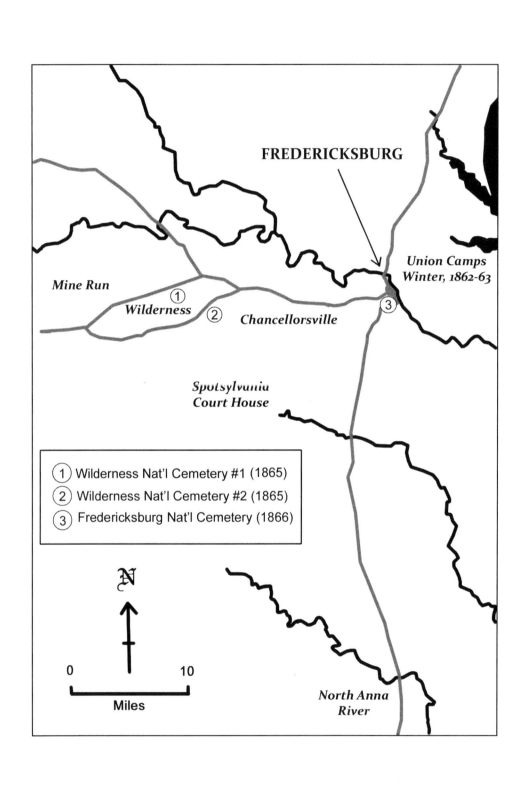

FREDERICKSBURG

Union Camps
Winter, 1862-63

Mine Run

① Wilderness

② Chancellorsville

③

Spotsylvania
Court House

① Wilderness Nat'l Cemetery #1 (1865)
② Wilderness Nat'l Cemetery #2 (1865)
③ Fredericksburg Nat'l Cemetery (1866)

N

0      10
Miles

North Anna
River

Heights, directly west of town. The battle resulted in more than 12,600 Union casualties, nearly 1,300 of whom died on or near the field of battle.[1]

Two days after the December 13, 1862, engagement, Major General William B. Franklin requested a truce for the purpose of caring for the wounded and burying the dead Union soldiers of his Left Grand Division.[2] His opponent, Confederate lieutenant general Thomas J. "Stonewall" Jackson, granted his request. Burial details hastily interred the dead in a series of long, shallow trenches located between the lines. "The Yankees merely scooped a shallow hole in the sandy bottom," recalled a North Carolina officer, "laid their dead in it, and threw earth on them, and sometimes did not more than cover them with earth as they lay on the ground."[3] Adjutant Evan M. Woodward of the Second Pennsylvania Reserves remembered that the troops "worked all night, the details from each army meeting half way between the pickets." He noted disapprovingly that "the Rebs stripped our men naked."[4]

Colonel Philippe Regis de Trobriand was in charge of the Union troops closest to the enemy. That evening his men disposed of ninety-two bodies, burying them in three rows just inside Union lines. "They were black, hideous, showing the most horrible wounds," he remembered. Night fell before Trobriand's men could finish the job. "At nine o'clock in the evening, we left without any noise, leaving the poor dead without burial," he wrote. "The rebels will bury them when they have time."[5] They did, although perhaps not in the manner he imagined. Pressed for time, the Confederates simply piled the corpses in a ditch beside the railroad and kicked dirt in on top of them.[6]

The December 15 truce pertained only to the troops in Franklin's command. Union soldiers who had died in front of Marye's Heights remained unburied until December 16, when the Army of the Potomac retreated to safety in Stafford County. Lee then sent a dispatch to Burnside requesting that he send troops back across the river to bury the Union dead. Burnside agreed, assigning the job to Major General Edwin V. Sumner, commander of the army's Right Grand Division. Sumner, in turn, detailed one field officer, one subaltern, and fifty enlisted men each from the Second and Ninth Corps to perform the grisly task. The detail crossed the Rappahannock on December 17. Although the party labored all day, it did not finish, and Sumner had to send a second party across the river the following day to complete the job. To make sure it did, he doubled the number of men in the detail to two hundred.[7]

Colonel John R. Brooke of the Fifty-Third Pennsylvania led the burial details. The detachments gathered at the Lacy house and then proceeded across the Rappahannock River under a flag of truce. Once across, a provost guard comprising men from the Thirteenth Mississippi escorted the unarmed Federals through the town to the plain leading to Marye's Heights. There a gruesome sight met their eyes. "As we approached the battlefield," wrote Private Nathaniel C. Deane of the Twenty-First Massachusetts, "the sight reminded me of a flock of sheep reposing in the field. But as we approached nearer, who can describe my feelings when I found them to be the dead bodies of our brave men, which had been stripped of their clothing. They were literally pieces of men, for those destructive shells had done their perfect work. It was the worst sight I ever beheld, and may I be spared another such a scene."[8]

While some soldiers went to work excavating a burial trench, the rest divided into groups and began gathering corpses. A soldier from the Fifteenth Connecticut noted with disgust that the unburied bodies "were frozen & most of them had turned black. Being naked, they exposed their frightful bloody wounds which had ended their lives. Oh it was awful!" Steeling themselves to their task, the Union soldiers placed the decomposing corpses on discarded boards and carried them to the ditch for burial. "We laid the poor fellows side by side in the trench & covered them with earth where they will remain

Burial of Union dead in front of Marye's Heights. Copy at *Fredericksburg and Spotsylvania County National Military Park.*

till the great Judgement Day," the Connecticut man recalled with a shudder. "O! What a dreadful war this is!"[9]

While the Northern soldiers went about this unpleasant duty, their adversaries taunted them by holding up clothing they had stripped from the dead bodies. "They told us they would fight us to the last man as long as we come on their soil," recalled one Union soldier.[10] In contrast to such brutish behavior was the quiet faithfulness of a Newfoundland dog observed by Private Charles C. Cummings of the Seventeenth Mississippi. The pet of a Union officer who had died in the battle, the dog held vigil beside his dead master until the burial party placed the officer in the ground. "With mournful mien and downcast countenance," wrote Cummings, the dog "followed the corpse to the trench, and when he saw the hostile dirt cover his master's remains in a hostile land he exhibited a human sympathy in his mourning, more so, than any there in human shape."[11]

Union soldiers interred 620 bodies on December 17 and 293 more the following day, burying them in mass graves with no attempt at identification. The battle was then four days old, and the corpses had started to decompose. It was important to get them in the ground as quickly as possible. In addition to those they buried, Brooke's men carried the remains of five Union officers back across the river to be sent north.[12]

To bury the corpses, Union troops dug trenches, placed the bodies side by side in them, and covered them with dirt. "The night before," wrote a Confederate soldier, "the thermometer must have fallen to zero, and the bodies of the slain had frozen to the ground. The ground was frozen nearly a foot deep, and it was necessary to use pick-axes. Trenches were dug on the battle-field and the dead collected and laid in line for burial," he observed. "It was a sad sight to see these brave soldiers thrown into the trenches, without even a blanket or a word of prayer, and the heavy clods thrown upon them."[13]

Union soldiers excavated two large trenches and several smaller ones.[14] The two large trenches lay parallel to one another and ran south from Hanover Street toward Allen Stratton's house. The western ditch was approximately 140 yards east of the Sunken Road and ended just west of the house. Six feet wide and sixty yards long, it held 130 bodies, some of which were layered up to three deep. The eastern trench accommodated 609 corpses. Originally excavated by Union troops on December 13 for protection against Confederate bullets, the ditch was six feet wide and one hundred yards long. One resident recalled that the burial party "piled and packed" the bodies into it "like dead mackerel in a barrel." In addition to the human occupants, at least one horse was buried there.[15]

Brooke's men did their job quickly but not well. Fredericksburg resident Edward L. Heinichen reported that burial of the bodies was "done so superficially, that parts of them after a short time showed above ground, & dogs brought home many a limb. Some corpses were entirely overlooked, & I recollect to have seen two of them untouched as late as the following April."[16] Many bodies were not buried at all. In order to save time, Union soldiers simply tossed corpses into the pit of Howison H. Wallace's icehouse at the edge of town.

Confederate major Heros von Borcke was "painfully shocked" at the lack of respect shown the dead in the icehouse. "The bodies of these poor fellows, stripped nearly naked, were gathered in huge mounds around the pit, and tumbled neck and heels into it," he recalled, "the dull 'thud' of corpse falling on corpse coming up from the depths of the hole until the solid mass of human flesh reached near the surface, when a covering of logs, chalk, and mud closed the mouth of this vast and awful tomb." Secondhand accounts place

Collapsed Wallace icehouse, the temporary tomb of dozens, possibly hundreds, of Union dead. *National Archives, Washington, D.C.*

the number of soldiers buried in the icehouse at anywhere from four hundred to eight hundred; however, this is probably an exaggeration. After the war, burial crews removed just fifty-two skeletons from the structure. Strangely, Colonel Brooke, who supervised the burial process, wrote nothing about the icehouse in his report. Given the lack of respect shown to those buried there, though, perhaps the omission is not so strange after all.[17]

In addition to the mass graves, the Union army excavated hundreds of individual graves. Edward Stephens, whose house adjoined the Sunken Road, found thirteen soldiers buried on his property, while his neighbor George Rowe counted no fewer than fifty-five burials on his lot. In town, nearly every yard became a cemetery. Brevet Major Hiram F. Gerrish examined Fredericksburg for Union gravesites in late 1865. He wrote that every lot in town had between one and seven graves on it, most of them lacking any identification.[18]

## Winter, 1862–63

Following the Battle of Fredericksburg, Union troops went into camp in Stafford County, north of the Rappahannock. Accidents, exposure, and disease claimed thousands of lives that winter. Soldiers buried their deceased comrades in informal cemeteries that sprang up near hospitals and camps. Unlike those who perished in combat, soldiers who died during the winter months usually received funeral services, headboards for their graves, and coffins. The chaplain of the Sixteenth New York described a funeral that took place in his camp a few days before the Battle of Fredericksburg.

> Lt. Barney came for me as soon as the coffin was done, part of which was made out of my saddle box, & we walked down & crossed the ravine & rode & entered the woods beyond & just on a knoll they had dug the graves[.] [T]hey lowered the coffin & then I read a passage from 1 Cor. 15:16–22 verse & some of the latter verses[.] . . . After that, I made a prayer. The colonel was there but we do not have a salute fired. They have dispensed with that, in these times. We placed a little board over the head with the name &c. so that the body can be found if the friends wish to remove it.[19]

If the deceased soldier was an officer or particularly well liked by his comrades, the entire regiment might turn out for his funeral. Such was the case of a soldier in the 137th New York who died in June 1863, just before the Army of the Potomac left Stafford County for Gettysburg. A semi-literate comrade described the ceremony:

> There was a man died out of Co H. He was an old man between fifty and sixty. He was a good old soldier but he couldent stand it here. There was three ladies to the funerl. It was the magers wife and two of the capt wives. I wish you could ben here. It was a sollom funerl. The drum corps marched ahead and played the death march and the chaplain and the capt of the Co next and the corpse next with the flag over it and then twelve men with their muskets and then the rest of the regt. We marched in two ranks. When we got to the grave they let the corpse down. Drum corps plaied while it was going down and then they sung and the chaplain prayed and then he spoke a fiew minuets. I never heard a man speak better. He give the old soldier a recamend [*sic*: recommendation].[20]

Ira M. Whittaker (grave #2086) stood at the other end of the age spectrum. A private in the Thirteenth New Hampshire, Whittaker was just sixteen years old when he died of measles at his Stafford County camp. Two soldiers fashioned a coffin for the boy made from three cracker boxes placed end to end; they nailed the boxes together using saplings instead of boards. A short, businesslike funeral followed. "A man's own company forms the usual procession on such occasions," a comrade wrote, "any friends joining who may choose to do so. A bottle well corked and sealed, and containing the man's name, regiment, home address, etc., is usually laid in the grave with his body. The burial is not prolonged: the slow march, the arms reversed, the muffled drum, the piercing fife, the dirge—often the Portug[u]ese Hymn, but more often the Dead March in Saul—the platoon fire over the grave, the quickstep march back to camp, two men left to close the grave, and all is done."[21] Because Whittaker's comrades took the trouble to place his name and regiment in a bottle, burial crews were later able to identify his body. Not all were so fortunate. Nearly half the graves unearthed in Stafford County after the war had no identification.[22]

Lieutenant Samuel S. Partridge, quartermaster of the Thirteenth New York, reflected on the hollow pageantry that attended that winter's funerals. Partridge happened to be writing a letter when a funeral procession passed his tent. He stopped his scribbling to describe the event.

Hark! I hear muffled drums and fifes wailing most dolorously that mournful, mournful, tremulous, dead march. A fellow died last night in camp, *only a private so nobody cares,* but the proper form of burial must be gone through with, according to regulations with as much punctilio, though less show and grandeur[,] as though it had been a general. . . .

Four drums, four fifes—Four men bearing a hospital stretcher and a corpse wrapped in a grey blanket. Eight soldiers with arms reversed, commanded by a Corporal and then a Lieutenant and a Chaplain in a long rubber coat. In a few minutes that grey blanket and its enfolded corpse will be resting in a muddy hole. The Corporal will march the escort of eight rank and file back at a shoulder arms and quick time, the muffles taken off the drum snares, and the drums beating furiously to Dick Sliters clog dance, or the devils wedding shrieked from the same fifes that just now uttered such dolorous notes, and tomorrow everybody will have forgotten the man that was buried. But perhaps in some far off humble household anxious days and sleepless nights will be spent watching for the wanderer who will never return, and [to] whom we, his fellow soldiers, his comrades, hard hearted wretches, calloused by many a similar scene, will never give a second thought. How little, very little, we think of the grief produced by wars calamities.

For every man who falls in battle, some one mourns. For every man who lies in hospital wards and of whom no note is taken, some one mourns. For the humblest soldier shot on picket, and of whose humble exit from the stage of life little is thought, some one mourns.[23]

In many cases, soldiers were buried in the nearest plot of ground without any regard to order. In some regiments, however, officers set aside land as a cemetery and buried their dead in orderly rows. The 107th New York's cemetery was particularly tidy. The regiment's commander, Colonel Alexander S. Diven, ordered the graveyard to be built on a pretty knoll that extended out into Aquia Creek. His men arranged the graves in rows divided by gravel walkways lined with holly. Each of the thirty-two graves received a headstone engraved with the deceased's name and a proper epitaph. Enclosing the grounds was a sturdy, if rustic, fence made of cedar and locust. At the entrance Diven erected a large block of stone identifying the cemetery as belonging to the 107th New York and beseeching those who visited the grounds not to disturb the graves. Today that stone is on display at Fredericksburg and Spotsylvania County National Military Park.[24]

Colonel Diven's cemetery reflected the best burial that a soldier could expect. More common were those performed by soldiers in the Twenty-Sixth New York. "We have had a death every day in our Regt lately," wrote Private William Paynton in February 1863 from his camp near White Oak Church. "Even now while I am writing, they are firing a volley over the new made grave of one of company Fs men. he died this morning with the scurvey, bro[u]ght on by so much salt food. a soldier's funeral is not as solemn as a citizens," he explained, "for here we dig a square hole, and wrap a mans blanket around him, and pitch him in, and cover him up with dirt. coffins is out of the question here. we cant carry them with us, nor we cant get the boards to make them. so we have to do without out them. it looks hard," he admitted, "but it cant be helped."[25] Sadly, far more soldiers received the hasty, unsympathetic burial Payton described than the dignified treatment accorded to the men of the 107th New York.

## Chancellorsville

In May 1863, the Army of the Potomac, now led by Major General Joseph Hooker, sallied across the Rappahannock River in another attempt to defeat Robert E. Lee. Leaving 27,000 men under Major General John Sedgwick opposite Fredericksburg to engage the Confederate leader's attention, Hooker crossed the Rappahannock upriver and consolidated the mass of his army at Chancellorsville, a large country inn ten miles west of town. Lee responded by dividing his army. While Major General Jubal Early continued to hold the Fredericksburg line in defiance of Sedgwick, Lee led the rest of his army west to confront Hooker at Chancellorsville. In five days of fighting, he again drove the Army of the Potomac back across the Rappahannock River. Hooker reported losing 12,145 men in the battle, 1,082 of whom were killed in action. In addition, the army's Sixth Corps lost 4,700 men at Fredericksburg and Salem Church, 493 of whom died during or immediately following the battle.[26]

In contrast to Burnside at Fredericksburg, Hooker did not send troops back across the Rappahannock River to inter the dead. Instead, he left the job to the Confederates, who disposed of the bodies by throwing them into trenches or burying them in shallow, unmarked graves. Many received no burial at all. When Union soldiers returned to Chancellorsville in May 1864 for the Overland Campaign, they found the bleached bones of their former comrades scattered throughout the woods. "We spent the night near these scenes," wrote Captain Charles H. Weygant of the 124th New York, and in many a letter written that afternoon there was inclosed a tiny wild flower, which the writer believed had been nourished by the soil enriched by his own blood, or by that of some friend or comrade who had there fought his last fight. It was a very easy matter to discover just where pools of blood had been, for particular spots were marked by the greenest tufts to be found upon the field. During the evening Colonel Cummins sent out a burial party to gather up the human bones which lay strewn over that portion of the field on which the majority of the brave boys of our regiment had fallen, and to hide them in a deep grave away from the gaze of curious human eyes.[27]

When members of the Twelfth Corps marched back through Chancellors-ville in 1865 on their way to the Grand Review, they too buried and marked the skeletons of former comrades who had died in the battle.[28] Given the hasty and haphazard nature of the burials at Chancellorsville, it is not surprising that few soldiers could be identified. In a postwar report to the quartermaster general, Major Gerrish indicated that just 82 of 664 graves—12.3 percent—had identification.[29]

# Mine Run

Lee used his victory at Chancellorsville as a springboard to invade the North. In June 1863 he dispersed a Union garrison at Winchester, Virginia, and for the second time in a year crossed the Potomac River into Maryland. Again he suffered defeat, this time at Gettysburg, just north of the Pennsylvania line. In three days of horrific combat, the Army of Northern Virginia incurred 28,000 casualties. Battered but unbowed, the Confederate army limped back to Virginia to recuperate. The Union army pursued it there and, after four months of skirmishing and maneuvers, brought Lee to battle on the western edge of the Wilderness, a sparsely populated, brush-choked area twenty miles west of Fredericksburg. After a small but inconclusive fight at a clearing known as Payne's farm, Lee took up a defensive position west of Mine Run, a tributary of the Rapidan River, and invited the Union commander, Major General George G. Meade, to attack. The Confederate position was even stronger than the one it had held at Fredericksburg, however, and Meade wisely chose to withdraw without renewing the fight. According to official returns, the weeklong campaign cost the Union army 1,653 casualties, of whom 173 died on or near the battlefield.[30]

Because the number of Union deaths at Mine Run was relatively small, burial accounts are hard to find. Today just eight soldiers positively identified as dying at Mine Run are buried in Fredericksburg National Cemetery.[31] However, due to the large percentage of unknown dead, as many as fifty soldiers from that battle may be buried there. The rest either were never found or were carried by comrades back across the Rapidan River.

## The Wilderness, Spotsylvania Court House, and North Anna

With another spring came another campaign and—for the North—another commander. In March 1864, President Abraham Lincoln appointed Ulysses S. Grant general-in-chief over all U.S. armies. Grant chose to make his headquarters with Meade's Army of the Potomac, thus, in effect, making it his own. His strategy, as he explained it, was simple: "to hammer continuously against the armed force of the enemy and his resources, until by mere attrition, if in no other way, there should be nothing left to him but . . . submission."[32]

The Union army left its camps in Culpeper County, Virginia, and crossed the Rapidan River, inaugurating six weeks of battles collectively known as the Overland Campaign. The two sides first clashed on May 5–6 in the Wilderness, the same impenetrable forest where they had earlier fought the Battles of Chancellorsville and Mine Run. On the opening day of the conflict, Grant took the initiative, attempting to overwhelm Lee by sheer force of numbers. The Confederate commander endured his opponent's blows, however, and struck back hard, turning both of Grant's flanks on the second day. Despite a staggering thirty thousand combined casualties, neither side could claim victory.

If anything, conditions for burying the dead were worse in the Wilderness than they had been one year earlier at Chancellorsville. The proximity of the two armies added to the incessant nature of the fighting left soldiers with little time or energy to inter fallen comrades. Moreover, brush fires consumed large tracts of forest, making the task of identifying and burying the dead all but impossible. When, after three days, the armies departed the Wilderness and moved to Spotsylvania Court House, they left thousands of unburied soldiers in their wake.

At Spotsylvania Court House the armies met again, this time in a savage struggle lasting two weeks. The fighting reached its peak on May 12 at a turn in the Confederate lines thereafter known as the "Bloody Angle." When the

Confederates fell back, Union forces briefly occupied the contested ground, now thickly carpeted with blue and gray corpses. To make the position tolerable, Northern soldiers threw the bodies of the slain into trenches formerly occupied by their foes and kicked dirt from the adjacent parapet down on them, just as the Confederates had done to the Union dead at Fredericksburg. Thus, remarked one soldier, "the unfortunate victims [had] unwittingly dug their own graves."[33]

Not all graves were so large and impersonal. At the conclusion of the Bloody Angle combat, William McVey took it upon himself to bury several of his friends in the 126th Ohio. "A. M. Pollock was laid in first," he explained to the father of one of the dead, "and your son, (T. Hervey) was laid on his (Pollock's) right, and Arnold on the right of your son . . . and on the right of Arnold was two of company C, Wharten and Brushear." A man named Thompson marked their graves with headboards, inscribing the names with paint made from a concoction of ink and gunpowder. McVey wrote two years after the event, by which time he could no longer recall how many headboards Thompson had erected. "I cant say wheather he put a board up to the head of each one or just to the heads of those that belonged to Company H, and one to the heads of those that belonged to company C, and then he hewed the side off a stump that stood near the grave, and wrote their names on it." Thompson must have written Hervey's, Pollock's, and Arnold's names on a single headboard, for they were later buried together in grave #3039 at Fredericksburg National Cemetery. Wharten and Brushear occupy unknown graves there. Like so many others, their headboards probably vanished before burial parties transferred their remains to Fredericksburg National Cemetery.[34]

The final clash at Spotsylvania occurred on May 19 on the Harris and Alsop farms adjoining the Fredericksburg Road. Union troops prevailed in the fight but at the loss of fifteen hundred men killed and wounded. Burials took place the following day. "Trenches were dug in the light soil some six feet wide and two or three feet deep, and the dead were laid side by side," recalled Captain Augustus C. Brown of the Fourth New York Heavy Artillery. "Care was taken to cover the faces of the dead with the capes of their overcoats or with blankets, and where the name, company, regiment, division or corps could be ascertained, the information was written in pencil on a board or smoothly whittled piece of wood, which was driven into the earth at the man's head."[35] Perhaps because it was their first battle, soldiers of the First Massachusetts Heavy Artillery felt obliged to say a few words over their fallen comrades before filling in the trench.

As the soldiers silently removed their caps, their chaplain stepped forward and said a short prayer. The brevity of his address and its manner of delivery, however, made it clear to Corporal Lewis Holt that the chaplain considered the exercise "a disagreeable duty" to be "got[t]en through with as quickly and easily as possible." When he finished his summary prayer, the men stepped forward to cover the dead. The dirt was "not thrown, but gently pushed in as though taking care not to hurt their poor dead comrades," remembered Holt. The ceremony concluded, the men wrote the names of their fallen comrades and the statement "Killed at Spotsilvania [*sic*] May 19th 1864" on strips of wood torn from boxes of hardtack and placed them at the appropriate spots along the burial trench. One day later, the regiment was miles away, following the dusty roads that led to the North Anna River.[36]

When the armies left Spotsylvania Court House, many of the dead remained unburied. A Confederate cavalryman wrote that "the dead Yankees are heaped up in piles half as high as a man, in front of our Breastworks, and all around on the Battlefield the dead yanks are lying just as thick as they can be, and none of them burried," adding, "they will all rotten on top of the ground." Another Confederate, an infantryman in Brigadier General Stephen D. Ramseur's brigade, was haunted by the ghastly upturned faces of the decomposing dead who lay between the lines. "Both parties seemed to be exhausted," he thought, "so much so as to prevent them from interring the fallen braves." A month after the battle, the First Maine Cavalry passed through Spotsylvania Court House and found "Federal and Confederate dead . . . lying around in all directions." The regiment halted briefly to bury the dead, but it could not have interred many for by nightfall it was at Guinea Station, fifteen miles away.[37]

Major David E. Cronin of the First New York Mounted Rifles was stationed near Spotsylvania Court House after the war and visited the Bloody Angle one year to the day after the battle, a month before government burial parties arrived. "It was a field impossible to describe adequately," he remembered,

> having been precipitately abandoned, by both combatants, after Lee's desperate but vain attempt to prevent the extension of Grant's left. It presented an awful picture of the magnitude and ferocity of the war. In some places the remains of the dead of both armies lay in mingled heaps, partly covered with mounds of brushwood, placed there by a few citizens remaining in the neighborhood after the battle, to prevent the ravages of wild hogs. In many other places the rain had washed

bare the shallow burial-trenches, disclosing hundreds of uniformed skeletons; but many bodies lay unsheltered, just as they had fallen.

One of the burial trenches along Major General Edward Johnson's front extended nearly an eighth of a mile and had been filled with corpses five and six deep. "The upper tier was exposed," wrote Cronin, "and skulls, skeletons, arms and legs were visible for hundreds of yards, or as far as a view could be obtained—to a distant wood." Many of the bodies on Johnson's front had not been buried at all and still lay where they fell. "Some had been shot as they raised their heads above our slight intrenchments; others as they mounted them," observed Cronin. "Many bodies lay between the lines which at one end were not twenty yards apart, and still others had lived to reach the enemy's parapet and fell over into his lines." Walking into the nearby woods, Cronin came upon a group of five Union soldiers exhibiting charred flesh—victims of a spot fire. He turned away from the sight in horror and disgust. "No enlightened man could dwell upon such a scene without deploring again and again, the backwardness of a civilization which renders possible the agony and horror of such a combat," he declared, even if they "died in the cause of Universal Progress."[38]

In his 1865 survey, Major Gerrish was able to identify 511 of 2,205 Union soldiers buried at Spotsylvania Court House—nearly twice the percentage of any other area battlefield. The higher rate—23.2 percent—may have had something to do with the Army of the Potomac's lengthy occupation of the ground.[39] Gerrish's burial statistics for Spotsylvania Court House did not include many men who had died as a result of the May 19, 1864, fighting at the Harris farm. After that engagement, ambulances carried 500 wounded Union soldiers back to hospitals in Fredericksburg. The ambulance train halted for the night just outside of town, at the foot of Marye's Heights. By the time it continued its tortuous journey the next day, many of the wounded had ceased to breathe. Soldiers buried the dead in a six-foot-wide, two-hundred-yard-long trench that ran north from modern Lafayette Boulevard. Located approximately one hundred yards east of the Sunken Road, the site of this trench, like those of the other two major burial trenches in front of Marye's Heights, is now covered by houses.[40]

Thanks to the efforts of Corporal Albert M. Downs of the Fifty-Seventh New York, as many as eight hundred Union soldiers who died at Fredericksburg in May 1864 received a decent burial. The Fifty-Seventh New York was then serving as provost guard in the town. After coming across a poorly fashioned mass grave, in which the dead were neither identified nor given a proper funeral, Downs took it upon himself to bury Union soldiers who had died in Fredericksburg after being wounded at Spotsylvania. He selected for his graveyard a parcel of land just west of town on the property of John J. Chew. Aided by five privates, Downs excavated several trenches, seven feet wide and twenty feet in length, each of which could accommodate twenty bodies buried two deep. At Downs's urging, Union surgeons tagged each corpse with a piece of paper giving the deceased soldier's name, company,

Burial of Union soldiers in Fredericksburg, May 1864. *Library of Congress.*

and regiment, information that Downs used to create individual headboards. Not content with simply giving his fallen comrades a decent burial, Downs shrouded each corpse in a blanket prior to its burial and arranged for delegates of the United States Christian Commission to conduct funeral services at each grave. Employees of Mathew Brady photographed Downs and his men at work in a well-known series of images taken on May 19–20.[41]

By then, the Union army was again on the move. At 10 p.m. on May 20, Major General Winfield S. Hancock's Second Corps marched to Milford Station, on the Richmond, Fredericksburg, and Potomac Railroad, in an effort to draw Lee into the open, where Grant could get at him. The ploy worked. Recognizing the threat Hancock posed both to Richmond and to his own line of supply, Lee abandoned his Spotsylvania trenches and raced south. However, rather than attack Hancock, as Grant had hoped, Lee bypassed Milford Station and headed directly for the North Anna River. Grant caught up with him there on May 23. In four days of fighting and maneuvers, the Army of the Potomac lost yet another twenty-six hundred men. Because most of them lay within Union lines, their comrades were able to bury them.[42] Such had not been the case with many of the Union soldiers killed in the Wilderness or at Spotsylvania Court House. A year would pass before they would receive a proper burial.

## 2. ❈ Postwar Burials in the Wilderness and at Spotsylvania Court House

The first postwar effort by the U.S. government to inter Union dead who remained unburied in Virginia took place in June 1865, just two months after Robert E. Lee's surrender at Appomattox Court House. Twenty-seven-year-old Brevet Major James M. Moore led the Union burial effort. Early in the war Moore had been a lieutenant in the Nineteenth Pennsylvania, but he later resigned his commission in order to accept an appointment as a captain in the Quartermaster Department. He spent the last two years of the war supervising the burial of Union soldiers who had died in and around Washington, D.C. He was an experienced man who knew his job.[1]

On June 7, 1865, Inspector General James A. Hardie set Moore on a new task, directing him "to take charge of the duty of the burial of the Union soldiers, portions of whose remains, it is reported, are lying exposed on the fields of the engagements at Wilderness and Spotsylvania and that vicinity." The two battlefields fell within the aegis of the army's Middle Military Division. Before leaving, Moore reported to the division's commander, Major General Winfield S. Hancock, for further instructions.[2]

Hancock assigned Colonel Charles P. Bird's First U.S. Veteran Volunteer Regiment to support Moore in this assignment.[3] Bird had been a captain in the Second Delaware in 1864 and had served under Hancock both in the Wilderness and at Spotsylvania Court House. Now, as the newly minted commander of the First U.S. Veteran Volunteers, he led a hodgepodge of officers and men who had reenlisted in the army after having served in other regiments.[4]

The First Regiment shuffled onto the transport USS *Hugh Jenkins* at Alexandria, Virginia, on June 8 and steamed down the Potomac River to Potomac Creek, arriving at a former Union army supply depot known as Belle Plain at 7:30 that night.[5] Moore met the regiment there the next day and led it on a twelve-mile march to Fredericksburg. On the way, it passed through southern Stafford County, an area made desolate by the Army of the Potomac's lengthy winter encampment there two and a half years earlier. An officer in Bird's regiment, Second Lieutenant William F. Landon, likened the barren, sparsely populated region to a "desert"—a "Virginia Sahara."[6]

Marching past White Oak Church, the First Regiment reached Fredericksburg late on the afternoon of June 9 and pitched its tents on the south side of the Rappahannock River, half a mile west of the town. Some soldiers wandered the streets of the shell-torn town; others hiked up Marye's Heights, where Union arms had suffered defeat on December 13, 1862. Private James Riley visited the tomb of Mary Washington, which he found "chip[p]ed up very badly by relic seekers and bullets." He and a friend then strolled through the town in search of "southern beauties," only to find that the women "looked upon us as if . . . we were of an inferior race."[7]

Everywhere Riley looked, destruction met his eyes. He found that "more than half of the town is burned and what houses are not burned are riddled with cannonballs." Graves dotted each lot. Unlike the Union soldiers who had perished in the Wilderness and at Spotsylvania Court House, most of those who had died at Fredericksburg had been buried immediately after the battle. Landon had fought at Fredericksburg with the Fourteenth Indiana, and he took the opportunity to search the town for graves of comrades who had fallen there. He found but one: Corporal John E. Hutchins of Company B, the "Old Post Guards."[8]

Landon and his comrades resumed their march at four o'clock the next morning, June 10, heading west along one of two roads: the Orange Turnpike or the Orange Plank Road. By noon, the First Regiment reached Chancellorsville, the site of another desperate battle. It halted there for two hours to allow the soldiers time to rest and eat dinner. The charred remains of the Chancellor house and the scattered remnants of blankets, knapsacks, and other equipment bore silent witness to the fierce struggle waged there. Passing on, the regiment reached the Wilderness Battlefield late in the afternoon. The soldiers bivouacked on the northern end of the battlefield at an abandoned goldmine—possibly the Woodville Mine. No sooner had they arrived than "a crowd of half-starved women and children" and a few men in Confederate uniforms flooded into the camp, hoping to trade garden vegetables for food that the soldiers carried in their wagons. "All the rations we could spare were freely given them," wrote Landon, but the demand far exceeded the supply, and many went away hungry. One item not in short supply was cherries. After downing their army rations, Riley and a friend gorged themselves freely on the wild fruit. "We liked to killed our selves (hog like) eating them," he recalled.[9]

## Gathering Union Remains on the Orange Turnpike

The First Regiment began collecting skeletons on June 12. Starting at the northern end of the battlefield, the soldiers slowly worked their way south, searching through "woods, thickets, fields, and swamps." After going a certain distance, they would halt, change direction, and then move forward again, marking the graves of those who had been properly interred and gathering up the remains of those who had not.[10] The woods were too thick for the passage of wagons, so one out of every four men had to carry a sack to hold the bones. Remains that lay in marshy ground had not fully decomposed. Too offensive to handle, they had to be buried where they lay.[11] Once the bags were filled, the soldiers carried them to Saunders field. "There," remembered Riley, "we had coffins and we emptied the bones out into a pile and some of us picked out bones enough of the various kinds to make 8 men and put them into one coffin and burryed them[.] [W]e burryed about 100 that day."[12]

Although required to bury only the Union dead, Moore and Bird took it upon themselves to inter Confederates whom they found too, a task that nearly doubled their workload.[13] Soldiers whose graves could be identified received a simple headboard. Such was the case of John W. Patterson, colonel of the 102nd Pennsylvania, who had died on May 5, 1864. Patterson's men had committed his body to the ground and marked his grave with whatever

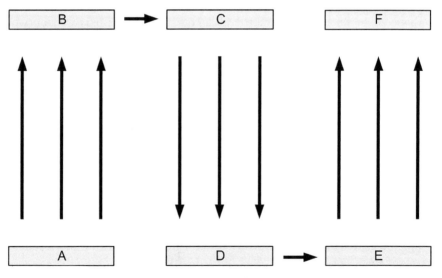

Method used by the burial party in searching for skeletons.

Skeletons in the Wilderness. *U.S. Army Military History Institute, Carlisle Barracks, Pa.*

wood happened to be available at the time. When Bird's men found Patterson's grave, more than a year later, they replaced the rough headboard with a tablet of their own. Patterson's family later recovered his body and took the tablet home with them as a relic of his death.[14] Patterson was more fortunate than most. Few soldiers had been buried, and fewer still had boards identifying their graves. "It was impossible to identify any of the bodies found unburied," insisted Bird, "they having been exposed [for] more than a year all traces of identification having been destroyed."[15]

After just one day on the battlefield, the First Regiment had collected thousands of bones and "a huge pile of grinning, ghastly skulls." To hold the remains, the soldiers constructed a cemetery south of the Orange Turnpike, near the western edge of Saunders field. The graveyard was sixty feet square and enclosed by a whitewashed fence made of horizontal planking. On one of the fence posts, workers nailed a board identifying the graveyard as "Wilderness National Cemetery No. 1."[16]

The First Regiment buried the dead in mass graves. Landon recalled placing ten skulls in each coffin and filling the rest of the container with bones. Once full, soldiers screwed lids onto the wooden boxes, and a "Corporal's Guard" lowered them into the ground, their occupants "unknown, but not unhonored nor unsung." By Landon's count, his regiment buried thirty-five coffins in this fashion, totaling 350 interments. However, his figure may be high. Bird reported burying 180 men in Wilderness National Cemetery No. 1, while Moore—perhaps erroneously—set the figure at just 108. Riley counted only 100.[17]

The men of the First Regiment arranged the graves in neat, orderly rows. Over each one they set a white wooden tablet with black lettering. Like those they erected elsewhere on the battlefield, the tablets were approximately ten inches wide and one and a half inches thick. They extended three feet above the ground and had gently rounded tops.[18]

## Gathering Union Remains on the Orange Plank Road

Having finished the job along the Orange Turnpike, Colonel Bird on June 13 shifted his camp four miles south. While his men were en route to their new camp it started to rain, and by the time they reached it, wrote Riley, "we was as wet as water could make us," adding, "We was the best representation of a lot of drowned rats [as] I ever saw."[19] The men pitched their "dog tents" in a large field just east of where the Brock Road crossed the Orange Plank Road.[20] On June 14, having settled into their new camp, the soldiers fanned out to look for additional graves. As before, the regiment erected neat tablets over the graves of every Union soldier that it found, known or unknown, and collected in sacks the remains of Union soldiers that had not been buried. The burial party interred Confederate soldiers too, but it marked the graves only of Southerners whom it could identify.[21]

The First Regiment buried the Union skeletons in a cemetery situated adjacent to the Orange Plank Road, less than half a mile west of the Brock Road intersection. The men called it Wilderness National Cemetery No. 2 to differentiate it from the one beside the Orange Turnpike. A whitewashed sign nailed to a tree identified the site.[22] The graveyard stood just east of a line of Confederate earthworks, where Union carnage had been most severe. Wilderness National Cemetery No. 2 was ninety feet square—50 percent larger than the graveyard constructed earlier along the Orange Turnpike. The soldiers enclosed the grounds with a white picket fence, different in appearance from the board fence they had erected around Wilderness National Cemetery No. 1. In contrast to that cemetery, which was constructed in a clearing, Wilderness National Cemetery No. 2 stood in the woods. Inside its enclosure grew no fewer than forty-five small oak trees.[23]

As they did at Wilderness National Cemetery No. 1, members of the burial party disagreed on just how many men they buried along the Plank Road.

Major Moore tabulated the number of soldiers there at 534, Colonel Bird thought they had buried 535, Lieutenant Landon set the tally at 650, while Private Riley counted just 400. "The bones of these men were gathered from the ground where they fell," Moore explained, "having never been interred; and by exposure to the weather for more than a year all traces of their identity were entirely obliterated."[24] Although most men buried in the cemetery had no recognizable identity, there were at least five exceptions: Captain Seth F.

Wilderness National Cemetery No. 2. *Orlando Poe Collection, U.S. Military Academy, West Point, N.Y.*

Johnson, Forty-Fourth New York; Sergeant Isaiah L. Gordon, Twentieth Maine; Private John Flanaghan, Ninth Massachusetts; Private John Hull, 149th Pennsylvania; and Private William C. Rogers, Fifth Michigan. Unlike their unknown comrades, who were packed ten to a coffin, each identified soldier received his own plot.[25]

Rain temporarily brought work at the cemetery to a halt. Undeterred by the weather, Landon went hunting for huckleberries in the swamps west of the Brock Road. He found bushes growing "as high as a man's head" and loaded with fruit. But as the lieutenant plucked berries from the branches, he stumbled upon a more gruesome harvest: the skeleton of a rebel soldier who had been shot through the head. Unlike other human skeletons that he had found, this one had not yet been plundered. Landon picked up the skull and shook it. The fatal bullet still rattled inside. But Landon was more interested in the man's gold teeth. With a callousness wrought by four years of war, he removed the gold and then proceeded to plunder his victim of every item he owned, down to his pocket comb. Before leaving, Landon "chucked" his victim's bones into a sinkhole and scraped a little dirt over them. He then mounted the man's skull on a stick in order to mark the grave for anyone who might come looking for it.[26]

A mile west of the Brock Road intersection stood the Carpenter farm, site of the Second Corps field hospital during the battle. Bird's men found four cemeteries there, one for each of the corps's four division hospitals. Soldiers who had died at the hospitals were "thickly planted" about the place, their graves marked by crude headboards fashioned from cracker boxes and other rough materials. A man named Akers occupied the farm. "This man Akers owns, or rather there are on his plantation about twenty negroes, mostly wenches and brats, with perhaps three rheumatic 'uncles,'" Landon informed a friend. "He has a son at home who was a lieutenant in the rebel army. Six acres in wheat and six in corn is all the crop they have to depend on for winter food—two worn-out horses and two cows compose their 'stock.'"[27]

## Gathering Union Remains at Spotsylvania Court House

The First Regiment completed its work on the Orange Plank Road in five days, and on June 19 it headed for Spotsylvania Court House.[28] It followed the Brock Road, the same route used by the Army of the Potomac in 1864. On the way it passed Todd's Tavern, a ramshackle frame building that had

Union graves on the Carpenter farm on the Wilderness Battlefield. *Library of Congress.*

been the site of some minor fighting in the campaign. The remains of eight soldiers lay within sight of the road; Bird and his men hastily committed the skeletons to the soil and continued on their way.[29]

A little farther on, the First Regiment came to the house of Katharine Couse. During the battle of Spotsylvania Court House the building had served as a Union field hospital, and for Landon its sight brought back memories as vivid as they were unpleasant. "I well remembered the rows of wounded soldiers I had seen stretched out here as we bivouacked on the same spot but little over one year ago, and listening all the night long to the deep groans of the wounded and dying heroes and shrieks and curses of those undergoing the torture of the probe or keen blade of the amputating knife. Many a poor fellow's bones rest here under the shade of the oak and pine," he wrote to a friend, "and few with boards to mark the spot."[30]

Across the road from the Couse house stood "Liberty Hill," the farm of Captain John C. Brown, a War of 1812 veteran. Here the Second Corps had gathered its strength before assaulting the Muleshoe Salient on May 12, 1864, an attack that led to the most savage day of fighting in American history. Among the casualties that bloody day was Landon's old commander, Colonel John Coons of the Fourteenth Indiana. Landon found Coons's grave after a three-hour search. Bending over, he pried open the coffin. Although the body had begun to molder, Landon recognized the colonel by his uniform, hair, and beard. A rough headboard over the grave confirmed the identity. With the help of another soldier, Landon transferred Coons's remains to a new coffin and buried it in Mrs. Couse's garden, beneath a small apple tree. He erected a headboard over that and other Fourteenth Indiana graves that he found so that family members could later locate the remains.[31]

The First Regiment established its Spotsylvania camp in rear of the Confederate works, at a point on the battlefield where the carnage had been particularly severe. Landon remembered the site as the "Death Angle," although it has come down to history as the "Bloody Angle." Either name is appropriate, for it had been a site of indescribable horror. For twenty-two hours Union and Confederate soldiers had struggled there, often in hand-to-hand combat, the torn and mangled bodies of the dead piling up two, three, even four deep around the works. After the fighting had subsided, Union soldiers tossed the dead into the trench and kicked dirt from the adjacent parapet down upon them.[32]

Moore and Bird found few men to bury at Spotsylvania. The Army of the Potomac had interred many of the dead at the time of the battle, and Joseph Sanford had taken care of the rest. Sanford owned a hotel at Spotsylvania Court House and was the village's most prominent citizen. In May 1865 he had made arrangements with Major General William T. Sherman, whose army was passing through the area en route to Washington, to bury Union soldiers whose remains still littered the ground. The innkeeper had tackled the job with energy. By the time Moore and his party reached the battlefield just one month later, they found but few unburied.[33] Moore intended to create a cemetery for the remaining skeletons, as he had done in the Wilderness, but the summer heat had rendered them so putrid that Bird's men could not bear to handle them. Bowing to necessity, Moore ordered the men to bury the skeletons where they lay, marking with headboards those who could be identified so that friends and family members could later find them. Existing graves were improved. According to Riley, the regiment "buried the bones of 500 and covered up 1000 more."[34] As in the Wilderness, it buried not only Union soldiers but Confederates too.

With the war now over, some Northern citizens had come to Spotsylvania in an effort to retrieve the remains of loved ones. The First Regiment met a woman who had been at the battlefield for three days searching for her dead son. During their final day at Spotsylvania, the men of the regiment found the young man's remains and consigned them to his mother's keeping.[35]

Confederate graves near the Bloody Angle. *Orlando Poe Collection, U.S. Military Academy, West Point, N.Y.*

# Return to Washington

Bird's men completed their task on June 24. They had been in the field for just over two weeks.[36] Before leaving the Bloody Angle on the twenty-fifth, a soldier nailed to a tree a board containing a stanza from Theodore O'Hara's poem "Bivouac of the Dead." In ornate script, it read,

> On Fame's eternal camping ground
> Their silent tents are spread
> And glory guards with solemn round
> The Bivouac of the Dead[37]

The return trip to Washington was uneventful. The First Regiment passed through Fredericksburg on Sunday, June 25, marched across the pontoon bridge there, and went into camp one mile beyond, in Stafford County. The next day the men marched through a pouring rain to Belle Plain, where they boarded a transport ship that carried them to Giesboro Point, near Washington. Members of the burial party had not taken a change of clothes with them, and by the time they set foot north of the Potomac they were, in Riley's words, "an awful dirty ragged set of sogers." Many had worn out their shoes and came back barefoot.[38]

In the course of the expedition, the First Regiment had buried nearly 1,500 skeletons, erected headboards over the graves of 785 known soldiers, and marked as unknown the graves of many more. "Our 'Skeleton Hunt' has ended," wrote Landon, "the heroes of the fierce and bloody battles of the Wilderness and Spottsylvania [*sic*], who offered up their lives in defense of their country's honor and her flag in those terrible conflicts, are now, at last, reposing in peace beneath the 'sacred soil' of the Old Dominion."[39]

Despite Landon's rosy assessment, the expedition had not been a complete success. Moore himself admitted as much. "Hundreds of graves on these battle fields are without any marks whatever to distinguish them," he informed General Hancock, "and so covered with foliage, that the visitor will be unable to find the last resting places of those who have fallen, until the rains and snows of winter wash from the surface the light covering of earth, and expose their remains." Bird took a more positive view of the matter. "It may be that a few were passed over," he admitted, "but from the extensive growth of weeds and underbrush, it was impossible to discover them."[40]

In coming months it was to become evident just how many skeletons the burial party had missed. Lieutenant Colonel Theodore Lyman visited Spotsylvania

Battlefield in April 1866, when the trees were still in bud, and was shocked at the number of bones he found scattered across the ground. "Not only are the remains not collected in a common cemetery," he noted critically, "but many marked graves have been overlooked. Only the scattered dead are marked and of those probably only a portion."[41] Writer John T. Trowbridge found a similar state of affairs in the Wilderness when he visited there in September 1865. Stepping into the woods, Trowbridge had found the skeletons of two soldiers lying side by side—the first of many such discoveries he would make. "It must have been that these bodies, and others we found afterwards, were overlooked by the party sent to construct the cemeteries," he mused. "It was shameful negligence, to say the least."[42]

Moore and Bird submitted reports of their expedition to Hancock upon their return to Washington. To his report, Moore appended the names of 722 soldiers whose graves he had marked. The list included at least a dozen Confederate soldiers.[43] The War Department later published portions of Moore's list in prominent newspapers throughout the North in order to give readers an opportunity to retrieve their loved ones' remains. The bones of Colonel Patterson, Colonel Coons, and many others were recovered in this manner.[44]

Unfortunately Moore's list contained numerous errors. A survey of thirteen names reveals no fewer than ten mistakes. While many of the errors were minor in nature, others were not. For instance, Moore recorded the interment of the Fourteenth Indiana's Thomas Gibson as "T. Gillison." Likewise, James Gallegher of the Eighth Ohio appeared as Joseph Gallough of the Fourth Ohio, and Anthony Magrum of the Eighth Ohio became A. Magerham of the Seventh Virginia. Given the frequency and flagrancy of such mistakes, it is remarkable that so many remains were claimed.[45]

The work done by Moore, Bird, and the men of the First Regiment remained intact for just one year. Confronted with the task of interring more than fifteen thousand Union soldiers in the Fredericksburg area, the War Department in 1866 decided to consolidate the graves of Union soldiers into a single cemetery located on Marye's Heights. Over the next two years, burial parties scoured the Fredericksburg region, bringing in wagonload after wagonload of human remains. Among them were the skeletons of men buried by the First Regiment in the Wilderness and at Spotsylvania Court House.

Today all traces of Wilderness National Cemetery No. 1 are gone, as are the individual plots of those once buried on Spotsylvania Battlefield. Only at Wilderness National Cemetery No. 2 does evidence of Moore's expedition remain. There, among the decaying leaves, one can still see shallow depressions in the earth whose regular alignment identifies them as former graves—haunting reminders of the great "Skeleton Hunt" of 1865.

## An Early Effort to Bury the Fredericksburg Dead?

It seems peculiar that General Hancock would order Major Moore to inter the dead on the Wilderness and Spotsylvania Battlefields but to ignore those he encountered at Fredericksburg and Chancellorsville. At Fredericksburg, the authorities may have felt that there was no need for a burial detail. After all, Major Generals Ambrose E. Burnside and William B. Franklin had buried their dead at the time of the battle. But what about Chancellorsville? Major General Joseph Hooker did not send burial parties back across the Rappahannock River in May 1863, as Burnside had done after Fredericksburg, instead leaving the task of interring the dead to the Confederates. That the job was inadequately done is shown by the many skeletons found by Union soldiers when they returned to the battlefield in 1864. Authorities in Washington must have known that skeletons of Union soldiers remained unburied at Chancellorsville, and yet they neglected to have Moore inter them. Is it possible that they made arrangements with others to bury the Union dead at both Fredericksburg and Chancellorsville?

Lieutenant Wiley Roy Mason indicates that such was the case. In an article titled "Notes of a Confederate Staff-Officer," Mason wrote that the U.S. government hired a contractor to inter the remains of the Union dead at all four Fredericksburg-area battlefields, agreeing to pay him for each skeleton that he recovered. According to Mason, the unscrupulous man found several hundred skeletons packed into the Wallace family icehouse on the outskirts of town. Not content with this bonanza, he tried to pad his profits by placing the remains of individual soldiers into more than one coffin. Mason discovered the fraud and reported it to Fredericksburg's post commander, Colonel Edwin V. Sumner Jr., son and namesake of the late general. Shocked at this "vandalism," Sumner revoked the man's contract.[46]

Sumner left Fredericksburg on July 17, 1865. If Mason's story is true, the episode must have happened earlier that summer, at approximately the same time that Moore was burying the dead at Wilderness and Spotsylvania Court House. But why would the army use two different methods to accomplish the same goal? Wouldn't it have been easier to simply have Moore's men inter the dead at all four places? And where did the contractor intend to bury the dead once he had unearthed them?

Although no evidence has yet been found to support Mason's claim that the government hired a contractor to exhume the remains of Union dead in Fredericksburg, it would explain the difference between the number of men supposedly buried at Wallace's icehouse and the actual number of skeletons unearthed there. Mason estimated that the structure held between four hundred and five hundred Union skeletons, a statement supported by at least five other sources. Yet when government workers entered the icehouse in 1866 to move those entombed there to the national cemetery, they found the remains of just fifty-two bodies. Did Mason and others exaggerate the number of skeletons buried there, or had someone—perhaps a government contractor—removed most of the skeletons at an earlier date? For now, at least, the mystery remains unsolved.[47]

# 3. ❀ A Call to Action

The call for the creation of national cemeteries in the South came, in part, from Northern citizens who had visited the Fredericksburg-area battlefields. Shortly after the war, a man named Joseph Williams accompanied a group of Northerners to Spotsylvania Battlefield, where he discovered the remains of Union soldiers buried in shallow graves. "The cleared land on which these bodies are so slightly buried," he reported to Secretary of War Edwin M. Stanton, "will doubtless be plowed this fall for wheat, or next spring for corn, and thousands of bones will thus be plowed up and exposed to view, and to the desecration of rebel plowmen and farmers, who will again spurn the hated Yankee, and manure his lands with the bones of his enemies. The timber land will in time also be brought under cultivation and an equal number of our fallen defenders be used to fatten the lands of our enemies." Williams urged the secretary to immediately purchase or seize battlefields throughout the South "so that no rebel should ever have the opportunity to plow up and desecrate our honored dead."[1]

On the heels of Williams's letter came correspondence from Charles Kronenberger, a man whose son had died at a Fredericksburg field hospital in May 1864. Kronenberger and his wife had just returned from the town, where they had searched in vain for their son's remains. "Instead of finding the graves marked as was expected," wrote the bereaved father, "there appeared about 400 buried in one lot and but 2 or 3 graves marked." Worse still, the owner of the lot told Kronenberger that he intended to erect a structure on the site. The father appealed to Stanton to prevent such action.[2]

Stanton forwarded Kronenberger's letter to Quartermaster General Montgomery C. Meigs, who in turn referred the matter to James M. Moore, who had recently been brevetted a lieutenant colonel. Although Moore had not personally inspected the site, he acknowledged that the burial grounds at Fredericksburg were "like all other places of the kind, where no care has been bestowed by the Government, in a very dilapidated and forlorn condition." Although a quartermaster had been stationed at Fredericksburg for more

36

than a year, Moore admitted, "no headboards have as yet been erected; nor any other steps taken by that Officer, to lay out a Cemetery, or improve and beautify, the present burial ground."[3]

Even Southerners seemed to agree that immediate action by the government was necessary to prevent desecration of Northern graves. On December 1, 1865, George E. Chancellor wrote to Stanton requesting a contract to create national cemeteries on the battlefields of Chancellorsville, the Wilderness, and Spotsylvania Court House. Chancellor offered to collect the Union remains, create headboards for the dead, and inter them in the cemeteries. Not only would he become caretaker of the three cemeteries he established, but he also would take charge of the two Wilderness cemeteries established earlier by Moore. Chancellor warned Stanton not to delay. "If [the bodies] are not taken up and car[r]ied to some bur[y]ing ground they will soon all be ploughed over by the Farmers as a great many of them are in the cultivated fields."[4]

The secretary referred the matter to Brevet Major General Daniel H. Rucker, chief quartermaster of the Washington Depot, who asked Moore for his comments. Moore agreed that immediate action was necessary in order to prevent desecration of the graves, but he felt that the government could do the work more effectively and at half the cost of Chancellor or any other private contractor.[5]

## Gerrish's Survey

Letters like those sent by Williams, Kronenberger, and Chancellor helped persuade the War Department that prompt action was necessary to prevent desecration of Union graves throughout the South. Stanton charged Meigs with preventing such desecration and seeing to the proper burial of the dead. In an effort to determine the scale of the task facing him, the quartermaster general on October 30, 1865, ordered his officers in the field to report on the number and location of Union graves in their districts.

Brevet Major Hiram F. Gerrish conducted a survey of the Fredericksburg region. In the town itself, he estimated that each lot contained between one and seven graves. Many of the graves were on land that property owners intended to cultivate in the spring. If the government wished to save those graves from desecration, it would have to act quickly. In addition to the town lots, Gerrish identified 115 parcels of land in the surrounding area that contained Union graves, which were widely dispersed and largely unmarked. He carefully listed the number of bodies, marked and unmarked, at each spot, identifying 8,018 graves in all.[6] The Fredericksburg Agricultural Fair Grounds, in front of Marye's Heights, topped the list with 1,363 burials, followed by the adjacent Stratton property with 560. Dr. Durrett's farm in Spotsylvania posted the third highest total in the region with 475.[7] Gerrish's totals, broken down by area, were as follows:

| Area | Marked | Unmarked | Total | Percentage marked |
|---|---|---|---|---|
| Stafford | 1,315 | 1,095 | 2,410 | 54.6 |
| Fredericksburg | 195 | 2,544 | 2,739 | 7.1 |
| Chancellorsville | 82 | 582 | 664 | 12.3 |
| Spotsylvania | 511 | 1,694 | 2,205 | 23.2 |
| Total | 2,103 | 5,915 | 8,018 | 26.2 |

Knowing that in June 1865 the First U.S. Veteran Volunteer Regiment had collected the remains of Union soldiers who had perished in the Wilderness and buried them in Wilderness National Cemeteries Nos. 1 and 2, Gerrish did not include the Wilderness Battlefield in his report. Even so, his total fell far short of the 15,300 burials eventually interred at Fredericksburg National Cemetery. The biggest obstacle in getting an accurate count was the large number of mass graves. "At one place near the City there are said to be 500 interred in one grave," he wrote, referring to the Wallace icehouse, "and at another place 800 are buried in a trench[.] none of them are marked[.] At other places there are trenches where a less number are buried. All through the City are scattered graves in door yards & gardens[.] some of them are marked but a greater number have nothing by which they can be designated." To get an accurate count of the bodies would require digging.[8]

In addition to his request that each officer report on the number and location of Union graves in their districts, Meigs asked them for recommendations on protecting the remains from desecration. Gerrish suggested that the government maintain the cemeteries created by Moore in the Wilderness and establish four additional cemeteries in the Fredericksburg area: one on the fairgrounds outside of town and others at the Phillips farm in Stafford County and at the Chancellorsville and Spotsylvania Battlefields. Creating four new cemeteries would not be as expensive as it appeared, he assured Meigs, as land in the county was much cheaper than land in town. But whatever Meigs chose to do, he had to do quickly, Gerrish warned, "as in many instances the

Headboards and what little fencing there is are being rapidly destroyed by citizens & negroes."[9]

## Watson's Letter

Meigs received Gerrish's report in March 1866. By then, a letter written by a man named Watson was circulating through Congress. Watson claimed to be a loyal citizen living in Fredericksburg and described efforts being taken by Northern citizens to erect a soldiers' monument on the fairgrounds behind the town. The mayor and city council, however, threatened to upset those plans by giving the land to the Agricultural Society. Watson viewed this as a deliberate attempt to disgrace the North's fallen heroes. "We ask whether it is intended by the United States that the remains of their soldiers shall be desecrated by rebel fairs and rebel gala parties congregating and trampling them under foot, and making jests at the expense of dead Yankees?" he demanded.[10]

There was more. Watson claimed that Southerners planned to dig up the bones of Northern soldiers and grind them into dust for fertilizer. In doing so, they would make good on earlier boasts "that if the North came down to subdue them, they would manure the land with their bodies." To prevent that from happening, Watson urged Congress to confiscate battlefields throughout the South, "making them United States lands forever, that they may never be plowed up or otherwise desecrated by the unrepentant rebels."[11]

At a distance of more than 150 years, Watson's warnings appear overwrought, but Washington officials took them seriously. The chairman of the House Committee of Military Affairs forwarded the letter to Secretary Stanton, who, on April 2, 1866, directed General Meigs to "take charge of and enclose . . . the fields at Fredericksburg, Va., on which the battle was fought . . . and hold the same as a National Cemet[e]ry and adopt measures to secure the graves from desecration." Federal troops seized the land eight days later. By May 1866, the government was ready to begin construction of a cemetery.[12]

## Occupation Troops

From 1865 to 1869, Fredericksburg belonged to the Military District of Northeastern Virginia and was occupied by Union troops. Brigadier General Charles Devens commanded the district in the summer of 1865; Major General James B. Ricketts and Brigadier General Thomas M. Harris succeeded him. District headquarters were in Fredericksburg.[13]

Within the District of Northeastern Virginia were several subdistricts. The Rappahannock Subdistrict had its headquarters in Fredericksburg. Colonel Edwin V. Sumner Jr. was post commander until July 1865, when Brigadier General Thomas M. Harris succeeded him. In August, Harris gave way to Brigadier General Samuel S. Carroll. Brevet Lieutenant Colonel H. A. Hambright of the Eleventh United States Infantry commanded the post in January 1866.[14]

Fredericksburg's garrison changed as frequently as its commanders. A battalion of the First New York Mounted Rifles occupied the town in the summer of 1865. It was replaced, in turn, by detachments of the Fifth Maryland, Ninety-Sixth New York, Eleventh Maine, Eleventh United States Regulars, Twelfth United States Regulars, and Twenty-First United States Regulars.[15] In warmer months of the year, the soldiers camped on Marye's Heights, but as the weather grew colder they moved into town, occupying buildings such the town hall, the Masonic lodge, and Citizens Hall. The occupation of Fredericksburg and its buildings formally ended on April 1, 1869, when the last Federal troops boarded a train for Richmond.[16]

When not on duty, the soldiers strolled through the town, played baseball, or took part in a "reading room association." In warmer months, they swam in the area's many rivers and waterholes. One soldier, Private David Trussel of Company G, Twenty-First U.S. Infantry, drowned while swimming off Marlborough Point in 1867 and is today buried in grave #3505 at Fredericksburg National Cemetery. At least four other soldiers are reported to have died in the Fredericksburg area between 1866 and 1868: one from a gunshot wound, another from typhoid, a third from sunstroke, and the last from injuries incurred when he fell off a horse.[17]

For the most part, the Federal soldiers created few disturbances; when they did, liquor was usually the cause. The soldiers did not get paid often and celebrated their sporadic wages by going on sprees. An 1868 article in the *Fredericksburg Ledger* noted that "the Federal troops at this place were paid of[f] last Friday evening," adding, "The 'boys' were quite lively at night."[18] Drinking sometimes led to violence. One evening, half a dozen soldiers broke into a Fredericksburg house, forcing the terrified residents to flee. Military authorities rounded up the offenders and clapped them in irons to await trail. On another occasion, a drunken soldier belonging to the First New York Mounted Rifles entered a Fredericksburg home and abused a man and woman who lived there. When he drew a saber and advanced toward the couple's son, the occupants shot him dead. To prevent such lawless behavior,

Major Henry C. Adams issued an order on January 3, 1866, forbidding the sale of intoxicating liquors to all soldiers in the Rappahannock Subdistrict. In addition, Adams ordered that all public houses close their doors at 10 p.m. and not open them at all on Sundays. Although well intentioned, his efforts probably had little effect in curbing the soldiers' bad behavior.[19]

The Eleventh U.S. Infantry was occupying Fredericksburg in late May 1866 when construction of the national cemetery began. While engineers prepared the ground at Willis Hill to receive burials, fifty men of the Eleventh Infantry began scouring the area for Union remains. A Major Johnston of the Quartermaster Corps supervised the work. Perhaps acceding to the demands of the city fathers, he made town lots and the fairgrounds his first priority. "The work is being rapidly pushed forward," the *Fredericksburg Ledger* reported approvingly on June 1. Within two weeks, Johnston and his men had interred the remains of more than fifty soldiers. Although the work was not difficult, it was highly unpleasant. In the first week alone, more than twenty soldiers deserted.[20]

## The Burial Corps

Soldiers of the Eleventh U.S. Infantry began collecting and burying Union remains at Fredericksburg in May 1866. Within one month, however, the government began hiring private laborers to do the job. Known as the Burial Corps, the laborers consisted of former slaves, Irish immigrants, and even Confederate veterans. The Quartermaster Department paid each man fifteen dollars a month plus lodging (tents) and rations.[21] Although they accepted the positions, few workers were content with their wages. In a letter to the War Department dated January 1, 1867, black teamsters complained that former Confederates earned twice the salary that they were making. According to their statement, Southerners in the Burial Corps had bragged that "they got 16 Doll[ar]s for killing" the Federals "and now they are getting 30 for putting them away." That was not the case, however, and the government dismissed the claim.[22]

The Irish workers complained too. Many had recently served in the Union army, where they claimed to have earned thirty dollars, twice the salary being paid to members of the Burial Corps. In May 1868, several of them petitioned President Andrew Johnson and General Ulysses S. Grant to double their wages to thirty dollars per month. "We earnestly entreat you to give the Soldiers a hearing," they appealed to Grant, "as there is destitution among men with families."[23] Grant sent the petition down the chain of command until it landed on the desk of Quartermaster James M. Moore, in charge of burial operations throughout Virginia. He argued against the increase. While acknowledging that Burial Corps workers earned somewhat less than men working for the railroad, Moore pointed out that they still made more than most farmhands in the state. Moreover, the men in the Burial Corps received free rations and lodging in tents. "Considering the entire sureness and punctuality of the pay of the Government as compared with private parties, the compensation paid to the laborers on this National Cemetery at Fredericksburg is considered sufficient, and no increase is recommended." Grant accepted Moore's advice and disapproved the workers' request.[24]

Despite their meager wages, Burial Corps workers found money to buy liquor at Fredericksburg's many drinking establishments. A newspaper reporter recorded a brawl in August 1866 "between citizens and citizens, between soldiers and citizens, and between soldiers and parties belonging to the burial corps." The following summer a group of laborers got roaring drunk at the Exchange Hotel. When asked to leave, they kicked up a ruckus, committing depredations for which the editor of the *Fredericksburg Ledger* thought "they deserved at least a night's lodging, at their own expense, in the calaboose." However, the Burial Corps was under military authority, and the civil authorities were powerless to discipline them. "We have two governments, civil and military," lamented the *Ledger,* "but the one seems to be in the way of the other. The ends of justice are seldom subserved when there is a divided responsibility."[25]

No records have yet surfaced to indicate the number of men who worked in Fredericksburg's Burial Corps, but if Chickamauga and Petersburg are any guides, the number must have been quite large. John Trowbridge visited Chickamauga in 1866 and counted precisely 217 Burial Corps workers in camp there—black soldiers and their white officers. At Petersburg, the Burial Corps consisted of approximately 100 men, forty mules, and twelve saddle horses. The Fredericksburg area had four times the number of Union casualties as Chickamauga and nearly twice as many as Petersburg. Given those figures, it is reasonable to assume that it had at least 200 Burial Corps workers and likely more.[26]

Members of the Burial Corps pitched their tents at the foot of Willis Hill, near the present-day Fredericksburg Battlefield Visitor Center. They called their temporary home "Camp Augur."[27] Joseph Hall owned the land on which the Burial Corps made its camp and later submitted a $365.00 claim to the army for damages that he had incurred. Hall charged the government $25.00 apiece for the removal and use of a stone fence, the removal of a chimney and foundation of his destroyed house, and the removal of a brick wall and

Burial party at Cold Harbor Battlefield, Virginia. *Library of Congress.*

the filling up of a well. In addition, he billed the government $200.00 for using two acres of turf to sod cemetery graves and $90.00 for occupying his property as a campground from September 1, 1867, to March 31, 1869. When the army insisted that Hall provide documentation to support his claim, he boosted the total to $392.00. His new invoice reduced the claim for sod from $200.00 to $150.00, but it increased the claim for stone from $25.00 to $85.50 and the claim for brick from $25.00 to $40.00. Hall claimed that the army took twenty-five perch of stone and eight thousand bricks, which it used to construct chimneys for fourteen huts.[28] Before paying any damages, the army demanded Hall provide proof of his loyalty to the Union during the Civil War. He refused. A dyed-in-the-wool secessionist, he argued that the army had confiscated his property after the war and that his loyalty to the Union was therefore irrelevant. Brevet Brigadier General Alexander J. Perry apparently agreed, for he recommended that Hall be compensated for his losses regardless of his loyalty. Hall finally received payment early in 1870.[29]

In its first six months of operation, the Burial Corps interred the remains of 2,442 soldiers at Fredericksburg National Cemetery. By the time it finished, less than two years later, it had buried the remains of more than 15,000 men.[30]

No detailed account of the Fredericksburg Burial Corps's operations has yet come to light, but it probably followed procedures similar to those employed at Chickamauga. When searching an area, a witness there observed, "a hundred men were deployed in a line a yard apart, each examining half a yard [*sic*] of ground on both sides as they proceeded. Thus was swept a space five hundred yards in breadth. Trees were blazed or stakes set along the edge of this space to guide the company on its return. In this manner the entire battlefield had been or was to be searched." When searchers came upon a grave, the entire line stopped until a team came forward to remove the body. "Many graves were marked with stakes, but some were to be discovered only by the disturbed appearance of the ground. Those bodies which had been buried in trenches were but little decomposed, while of those buried singly in boxes, not much was left but bones and dust."[31]

At Petersburg, the Burial Corps divided into teams, each led by a scout. The scout located graves in his sector, supervised the disinterment of the remains, and attempted to identify them. Each team placed the remains it found in rough coffins made of yellow pine and sent them to Petersburg for burial. If it found a headboard with the remains, it nailed the board to the coffin to help officials later identify the soldier. The scout oversaw transportation of the remains to the national cemetery, supervised their interment there under the guidance of the cemetery superintendent, and recorded all information pertinent to their recovery and burial.[32]

## Identifying the Dead

Identifying the dead could be a daunting task. Many soldiers had been buried in mass graves or had not been buried at all. Even those fortunate enough to receive a marked grave often had their wooden headboard burned for fuel by local residents.[33] The U.S. Army did not issue dog tags in those days, and few soldiers purchased them with their own funds. Consequently, the identities of 83.5 percent of the Union soldiers buried at Fredericksburg are unknown, and information on many of the remaining 16.5 percent is incomplete or in error. By contrast, 45.5 percent of Union soldiers interred nationwide by 1870 were unknown.[34]

The Burial Corps did its best to identify the remains. Its first task was to determine if a soldier had belonged to the Union or the Confederate army. That was relatively easy. Samuel Weaver supervised the interment of Union soldiers at Gettysburg National Cemetery and described the process.

In the first place, as a general rule, the rebels never went into battle with the United States coat on. They sometimes stole the pantaloons from our dead and wore them, but not the coat. The rebel clothing is made of cotton, and is of a grey or brown color. Occasionally I found one with a blue cotton jean roundabout on. The clothing of our men is of wool, and blue; so that the body having the coat of our uniform on was a pretty sure indication that he was a Union soldier. But if the body were without a coat, then there were other infallible marks. The shoes of the rebels were differently made from those of our soldiers. If these failed, then the underclothing was the next part examined. The rebel cotton undershirt gave proof of the army to which he belonged. In no instance was a body allowed to be removed which had any portion of the rebel clothing on it. Taking all these things together, we never had much trouble in deciding, with infallible accuracy, whether the body was that of a Union soldier or a rebel.[35]

At Fredericksburg the procedure was much the same. When a soldier's remains were found at the Bloody Angle in 1922, a quartermaster supply officer instructed Superintendent Frederick Wagner "to inspect said remains and if you are satisfied by such evidence as army button or scrap of uniform that the remains are those of a diceased [*sic*] Union Soldier you will have them placed in a suitable box, removed to the cem[etery] and properly interred."[36]

Once burial crews determined that a grave belonged to a Union soldier, they carefully searched the remains for clues to his identity. "They were discovered in various ways," remembered Weaver. "Sometimes by the pocket diaries, by letters, by names in Bible, or Testament, by photographs, names in pocketbooks, descriptive list, express receipts, medals, names on some part of the clothing, or on belt, or cartridge-box, &c., &c."[37] Members of Fredericksburg's burial parties used similar methods. Private Thomas Elam explained to Hayes A. Walker, the son of a deceased soldier, that "it Gave me Great pleasure indeed to Examine very Close all bodies found and see if i Could not Identify them and if so i would write to their friends and inform them where the body Could be found as I would have liked for the same thing to be done by my remains if i had been so Unfortunate as to be Killed during the war." In the case of Walker's father, Elam had found a packet of letters on the body, giving the owner's name and regiment.[38]

Information gleaned from a soldier's headboard, clothing, or belongings was frequently incomplete. A headboard might contain a soldier's name but not his unit, for instance, while a letter found in a soldier's pocket might contain his initials and regiment but no name. In an effort to fully identify such individuals, Superintendent Charles Fitchett in 1874 sent information on partially identified soldiers to adjutants general in the Northern states, asking them to compare clues found on the bodies with information located in the their files. Unfortunately, his efforts yielded little new information.[39]

Clerical errors complicated matters still more. In one early register, a cemetery clerk made two copies of the burials in division D, section C. In the first list, he identified one soldier as C. H. Jones; the second time around he identified the same man as A. H. Jones. More egregious was an error pertaining to grave #160. In that case, the clerk initially identified the man as George Dwayne. When copying the list at a later date, he listed the man's name as George Sawyer. Such errors were common, but we should not judge too harshly. Transcribing thousands of names by hand was mind-numbing work, and even the most diligent clerk was bound to make mistakes.[40]

Officials in the Quartermaster General's Office, by contrast, had no excuse for their carelessness. On several occasions, cemetery superintendents wrote to their superiors complaining of errors. Names were misspelled, units were misidentified, dates of death were wrong, and information on soldiers' discharge papers did not match that in the grave registry. It was all very maddening. "Discrepancies of this kind cause error in inscriptions on head stones," complained one frustrated superintendent, "and I wish to avoid trouble of this nature."[41]

The Burial Corps began its work at Fredericksburg in June 1866 and finished by the fall of 1868. An inspection of Fredericksburg National Cemetery conducted on October 21, 1868, found a total of 15,128 interments.[42] Its task completed, the Burial Corps disbanded in 1868. One year later, on April 1, 1869, the last military troops left Fredericksburg too. For the first time in eight years, the area would be free of Federal troops.[43]

# 4. ✦ The Creation of Fredericksburg National Cemetery

revet Major Hiram F. Gerrish's supervisors in the Quartermaster Department wisely ignored his proposal to create four new national cemeteries in the Fredericksburg area in addition to the two already existing in the Wilderness. Instead, they ordered the construction of a single large cemetery at Fredericksburg, where workers would have easy access to river, rail, and road transportation. But exactly where in Fredericksburg would it be? And what would be its design? Fredericksburg had a small but vocal Unionist community that had strong views on the matter. As early as October 1865, they advocated creating a cemetery on the fairgrounds at the foot of Marye's Heights and erecting a soldiers' monument there. The confiscation of the Agricultural Fair Grounds by the U.S. Army brought that plan closer to fruition. But then Brevet Lieutenant Colonel James M. Moore weighed in. Moore was the Quartermaster Department's regional representative on matters pertaining to national cemeteries. On May 23, 1866, he informed Quartermaster General Montgomery C. Meigs that the Agricultural Fair Grounds land was unsuitable for burials. The water table there was just three feet below the surface of the ground, and the site was subject to runoff from the nearby heights. He recommended instead that the government place its cemetery on Willis Hill, at the southern end of Marye's Heights.[1]

Moore's proposal to build a cemetery on Willis Hill did not sit well with local Unionists, who continued to press the secretary of war to locate the cemetery on the city's Agricultural Fair Grounds. They argued that the fairgrounds were the most logical place for the cemetery since many of Union dead were already buried there and would not have to be moved. In addition, the fairgrounds offered ample space for a large cemetery, stood in full view of both the railroad and the town, and could be purchased from a Union man at a cheap price. Willis Hill, by contrast, was "almost out of sight of the town" and was ground on which Union soldiers "did not fight." If we read between the lines, their real objection to Willis Hill seems to have been its distance from the town. They wished to antagonize local residents by erecting a huge

Brevet Lieutenant Colonel
James M. Moore. *National
Archives, Washington, D.C.*

monument on the plain that would constantly remind them of the North's
ultimate triumph. A monument placed atop Marye's Heights simply would
not have the same impact.[2]

The *Fredericksburg Ledger* supported their view. In an article published on
June 8, 1866, the Unionist newspaper opined that "the Fair Grounds would
have been a much more appropriate spot for the Federal dead, as it was there
they made their ensanguinary effort to capture the heights." Willis Hill, on
the other hand, had been a Confederate stronghold in both the Fredericksburg
and Chancellorsville campaigns. As Southern soldiers had died defending
the hill, it seemed more appropriate that they, rather than Federal soldiers,
be buried there.[3] Unfortunately, Secretary of War Edwin M. Stanton did
not see it that way. A practical man, Stanton saw no sense in constructing
a cemetery on ground with a shallow water table. He authorized Moore to
build the cemetery on Willis Hill, as proposed. Disappointed at not getting
their way, the local Unionists scrapped their plans for a soldiers' monument.

Willis Hill had a long history of human habitation. In the eighteenth
century the Willis family had constructed a cemetery and several buildings
there. Although the buildings did not survive the 1862 and 1863 fighting, the

cemetery was still intact. The Willis family sold the hill to Robert S. Chew and John S. Wellford in 1821. Wellford took exclusive possession of the property in 1830; when he died in 1852, his executor deeded the property to John Howison. Howison held onto the land for just two years before selling it to William M. Mitchell in 1854. In 1860, on the eve of the Civil War, Mitchell's trustee sold the property to Douglas H. Gordon.[4]

In 1867, Congress authorized the secretary of war to purchase land needed for national cemeteries. If the government could not agree with the owner on a price, Congress authorized the secretary to confiscate the land, paying the owner its appraised value as later determined by a court of law. Using that authority, Moore condemned eight acres of Gordon's 23.5-acre tract, offering to pay him $125 an acre for the land. Gordon initially agreed to the price but later thought better of the deal, offering instead to sell the government the entire 23.5-acre tract for $300 an acre. The army rejected the offer, deeming the property to be worth no more than $150 an acre. Gordon reduced his asking price to $200 per acre, but he refused to go any lower.[5]

The two sides had reached an impasse. According to its congressional mandate, the army was obliged to settle the dispute in a court of law. However, the army's inspector of cemeteries warned his superiors against such a course. The court's decision would hinge on the appraised value of the property, he explained, and it would be difficult for the government to get a fair appraisal in Virginia. As an example, he pointed to Culpeper National Cemetery, where the government recently had to pay $250 per acre for land that was worth no more than 20 percent of that price. The government had been gouged once; the inspector did not want that to happen again. To avoid such an outcome, he advised Secretary of War John Schofield to settle out of court. Schofield took his advice, agreeing to pay Gordon $250 an acre for 12.005 acres of land—a total of $3,001.25. The parties formally signed the deed on November 5, 1868.[6]

## The Cemetery Design

Construction of Fredericksburg National Cemetery began in June 1866, two and a half years before the government formally settled its claim with Douglas Gordon. While workmen spaded the ground, engineers staked out the design.[7] The cemetery has eleven sides and is asymmetrical in shape. Its northern and eastern sides are relatively straight, whereas the southern and western sides, following the contours of the winding bluff that overlooks Hazel Run, are broken and irregular.[8] The plateau, which rises one hundred feet above the surrounding plain, has gentle undulations but is reasonably level.[9] Its southern and eastern slopes, by contrast, fall sharply away and are subject to erosion after heavy rains. An inspector, visiting the site in 1882, thought the cemetery "the most picturesque spot I have yet visited."[10]

The War Department originally condemned just eight acres on the summit of the hill. To prevent erosion, however, it took possession of the hill's eastern slope about a year later, cutting it into parallel terraces—eight north of the entrance road and nine south of it.[11] The terraces are between eight and ten feet tall with terrepleins at their bases measuring between fourteen and seventeen feet in width. Once they created the terraces, workers carefully sodded the hillside and placed brick gutters at the foot of each terrace to carry away excess water.[12]

The cemetery entrance stands at the northern end of the east wall, leading onto what was then called the Spotsylvania Court House Road. Within the cemetery gate, a carriageway leads to a crest. Halfway up the hill, the carriageway divides, creating a triangular, grassy plot unoccupied by graves. The two branches continue up the hill in opposite directions until they reach the

Distant view of Marye's Heights showing rows of cedar trees bordering the steps on the front slope of the hill and buildings on the far right. *Historic Fredericksburg Foundation, Inc.*

plateau. Once there, they run along the brow of the hill in opposite directions until they reach the enclosing wall. The road branches then run along the inside of the wall until they meet, thus encircling the plateau.[13]

According to the National Cemetery Administration, most national cemeteries created after the Civil War "were variations on a circular plan or a square or rectangular grid," featuring "a central flagpole and burial sections defined by paths, roads, and graves."[14] Fredericksburg National Cemetery neatly fits that description. At the top of Willis Hill, engineers laid out a series of grassy avenues at right angles to one another. The avenues dissect the property into parcels known as sections. Although the sections themselves are uniform in neither size nor shape, their graves lie in parallel rows.[15] Near the center of the plateau, at the intersection of two avenues, engineers constructed a circular mound for the flagstaff. At the southern end of the property was a second, larger mound that was set aside for a future soldiers' monument.[16]

## The Original Identification System

When the army first built the cemetery, it did not assign individual numbers to the graves. To make it easier to locate a specific plot, officers divided the graves on the hill's plateau into four divisions. Division A stood in the cemetery's northeast quadrant, division B in the northwest quadrant, division C in the southwest quadrant, and division D in the southeast quadrant. They then subdivided each division into smaller parcels called sections. (For the purposes of this volume, parcels will be identified by the division letter followed by the section letter. For instance, division A, section C, will be shown as parcel AC.) Their plan seems to have been to have four sections per division, with the sections arranged in the shape of a square. Section A of each division would stand at the center of the cemetery, closest to the flagstaff (marked below by the letter *X*), while section D of each division would stand at the cemetery's four corners, farthest from the flagstaff. Sections B and C would occupy the remaining two positions. The resulting pattern looked like this:

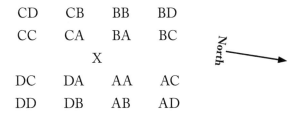

Under this plan, the easternmost parcels—DD, DB, AB, and AD—should have encompassed graves on the eastern slope of the hill. However, the decision to construct terraces there prompted the army to identify graves on the hill slope by terrace rather than by section. Consequently, sections DD, DB, and AD do not exist. Section AB does exist but at a different location, as described below.[17]

At the same time that it eliminated the four easternmost parcels, the army added two tiny sections on the rolling ground between parcels CC and CD. In an effort at continuity, officials designated those sections CE and CF. At the same time, they added a new parcel at the far western end of the cemetery, adjacent to parcels BB and BD. Logically, they should have called this section BE, or possibly EA, but logic played no part in the decision. Instead they identified the new parcel as division A, section B, despite the fact that it stood apart from the other sections in that division. When all was said and done, division A had three sections (A through C), division B had four sections (A through D), division C had six sections (A through F), while division D had just two sections, lettered A and C. The result was an organizational jumble (see fig. 4.3).

From the beginning, certain sections had distinct characteristics. Those that lay along the cemetery's north wall (AC, BC, and BD) contain both known and unknown graves culled from multiple battlefields. Unknown graves occupy nearly every plot in parcels AB and CE. Most soldiers buried in sections AA and DA died at Fredericksburg, while most of those buried in parcels CD, CE, and CF perished at Spotsylvania. Sections BB and CB, by contrast, largely contain soldiers originally buried in Stafford County. Parcels BA and CA are notable for having plots with ten, eleven, or even twelve skeletons in them, while ninety-two of the ninety-five graves in section CD contain precisely four bodies.[18]

Avenues originally separated the sections, but following the Spanish-American War cemetery officials began putting graves in some of the avenues. Beginning around 1898, they filled up the short avenues that separated parcel CD from parcel CE, and parcel CE from parcel CF. Then, in 1920, they began filling the longer north-south avenue that separated parcel CA from CB, parcel BA from BB, and parcel BC from BD. Consequently, these sections, which once enjoyed distinct borders, now merge.

With America's entry into World War II, the army began searching for additional places to bury its dead. It asked the National Park Service to submit

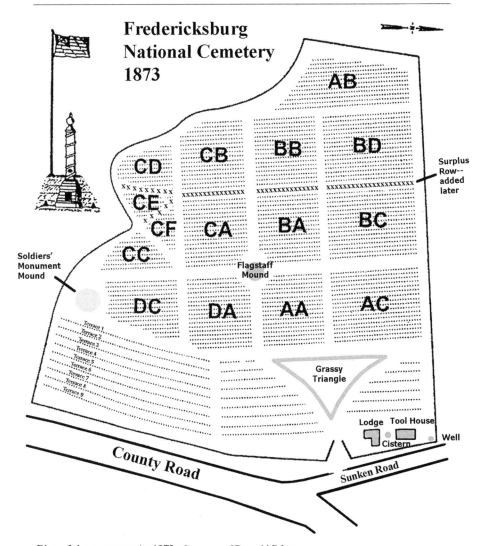

**Fredericksburg National Cemetery 1873**

AB

CD    CB    BB    BD

Surplus Row-- added later

CE
CF    CA    BA    BC

CC

Soldiers' Monument Mound

Flagstaff Mound

DC    DA    AA    AC

Terrace 1
Terrace 2
Terrace 3
Terrace 4
Terrace 5
Terrace 6
Terrace 7
Terrace 8
Terrace 9

Grassy Triangle

Lodge   Tool House
Cistern              Well

County Road

Sunken Road

Plat of the cemetery in 1873. *Courtesy of Donald Pfanz.*

a list of plots available in the national cemeteries that the agency administered. In response, Fredericksburg and Spotsylvania County National Military Park identified 104 unused grave sites: 72 of them stood at the site originally set aside for a soldiers' monument, 19 stood along the west wall in parcel CD, 10 stood along the west wall in parcel AB, and the remaining three stood near the north wall, where an avenue once separated parcel BD from parcel BC. The army used few, if any, of these plots.[19]

## The Carriageway and Avenues

Fredericksburg National Cemetery has three types of roads. The main carriageway begins at the front gate, divides at the triangle, and then circles the plateau, running along the inside of the enclosure. Inside the carriageway a series of avenues run at right angles to one another, dividing the cemetery into sections. Finally, two steep roads—called the North Road and the South Road—run along the edge of the terraces, adjacent to the brick wall. The North Road was particularly important, for at one time it provided the only legitimate access to the maintenance buildings.

When they were first constructed, the carriageway and avenues were fifteen feet wide and paved with gravel.[20] Despite having brick drains on either side, the main carriageway washed out after heavy rains, creating gullies up to 150 feet in length on the hill's eastern slope. The steep 1:5 grade of the slope was to blame. So too was the high volume of carriage traffic, which cut ruts into the soft surface. One cemetery inspector thought Fredericksburg's drives were more heavily used than those of any cemetery he had visited.[21]

Sometime between 1878 and 1880 the army scattered soil over the gravel avenues and seeded them with grass. The only surface left in gravel was a short walkway running from the main gate to the lodge.[22] Cemetery inspector James Gall Jr. had great hopes for the new grassy surface. He believed the avenues would sport a handsome carpet of grass as early as the summer of 1884.[23] Unfortunately, his optimistic prediction did not pan out—at least not as far as the main carriageway was concerned. In 1884, Major C. W. Foster reported that runoff on the cemetery's steep eastern slope, combined with surface drainage from the lodge, had created gullies in the carriageway below the point where it forked. Even at the top of the hill, the grass was not taking hold. Foster reported stretches of up to fifty feet in length where there was no vegetation whatsoever. Superintendent Charles Fitchett earlier opined that the army had spread too little soil over the gravel surface, but Major Foster believed heavy carriage traffic was to blame. To support his theory, he pointed to the side avenues. Carriages were forbidden there, he noted, and the grass was doing well. His solution was to pave the lower end of the carriageway and ban vehicles from the grounds.[24]

Civil engineer W. H. Owen inspected the cemetery in 1886. Although he did not support Foster's prohibition on carriages, he did agree that the carriageway leading up the hill should be paved. "The grade is steep & the gravel washes badly," he reported. "It is expensive to keep in order & seldom looks well." Owen recommended paving the carriageway with small cobblestones from the entrance gate to the crest. In addition, he suggested installing a drainage basin at the point where the road forked. Rather than washing out the road, water running down the slope would enter the basin and leave the cemetery by means of a pipe placed under the carriageway. Owen's superiors adopted his suggestion regarding the drainage basin, but they resisted recommendations to pave the carriageway. As late as 1909, the lower third of the carriageway surface consisted of a curious mixture of stone, gravel, clay, and and ashes. Only in later years would concrete be added.[25] Meanwhile, the rest of the cemetery was undergoing changes that would improve its appearance and give it the permanence that it had hitherto lacked.

# 5. ❀ Toward a More Permanent Cemetery

When the Quartermaster Corps first set about the task of interring the dead, speed was its foremost consideration. Economy was second. The U.S. government had hundreds of thousands of soldiers to bury, and it wanted to inter them as quickly and cheaply as possible. It should come as no surprise, then, that early structures at Fredericksburg and other national cemeteries were made of wood, a material both cheap and easy to find. Unfortunately, wood rots. Untreated wood rots quickly. Within five years, cemetery superintendents throughout the country were reporting that their fences, lodges, stairways, and headstones—even their gutters—needed to be replaced. Faced with the prospect of making such replacements every five years, the government decided on a wise, if expensive, course of action: it would replace the cemeteries' wooden elements with ones made of brick, stone, and iron   materials that would last. Between 1871 and 1875, Fredericksburg National Cemetery underwent a major facelift that ultimately saved the government money and gave the cemetery the appearance that it enjoys today.

## Enclosing the Cemetery:
## The Cemetery Wall and Front Gate

When it first created Fredericksburg National Cemetery, the army enclosed it with a whitewashed picket fence to keep out pigs, dogs, cattle, and other animals that might disturb the graves. It did not work as well against horses. On either side of the gate the fence was just three feet high, leading Superintendent Charles Fitchett to complain that horses frequently jumped over it "trampling flowers, drains and hedges."[1] Although the fence was primarily functional in nature, it was not without adornment. At the entryway stood two massive gateposts made of cedar, ornately chiseled to look like stone. Connecting the gateposts was a rounded arch inscribed "National Cemetery" surmounted by an urn. That gate stood several yards farther west than the current one—at a point roughly opposite the walkway that now leads to the

Early view of the cemetery showing the steep terraces, picket fence, one-story wooden lodge, and original flagstaff. *Harper's Weekly Magazine, October 26, 1867.*

Original gate and flagstaff. *Courtesy of Jerry and Louise Brent.*

cemetery lodge. It may have been the inspiration for the gate at Fredericksburg Confederate Cemetery, which it closely resembled.[2]

The army replaced both the fence and the gate within ten years. In 1873, Superintendent Fitchett wrote that the wood had decayed to the point where nails would no longer take hold. On the south side of the cemetery, earth had washed out from under the fence, creating holes large enough for pigs and hogs to enter, while on the east side the ground was so soft and spongy that the lower terrace had twice washed down into the public road. Major Oscar A. Mack corroborated Fitchett's assessment. In a report submitted one month later, the inspector wrote that "the fence is in poor condition, the posts being very generally rotten."[3]

Recognizing the need for a more durable barrier, the Quartermaster Department solicited bids from contractors to build a new enclosure of stone, iron, or brick. It awarded the contract to Fredericksburg businessman George W. Wroten, who began work on the wall in September 1873.[4] According to the terms of the contract, Wroten was to build a brick wall seven feet high and approximately three thousand feet long. Included in the price were four cut stone gateposts, two small iron gates, and one large iron gate. He was to begin work no later than October 1, 1873, and to complete the job in five months. For his efforts, the government agreed to pay him $2.64 per lineal foot, or roughly $8,000.00.[5]

Wroten began work on the wall in September 1873. Before construction began, civil engineer G. D. Chenoweth surveyed the lot and staked out lines for the new enclosure. Chenoweth oversaw Wroten's contract for the Quartermaster Department, and he held the contractor's feet to the fire. He condemned 430 feet of the wall's foundation because the contractor had used inferior brick, compelling Wroten to rebuild it. Later, when Wroten's crew broke the existing picket fence, Chenoweth demanded that they treat it with greater care. And when they damaged the gravel avenues and brick gutters, Chenoweth urged the Quartermaster Department to charge the contractor for the repairs.[6] Chenoweth's most frequent complaint was the contractor's lack of progress. According to the terms of the contract, Wroten should have completed the wall by February 28, 1874, but he was only halfway finished when the deadline passed. Chenoweth attributed the delay to the contractor's lack of energy. "I think Mr. Wroten will bear a great deal of pushing," he informed Quartermaster General Montgomery C. Meigs.[7]

Wroten's performance improved in 1874 despite several challenges. Because of the steep slope of the ground, the wall along the south side of the cemetery had to be built in short sections vertically offset from one another. And be-cause of the sharp escarpment and loose soil there, the foundation along the south wall had to be deeper than normal—as much as six feet into the earth. "It will not be safe to build it in any other way," Chenoweth informed his superiors. More unstable still was the soft blue clay along the eastern wall. To reach solid ground there, Wroten had to dig down fully seven feet. When he did so, water percolating down the hill seeped into the foundation trench, filling it with water. To drain off the water, Chenoweth recommended placing a two-inch tile pipe in the bottom of the trench that would carry the water into a ditch along the Spotsylvania Court House Road.[8]

By the fall of 1874 the wall was finished and Wroten was ready to install the new gate. At Chenoweth's instructions, he moved the gate a few yards east, to its present location. Simpler than the original gate, the new portal featured four gray granite columns in the shape of thick obelisks, each standing five feet eight inches high.[9] Between the columns hung four wrought-iron gates. The center portal was eight feet six inches wide and featured a double gate that was used for vehicular traffic. The side portals featured single gates, three feet ten inches wide. Although both were designed for pedestrian use, the southern gate appears to have gone out of use by the early 1900s. A photograph taken in 1903 shows a walkway leading up the hill from the northern gate. The southern gate has no such path, suggesting that then, as now, it served a purely decorative function.[10] Sometime after 1906 the army affixed to the center gateposts small shields, probably made of bronze and bearing the words "U.S. National Cemetery." It applied gold leaf to them in 1912 and again in 1922. One shield remains in place to this day.[11]

Wroten completed the project during Christmas week 1874, ten months behind schedule.[12] Within six months, problems began to appear. The con-tractor had pointed the walls with mortar made of lime. Lime absorbs water, and during the winter it expanded and cracked. By spring, pieces of mortar had started to fall out of the joints in the pillar caps and in the top three courses of the wall. The Quartermaster Department tried to get Wroten to re-point the affected areas with cement mortar at no charge, but he refused. He had warned the department about the dangers of using lime mortar when the construction project first started, but it had spurned his counsel. If the department wanted him to fix the problem now, it was going to have to pay him for it.[13]

The army made the repairs the following year, although it is unclear whether it employed Wroten to do the work. Whoever it was, he or they did not do a

Cemetery lodge and entrance gate, 1906. A decorative urn stands just inside the gate. *Fredericksburg and Spotsylvania County National Military Park.*

good job, for by 1884 much of the mortar was falling out, particularly along the coping.[14] Rather than employing a contractor to fix the problem, Superintendent Andrew J. Birdsall supervised day laborers in repairing the wall. As a former stonemason, Birdsall was fully qualified to oversee the project. When he and his workers finished the work in 1887, an inspector pronounced the wall to be "in excellent condition."[15]

Since its construction, workers have re-pointed the cemetery wall many times, most recently in 2004–5. At times, it has needed more substantial repairs. In 1942, a portion of the lowest terrace failed, knocking out a ten-foot section of the eastern wall, and on at least four occasions—once in 1920, twice in 1930, and once again in the 1990s—vehicles driving south of Lafayette Boulevard have taken the turn too fast and damaged the wall. Both of the 1930 accidents took place around Memorial Day, leading one to wonder whether the decoration of the graves may have distracted the drivers and contributed to the accidents.[16]

## The Side Gate

Over time, the earth around the graves and headstones in Fredericksburg National Cemetery settled, leaving the ground surface uneven and unattractive. To fill the unsightly depressions, the government took topsoil from a narrow strip of land it owned just outside the cemetery's west wall.[17] When it exhausted that source, it signed a five-year lease with John G. Lane for the use of a 0.75-acre parcel of land immediately north of the cemetery. Some soil excavated from Lane's land may have come from earthworks built on Willis Hill during the Civil War.[18]

Because the only entrance to Fredericksburg National Cemetery was along the Spotsylvania Court House Road, cemetery workers had to load the soil onto a cart, haul it down Willis Hill, transport it along the road, and then carry it back up a steep slope into the cemetery. To avoid this unnecessarily long and strenuous trek, the Quartermaster Department wisely decided to build a gate at the crest of the hill on the north wall. The opening, which was likely constructed in the winter of 1882–83, was twelve feet across, just wide enough for a horse and cart to comfortably pass through. A double gate made of painted wood covered the opening from 1918 until 1927, after which the army replaced it with one made of iron.[19]

## The Terrace Steps

When the army first built the terraces, they featured two sets of wooden steps, one adjacent to the south road and the other located near the center of the south terrace—the same positions that they hold today.[20] By 1873, the steps had started to decay. Inspector G. D. Chenoweth recommended eliminating the center stairway and replacing the wooden steps bordering the south road with ones made of either stone or iron. Six months later he submitted a second report in which he advocated constructing three sets of granite stairs, two on the south terraces and one on the north. Total cost for the project was $2,600.[21] That was more than his superiors in the Quartermaster Department wished to pay, however, and they asked Chenoweth to solicit estimates on brick steps. Altogether he submitted seven bids, two for granite steps and five for brick. The brick steps ranged in price from $900 to $1,600. The bids on the granite steps came in at $1,575 and $1,625, 75 percent more than the brick. His superiors went with the cheaper option.[22]

Construction of the brick steps took place in the spring of 1875. The contractor built two sets of steps on the southern terraces, replacing the wooden steps that were already there. The steps were four feet wide, ten inches deep, and nine inches high. At the same time, the Quartermaster Corps replaced the wooden steps leading from the carriageway to the plateau in front of the lodge with ones made of sandstone and extended the brick walk "so as to conform to the curvature of the main carriage-way." Plans to construct steps on the northern terraces apparently were set aside due to budgetary constraints.[23]

## Headboards and Headstones

### Original Headboards

The most important feature of any cemetery is its grave markers. Soldiers buried at Fredericksburg National Cemetery between 1866 and 1873 received rounded, wooden headboards over their graves. Identified soldiers had a grave to themselves, while most unidentified soldiers shared a grave with at least one other soldier. The tablets of identified soldiers contained their name, unit, date of death, and original burial location. Elisha Mowry's headboard was typical:

E. MOWRY

Cº F II CONN.

DECEMBER 10, 1862

REMOVED FROM

PHILLIPS FARM

More unusual was the headboard of Warrenton G. Roberts, a first lieutenant in the Twenty-Eighth United States Colored Troops:

Sacred to the Memory
of
W. G. ROBERTS
—IST LIEUT. U.S.A.—
Who departed this life March 25, 1867
at Fredericksburg, Va.
in the 20th year of his life

Several lines of text followed. Roberts had been severely wounded at the Crater, near Petersburg, losing his left hand and parts of his left arm and hip. Miraculously, he survived his wounds and became an officer in the Sixteenth

Veteran Reserve Corps. He died of consumption on March 25, 1867, at Fredericksburg. He probably knew the Union officers supervising the burials, which may explain the elaborate inscription on his headboard.[24]

Headboards of unknown soldiers gave the number of soldiers buried in the grave and identified the place from which the remains had come. Typical was a headboard [25] that read:

3

UNKNOWN

U.S.

SOLDIERS.

REMOVED FROM

FAIR GROUNDS.

Original wooden headboards. Warrenton Roberts's headboard appears in the right foreground. *Courtesy of Jerry and Louise Brent.*

If a soldier was an officer, his rank appeared on the first line of the inscription. The headboard of an unidentified captain in the Forty-Ninth New York Volunteers read:

CAPT.

UNKNOWN

__49. N.Y.V.

DIED MAY_1864

REMOVED FROM

MCCOOLS FARM

The underscoring to the left of the regiment number stood where the soldier's company should have been and indicated that the captain's company, like his name, was unknown.[26]

## *Replacing Headboards with Headstones*

In the 1870s, Fredericksburg's wooden headboards gave way to granite markers.[27] As usual, the driving force was economics. Wooden headboards exposed to the elements lasted no more than five years. As early as 1866, Brevet Brigadier General J. J. Dana reported that "public opinion seems to be turning in the direction of a more permanent mode of marking the graves than by wooden headboards." Dana firmly believed that "the sentiment of the nation will not only sustain the expense of marble or other permanent memorials, but, moreover, that it will be likely to demand it in a few years, if not now established." He felt that the Quartermaster Department should make the switch immediately, while it had a large number of officers, troops, and laborers to do the work, rather than wait for the boards to deteriorate.[28]

But the army did not heed Dana's advice, and for the next few years headboards in national cemeteries worsened. By 1873, an officer inspecting Fredericksburg National Cemetery noted that many of the boards were "a good deal decayed, and quite a number have fallen down."[29] At $1.23 apiece, the cost of erecting new headboards at Fredericksburg would exceed $8,000.00. Nationwide, the total would run upward of $70,000.00. Faced with those figures, the War Department wisely, if belatedly, chose to replace the wooden headboards with ones made of more durable materials.[30]

On May 7, 1865, Secretary of War Edwin M. Stanton appointed a board of officers to select the material and design for permanent headstones. The board recommended hollow cast-iron markers coated in zinc as the most durable and economical alternative, a solution favored by Quartermaster General Montgomery Meigs. Public opinion, however, favored stones made of marble or granite. For seven years the issue remained unresolved. Congress finally settled the matter on June 8, 1872, deciding on granite markers and amending section 1 of the National Cemetery Act to require the secretary of war to mark each grave with "a small headstone, with the name of the soldier and the name of the State inscribed thereon, when the same are known." In addition, he was to place a number identifying the plot on the stone.[31]

The Quartermaster Department calculated that it would need precisely 253,088 stones for its cemeteries throughout the nation: 147,694 granite slabs for the known dead and 105,394 granite blocks for the unknown. Virginia alone required 30,000 stones for its twelve cemeteries. Of those allotted to the Old Dominion, Fredericksburg claimed the largest share with 6,603.[32]

Congress gave the secretary of war ninety days to solicit bids for the construction and erection of the headstones. The secretary had to place advertisements in no fewer than twenty newspapers for a period of sixty successive days. Contracts at each cemetery would be awarded to the "lowest responsible bidder." To ensure that they completed the jobs satisfactorily, contractors had to post bond. Congress appropriated $1 million for the project, of which the Quartermaster Department spent just $786,360.[33]

The Quartermaster Department unsealed the bids in Washington, D.C., in September 1873. Rather than award the contract to a single company, it divided the work among several firms. At Fredericksburg, Major Edward P. Doherty of Washington, D.C., won the contract. According to the *Fredericksburg Ledger*, Doherty received $3.95 for each granite slab and $3.50 for each granite block that he produced.[34] G. D. Chenoweth, the civil engineer who had overseen George Wroten's contract for his work on the cemetery walls, supervised Doherty's work too. He copied the information written on the headboards, assigned each grave a number, and then gave the list to Doherty, who manufactured the stones.[35]

Chenoweth was a hard man to please. In March 1874 he inspected the slabs and blocks of stone that Doherty proposed using at Fredericksburg and rejected them as "wholly unacceptable." Two months later, when Doherty brought a new shipment of stones to Fredericksburg, Chenoweth recognized the stones as ones that he had rejected earlier at a national cemetery in Richmond. He rejected them again.[36]

Doherty's blocks for unknown-soldier graves did not meet the government's standards, either. Quartermaster Department officers made it clear that the blocks should be six inches square and flat on the bottom. Yet when Doherty delivered the first six hundred blocks, they were "very roughly split out . . . with very irregular outlines." Instead of being flat on the bottom, they came to a narrow point. Doherty tried to browbeat army officials into accepting them, but his bullying tactics backfired. While Major Oscar A. Mack admitted that the pointed bottoms really wouldn't make any difference, he thought the department should insist that Doherty meet the terms of the contract, if only as a matter of principle. "Had not Mr. Doherty been so persistent in trying to force upon the Govt. work that is not up to the standard required, I should feel more disposed to recommend some modification of the specifications," he wrote, "but the conditions required for the bottom of the block ought to be insisted upon." Chenoweth had rejected the entire shipment of granite blocks, and Mack supported him in his decision. "I presume this inspector has rejected some blocks that he might have passed, had the lot been generally good," explained Mack in July 1874, "but there is nothing strange in that. In some kind of Govt. supplies, when a certain percentage is bad, the whole is rejected."[37]

A couple of weeks later, Doherty delivered a new shipment of headstones to the cemetery, but Superintendent Fitchett—acting under orders from the department—refused to accept them until Doherty removed the defective stones that he had delivered earlier. Again Doherty bullied and blustered, but again the government held its ground. "When the blocks pronounced as wholly unacceptable have been removed & the number of accepted ones shall have reached 1000," the department wrote Fitchett, "the erection thereof may be commenced." Three weeks later, the issue was still unresolved. For now that is all we know, for the written record disappears.[38]

## Headstones for Identified Civil War Soldiers

Unlike the wooden headboards, the granite headstones had one pattern for identified soldiers and another for unidentified soldiers. Headstones for identified soldiers have a slab design with a slightly rounded top. They are ten inches wide and four inches deep and extend approximately one foot above the ground and two feet below it. Chiseled into the face of the stone are two lines. On the top line is the soldier's name and, if an officer, his rank. On the bottom line are letters indicating the state for which the man had fought. Rank and state designations are always abbreviated, and first names are often abbreviated as well.[39]

The manufacturer employed three types of font styles. He used capital letters for initials in a name, for the first letter of each word or name, and for each letter in the state abbreviation. He used small capitals for all but the first letter of first and last names. Finally, he applied lowercase lettering for all but the first letter of a soldier's rank. The grave number was chiseled into the top of the stone. If a soldier had a short name, it was written on the front of the stone in a straight line, parallel with the ground (fig. 5.5). But if the soldier's name (and rank) was too long to fit on the stone, masons curved the ends downward, cradling the state abbreviation between the two ends. That was fine for states like Vermont or Pennsylvania, whose state abbreviation was just two letters long. But states featuring longer abbreviations would not always fit between the curved ends of the upper line. In those instances, masons inscribed the state abbreviation below the drooping ends.

## Headstones for Unidentified Civil War Soldiers

The graves of unidentified soldiers feature a granite block, six inches square and thirty inches long. Only the top four inches—the part that appears above the surface of the ground—are finished. The top of the stone is flat and bears two numbers: a grave number and a second figure indicating the number of soldier remains buried in that plot. Headstones displaying only the grave number hold the remains of just one soldier.[40]

## Civil War–Style Headstones

No sooner had the Quartermaster Corps ordered Fredericksburg's headstones than Secretary of War William W. Belknap altered the design. In 1873, Belknap directed that future headstones feature a sunken shield in which the grave number and the soldier's name, rank, and state would appear in bas relief. Because they were ordered prior to Belknap's directive, most of Fredericksburg's headstones do not conform to this design. Only Civil War veterans buried after 1897 received the so-called Civil War design mandated by Belknap. Ironically, most soldiers at Fredericksburg who received that type of headstone were not Civil War veterans at all but men who had served in the Spanish-American War. When the square granite blocks that had formerly marked the graves of unknown Civil War soldiers were discontinued on October 21, 1903, those soldiers likewise received headstones based on Belknap's sunken shield design.[41]

## General-Style Headstones

During World War I, the War Department adopted a new style of headstone for all graves except those of Civil War and Spanish-American War veterans,

Four principal types of headstones in the cemetery: those for identified (*top left*) and unidentified (*top right*) Civil War soldiers; those with a shield emblem, used mostly for Spanish-American War veterans (*bottom left*); and the so-called general-style stones, used on the graves of World War I and World War II soldiers (*bottom right*). *Fredericksburg and Spotsylvania County National Military Park*

which continued to receive markers of Belknap's design. "General" headstones, as the new generation of markers was called, were made of white marble. They were forty-two inches long, thirteen inches wide, and four inches thick with inscriptions that featured the soldier's name, rank, regiment, division, death date, and state. Like the Civil War headstones that preceded them, the top two feet of the general headstones stand above ground, making them twice as tall as the "slab" stones erected over the graves of known Civil War soldiers and six times as tall as the granite blocks marking the unknown graves.[42] At Fredericksburg, all government-funded headstones for World War I and World War II veterans are of this design. At least five Spanish-American War veterans also received general headstones, possibly by mistake.[43]

In 1922, general-style headstones began to carry emblems identifying the soldiers' religion: a Latin cross for Christians or the Star of David for Jews. Later in the century, the government added symbols for other faiths. Circles surround the religious emblems in the older stones; in more recent ones, the circle is absent. At Fredericksburg, all general-style headstones bear the Latin cross with the exception of Walter D. Heislup (#6691), whose marker has no religious emblem.[44]

*Private Headstones*

Regulations permitted family members to erect a private headstone over the grave of loved ones so long as they received prior approval from the War Department and paid for the stone with their own funds. Fredericksburg has eighteen such stones, only two of which belong to soldiers who died in the Civil War. The others belong to veterans who died in Fredericksburg after the war, and six of those belong to cemetery superintendents or their spouses. They are located along the brow of the hill, on or adjacent to south terrace #1.

The two soldiers with private headstones who died during the Civil War are Colonel Joseph A. Moesch (grave #6618) and Sergeant Edward L. Townsend (grave #2292). Moesch's memorial will be described in chapter 7. Townsend belonged to Company I, Twenty-Fifth New Jersey. His parents erected the stone within five years of the cemetery's creation at a cost of approximately twenty-five dollars. Unfortunately, they made the marker out of limestone, and it eroded quickly. By 1927, its inscription had become so worn that Superintendent James McCall could not correctly read Townsend's first name. He recommended that the stone be replaced.[45]

Unknown to McCall, a backup was already in place. A short distance to the north, at grave #2660, is a slab-style headstone that marked the original

Two of the eighteen privately funded headstones at Fredericksburg National Cemetery. These belong to Superintendent Richard Hill (*right*) and his wife, Mary Ann, and son, Arthur (*left*). *Fredericksburg and Spotsylvania County National Military Park.*

location of Townsend's grave. Either cemetery workers left the stone in place after they moved Townsend's remains, or the private stone is simply a memorial and Townsend is still buried under the original stone. Either way, the New Jersey sergeant has the distinction of being one of just five soldiers in the cemetery to have two plots. The others are Corporal Reuben Robinson of the Forty-Eighth Pennsylvania, whose headstone marks both grave #3527 and grave #5595; Private Pierre Blondin Van Ness of the Sixty-Seventh New York, whose remains supposedly lie in both graves #5387 and #5396; Corporal William Vandyke of the 148th Pennsylvania, who has headstones at plots #550 and #3441; and Private John Collins of the Ninth New Hampshire, who is listed as being in both graves #3136 and #4279. Unlike Townsend, the names of the other four men appear twice on the *Roll of Honor*, indicating that they had two headstones from the start. Obviously, at least four of the eight graves contain the remains of other soldiers.[46]

It is ironic that five men have their names on two headstones in a cemetery where nearly thirteen thousand men lie in anonymity. Such, however, was the haphazard nature of soldier identification in the 1860s. In our modern age of dog tags, dental records, and DNA, such misidentification or lack of identification is unthinkable. During the Civil War it was commonplace.

# 6. ❧ The Superintendent's Lodge and Other Buildings

The 1870s was a period of change at Fredericksburg National Cemetery, as the original wooden elements gave way to replacements made of brick and stone. The superintendent's lodge likewise was transformed from a one-story wooden structure to a two-story structure made of stone. Other changes followed, including the addition of a cellar, kitchen, and bathroom and the installation of indoor plumbing, electricity, and telephone service. Several buildings directly behind the lodge made up the cemetery's work area; all of them are now gone except for a 1960s maintenance building. Together with the lodge it reminds us that, while the cemetery is the final resting place for the dead, it has also been a home and place of work for the living.

## The Superintendent's Lodge

Quartermaster General Montgomery C. Meigs recognized as early as 1866 the need to hire individuals to protect and maintain the country's new national cemeteries. Such men required a place to live. To that end, Meigs proposed "to erect permanent buildings of brick or stone at each principal cemetery, for the preservation of the records, & habitation of the keeper." Until such houses could be built, he authorized Brevet Lieutenant Colonel James M. Moore "to put up a temporary wooden shelter at each place for the Sexton or Watchman in charge, provided sufficient accommodation cannot be had in tents." Congress codified Meigs's decision in 1867, directing the secretary of war to appoint superintendents to administer the national cemeteries and to construct "caretaker lodges" for them. The lodges were to be placed at the cemetery entrances, where visitors could easily find them.[1]

At Fredericksburg, the original superintendent's lodge was made of vertical wooden timbers underpinned by oak cordwood. It stood just inside the cemetery gate, on the lowest terrace north of the carriage drive, near the current house.[2] Built in 1866, the wooden lodge stood for just five years before engineers moved it and the adjacent toolhouse fifty feet north to make room for a new structure made of stone.[3] The stone lodge was much heavier than the wooden one—engineers had to dig down nine feet to find solid ground on which to build its foundation[4]—and was made of sandstone blocks, some reputedly taken from the historic stone wall that bordered the Sunken Road.[5] It was built in the Second Empire style using plans designed by architect Edward Clark.[6] Originally, the building had just one story and no cellar. The roof was flat and, in the opinion of at least one inspector, was too low for its ground plan.[7]

In accordance with Clark's design, the caretaker's house had the shape of an L and contained just three rooms: a kitchen, a living room, and an office, each measuring sixteen by fourteen feet. However, early superintendents established the kitchen in the toolhouse out back, enabling them to double their living space inside the house. Between its two arms, the building cradled a porch. Originally the porch was open, but the government added a railing to its east side in the early 1900s and placed a screen around the entire porch in 1926. The screen was later removed.[8]

Conspicuously missing from Clark's design were bedrooms. Such a lodge might have sufficed for a bachelor, but for a man with a family it simply would not do. In 1873, the government contracted with Jonathan C. Comfort of Shiremanstown, Pennsylvania, to add a second story, thereby doubling the number of rooms in the house from three to six.[9] The refurbished house had a mansard roof with slate tiles.[10] Although the roofs of many cemetery lodges featured patterns formed by colored tiles, Fredericksburg's lodge did not originally have such designs.[11]

Once expansion of the lodge was completed, the superintendents and their families slept upstairs, freeing up the central room for other purposes. The kitchen remained apart from the lodge until 1881, when the government constructed a new maintenance building. At that point, the cooking stove moved to the center room of the lodge. Although the stove provided welcome heat in winter, it made the house uncomfortably hot in summer. Superintendent Charles Fitchett appealed to his superiors to create a "summer kitchen" in the new maintenance building or, better yet, to add a kitchen onto the north end of the lodge, away from the bedrooms and living quarters. The authorities did as he proposed, but not until 1905, long after Fitchett had moved on to his next assignment.[12] Once constructed, the room featured an eighteen-by-thirty-inch sink with thirty-gallon water tank and an army range for cooking.[13] Over the kitchen was a large bathroom. The room came with a bathtub and sink, but because the building lacked a sewage system it had no toilet until 1921. Other

Superintendent's lodge adorned with roses. Superintendent M. M. Jefferys and his wife stand on the porch. *Fredericksburg and Spotsylvania County National Military Park.*

additions made in 1905 included the construction of a new chimney, a large atrium window for the north room, and possibly a back porch.[14]

Central heating came to the lodge in 1929. A furnace installed that year ran on coal and utilized a thirty-gallon hot water tank. To accommodate the new system, the Quartermaster Department hired J. George Bensel Company of Baltimore to construct a cellar under the house.[15] The blueprints called for the contractor to install a coal bin on the cellar's east side, but the Quartermaster Department moved the bin to the opposite wall when Superintendent James McCall pointed out that the only access coal trucks would have to the house would be on its west side. At one time there were coal chutes on both sides of the building, though only the one on the east is now visible from the outside. The National Park Service may have covered up the western opening when it replaced the coal-burning furnace with one fueled by oil.[16]

Two sets of stairs led to the basement: an interior stairway made of wood and an exterior stairway made of concrete. The interior stairway stood directly below the steps leading to the second floor in a space today occupied by the first-floor coat closet. The exterior stairs bordered the north wall of the building's east wing and are still in use.

The last major change to the lodge took place in 1929, when the government replaced the wooden floor of the back porch with one made of cement.[17] It later enclosed the porch, creating an anteroom on the north side of the kitchen. The new room was partitioned to create two spaces: a mudroom (or laundry room) on the east side and a small toilet on the west. This change took place sometime after 1940, during the National Park Service's ownership of the property.[18]

## The Maintenance Building

In 1866, when work on Fredericksburg National Cemetery first began, the army built a wooden toolhouse behind the superintendent's lodge. The toolhouse stood just north of the lodge, in the vicinity of the current maintenance building. To make room for a stone lodge, the army in 1871 moved the wooden lodge and toolhouse back about fifty feet.[19] A map drawn in 1873 shows just one structure behind the stone lodge, however, indicating that the army had either combined the two original buildings or torn down the toolhouse. The building that remained stood north of the stone lodge, near the current maintenance building but slightly west of it—in the area today covered by the asphalt drive.[20]

The army remodeled the original wooden lodge and used it as a toolhouse, kitchen, and earth closet (privy).[21] Inspector Oliver Cox examined the structure in 1875 and was shocked to find that the earth closet was in the tool room rather than in its own separate room. To give those using the facility some privacy, he advised erecting walls around it. A brick chimney stood at the end of the building. To provide access to the earth closet, Cox recommended removing the chimney and putting a door in its place.[22]

At the time Cox wrote his recommendation, he was tearing out the cemetery's brick gutters. Removal of the drains left him with sixty thousand to eighty thousand bricks, which workers stacked outside the cemetery's rear wall. The toolhouse was getting older, and in 1879 Major C. W. Foster suggested using the bricks to construct a new building. Superintendent Fitchett heartily endorsed the proposal. Writing to the Quartermaster Department in April 1881, Fitchett noted that the log building was old and in bad condition, its frame having been weakened over the years by its transfer from one part of the cemetery to another. Even if repaired, he argued, it would not last more than a few years. The old building was an eyesore, he complained, a disgrace to the cemetery. It had served a practical purpose in earlier years, he admitted, but now that the cemetery had a "pretty Lodge, handsome Wall and beautiful grounds," the old log building simply did not fit in. More important, the building was a firetrap. Should it catch fire, Fitchett warned, embers might blow onto the stone lodge and destroy both buildings. To prevent such a mishap, he recommended that his superiors adopt Foster's suggestion and construct a new toolhouse out of bricks salvaged from the old gutters. Any leftover bricks could be used to add a brick kitchen to the lodge.[23]

The Quartermaster Department agreed to build the brick toolhouse but not the kitchen, which it moved to the center room of the lodge; the family may also have used that room for dining. It sold the log toolhouse and started work on the new brick maintenance building around October 1, 1881.[24] The new structure stood twenty-five feet north of the lodge and on a direct line with it. A tin roof sloped downward from a tall west wall to a much shorter east wall. Bordering the roof, like twin staircases, were the terraced rooflines of the north and south walls, both of which featured massive capitals. A fireplace with a tall brick chimney stood in the center. The building had three rooms: a wagon shed occupied the center position, flanked on the south by a tool room and on the north by a stable. A privy stood in the northeast corner of the building, next to the stable. Two rooms had concrete floors, and there appears to have been three windows, one apiece on the north, south, and east walls. At least one window had louvered slats. Access to the privy was by a separate door on the structure's north side. With the construction of a sewer line to the maintenance building in 1921, a sink was added and the privy was upgraded to a toilet.[25]

Thwarted in his efforts to add a kitchen to the lodge, Fitchett petitioned the Quartermaster Department for permission to establish a summer kitchen in the new maintenance building. One would think that Fitchett would prefer having the kitchen inside the lodge, but that was not the case. The stove generated a tremendous amount of heat, which radiated upward into the second-story bedrooms. While the occupants undoubtedly welcomed the additional heat in the winter months, they found it intolerable in summer. Fitchett went so far as to insist that the stove made the lodge "unfit for human habitation" in the summer and claimed that the intense heat had made each member of his family sick. To remedy the situation, he asked for permission to move the cooking stove into the tool room, at least during the summer months. The stable was empty, he argued, and the equipment in the tool room could be moved next door to the wagon shed.[26]

Fitchett's superiors rejected his request. Fredericksburg National Cemetery was scheduled to get a draft animal and cart. When that happened, the animal would stable in one room, the cart and other equipment would occupy the second room, and tools would fill the third room. There simply would be no space in the maintenance building for a kitchen too.[27] But Fitchett refused to give up. When Major Richard Arnold inspected the cemetery in May 1882, the persistent superintendent renewed his request to attach a brick kitchen to the lodge. Again he stressed the harmful effect that the stove was having on the health of himself and his family. Arnold, however, was not impressed by his arguments. "The reasons given for this additional room will apply with much more force to all cemeteries south of this position," he wrote, "and none have been asked for to my knowledge." The department again denied Fitchett's request.[28]

Although the kitchen remained in the lodge during Fitchett's tenure, his efforts bore fruit for later superintendents. By 1888, the army allowed Fitchett's successors to keep a summer kitchen in the maintenance building, a practice that continued into the twentieth century.[29] The kitchen probably stood in the south room, and because the lodge had no cellar at that time, the army permitted the superintendent's family to store personal belongings there as well. Tools and fuel were stored in the center room, while the stable and privy occupied the building's north room.[30] The building's function changed slightly over the years but not much. In response to a questionnaire issued by the Quartermaster Department in 1909, Superintendent M. M. Jefferys stated that the building was being used as an "outkitchen, washhouse, Storageroom, tool house, Stable and privy."[31] The National Park Service replaced it with the current cinder-block structure in 1960.[32]

## The Cart House and Woodshed

To make room for the summer kitchen, superintendents had to park the government dump cart out of doors. Weather was hard on the cart, though, and in 1888 civil engineer William Owen recommended building a small cart house. The 14'3" × 10'3" wooden structure sheltered the cemetery cart, lawn mowers, and fuel. Situated against the north wall, just a few feet from the cemetery's northeast corner, the building stood until 1926, when an inspector condemned the deteriorating structure and it was removed.[33]

A woodshed was adjacent to the cart house. Built sometime before 1906, this 21'9" × 9'9" wooden structure stood just north of the maintenance building, between it and the well. Workers whitewashed the building and placed a tin roof on it in 1907. The roof, like the walls, was painted.[34] The woodshed held the timber and coal necessary to heat the lodge and maintenance building.

At times, superintendents stored feed for the cemetery's horse there too.[35] But by 1922, the horse was gone and the building was no longer needed. An inspector described the woodshed as "unsightly, out of plum[b] and tumbled down" and recommended that it be replaced at once. Authorities razed the structure in the fall of 1924 and stored the wood in the maintenance building, next to the tools.[36]

## Driveway and Walkways

The 1867 "Act to Establish and to Protect National Cemeteries" stipulated that the caretaker's lodge stand just inside the cemetery entrance so that superintendents could monitor who came onto the property and offer assistance to those requiring information. At Fredericksburg, this provision was impractical because the ground inside the cemetery gate was situated on a steep slope. Nevertheless, the army built the lodge there anyway and squeezed the maintenance building in behind it. Graves crowded the buildings, approaching to within twenty-five feet of the lodge and forty feet of the maintenance building.[37]

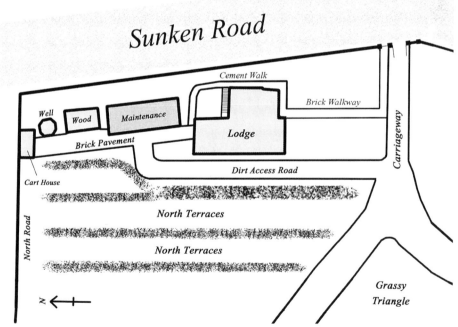

Plan of the cemetery buildings as they appeared in 1911. *Courtesy of Donald Pfanz.*

The only access to the maintenance building was by a steep road that ran along the north wall. A man could ascend the hill well enough, but it was too steep for a horse or mule to climb while drawing a cart. To reach the summit, the animal had to tread across graves immediately west of the lodge and then take the carriageway to the top. To rectify this situation, the army in December 1888 removed thirty-five graves from the terrace just above the lodge and reburied them on the next two higher terraces, inserting them between already existing graves. It then constructed a gravel road from the maintenance yard to the carriageway along the south side of the lodge. That road still exists. Unlike the current road, however, the 1889 road stopped short of the north wall, turning abruptly east at a point directly opposite the maintenance building. Not until the twentieth century did the army extend the road all the way to the north wall. Workers had to move additional graves to make room for the extension. As before, they transferred the graves to the adjacent terraces.[38]

When the army first built the cemetery, it enclosed the grounds with a picket fence. The main gate stood much farther west then than it does now, and to reach the lodge, visitors had to pass through a small portal situated just outside the main gate. In 1874, when contractors replaced the picket fence with a brick wall, they moved the main gate to its current location. A brick walkway led up the hill from the north pedestrian gate. A short distance up the slope, it made a ninety-degree turn to the right and ran back to the lodge. The walkway wrapped around the east side of the building and by 1911 terminated at a work area paved with brick, next to the back porch. The entire walkway was made of brick until about the 1890s, when cement replaced the bricks between the southeast corner of the house and the back porch. The rest of the walkway remained paved in brick until the twentieth century, when it too was changed to cement.[39]

## Utilities

### Heating

By its very nature the stone lodge was a cold, damp structure. Nearly three decades into the twentieth century, a superintendent complained that "a constant fire is necessary to make it habitable."[40] Edward Clark's plans called for each lodge to have two chimneys: one for the living room fireplace and the other for the office stove. At Fredericksburg, these corresponded to the south and east rooms. Both chimneys appear in an 1874 photograph of the lodge. At some point after 1939, the National Park Service boxed in both features with drywall and removed the fireplace chimney. The chimney for the east room's flue is still present.[41]

Curiously, Clark's plans did not indicate any source of heat for the center room, which he designated as a kitchen and which was used throughout the year as such from 1881 to 1905. Presumably superintendents heated this room by means of a stove placed against the room's south wall, the smoke of which vented through a pipe cut into the back of the office chimney.[42] That the kitchen had a stove is certain, for in 1886 Inspector W. H. Owen reported that the chimney there smoked badly as a result of it being lower than the adjacent ridge. To keep the chimney from smoking, Owen recommended installation of a hood.[43] In 1905, the army added a new kitchen on the north end of the lodge, and the center room became simply a dining room.

By 1905, then, the lodge had four rooms on the first floor: a kitchen in the north room, a living room in the east room, an office in the south room, and a dining room in the center. Just two of these rooms had a source of energy. The kitchen contained an army range for cooking, and the living room had a Latrobe stove for heating.[44] The office had a fireplace, but it may have ceased to function. In any event, it appears to have been a cold room. Upon taking charge of the cemetery in 1922, Superintendent Frederick Wagner asked his superiors to install a coal-burning stove there, but they denied his request. Regulations permitted each lodge to have one cooking stove and one heating stove, and Fredericksburg already had its allotment. Unable to squeeze an extra stove out of his superiors, Wagner switched rooms, turning the south room into his living room and making the east room his office. He was the only superintendent to adopt that arrangement.[45]

Fredericksburg superintendents used both wood and coal to heat the lodge. Each year the superintendent received four cords of hardwood and 14,450 pounds of anthracite coal.[46] In 1924, the cost for heating the lodge and the adjacent maintenance building was $156: $40 for wood and $116 for coal.[47] The cemetery's coal consumption increased with the addition of central heating to the lodge. The heating system, which had a pump, air compressor, and expansion tank, was completed in the summer of 1929. It utilized anthracite coal, which suppliers deposited into a bin located on the west side of the house. As a result of the new system, the army cut Fredericksburg's firewood allotment in half, from four cords a year to just two.[48]

## Water

Like heat, water was a necessity at the lodge. The cemetery required a good deal of water, not only for human consumption but also for watering trees and shrubs during the dry summer months. A natural spring flowed from

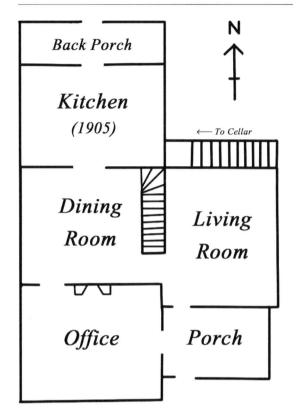

Lodge floor plan.

the ground near the eastern base of Willis Hill, but it was neither convenient nor sufficient for the cemetery's needs. In 1868 workers dug a well near the entrance, but workers destroyed it during construction of the stone lodge.[49] To replace it, the army excavated a new well in the northeast corner of the cemetery, north of the wooden toolhouse. The well appears indistinctly in the background of an 1873 photograph of the lodge.[50] Workers made the well thirty-five feet deep, curbed it in brick, and covered it with a wooden platform.[51] For almost a dozen years, it provided the superintendent and his crew with "good water," but by 1882 it was in need of repair. In that year, workers repaired the well's brick curbing and installed a new pipe and wooden pump. The following year they replaced its rotting wooden platform and constructed over it an octagonal cover, replete with latticed sides and a tin roof. An inspector considered the cover "a neat substantial structure" that "improves the appearance & convenience of the well surroundings."[52]

The well remained in use for half a century, an iron force pump replacing the original wooden pump around 1888.[53] By the 1920s, however, the well had outlived its usefulness. The cemetery had tapped into Fredericksburg's water system more than twenty years earlier, and the well was no longer used. In 1921, Superintendent Thomas B. Robinson reported that the wooden platform had rotted and fallen into the well, making its water unfit to drink. By 1923, the entire well house was in decay and the well itself had partly caved in. With the approval of his superior, Robinson's successor, Superintendent Frederick Wagner, sold the pump, demolished the well house and filled the shaft with ashes. Today no evidence of it remains.[54]

A cistern supplemented the cemetery's water supply. An inspector had recommended the construction of a cistern as early as 1871, and the army may in fact have built one at that time, for a large, round structure appears between the lodge and the toolhouse in an 1873 plat of the premises. If the unidentified feature indeed represents a cistern, however, the army must have removed it during the construction of the brick maintenance building in 1881, because the following year Major Richard Arnold explicitly stated that there was no cistern on the grounds.[55] The army rectified that deficiency six years later, constructing a new cistern on the site. Inspector W. H. Owen argued that a cistern was necessary for the health of the superintendent and his employees, as water drawn from the cemetery's well, being just fifty feet from graves, could not "afford wholesome water." The cistern held eleven thousand gallons of water and was probably built in accordance with plans drawn up by the Quartermaster Department.[56] The underground reservoir must have stood close to the brick maintenance building, as there was no other place for it, but exactly where it stood is open to conjecture. Superintendent M. M. Jefferys filled the cistern with dirt in September 1905, once city water was introduced at the lodge.[57]

The introduction of city water in 1897 ended Fredericksburg National Cemetery's dependence on wells and cisterns. Initially, water appears to have gone just to the maintenance building, but the city extended water service to the lodge in 1905 after the army added a kitchen and lavatory onto that building. The water line entered the property from the Sunken Road and ran along the northern edge of the carriageway. The pipe to the lodge branched off the main line just below the maintenance road and ran north, between the road and the lodge, until it reached a point opposite the kitchen (north room). There it entered the house and divided, one pipe filling a thirty-gallon tank in the kitchen and another running to a bathtub in the room above.[58]

City water was not without its own problems, however. Sometimes it came out of the spigot yellow, as I, a later resident of the lodge, can attest; at other times it did not come out at all. In October 1927, Superintendent James McCall complained that he had been without water all day, whining that "it is impossible for me to get along under such conditions." Three months later, the water dried up again. "In order to get any for use I have had to carry water nearly 1/2 of a mile through 6 inches of snow," McCall groused. "Your office cannot reasonable [*sic*] expect me at 62 years of age, to carry water up these steep grades. I am unable to cope with such a condition and something must be done by your office to relieve the situation." What he expected his superiors to do, he did not say.[59]

The city provided water not only for bathing and drinking but also for irrigation. During the cemetery's early years, workers had had to haul water from the well to the top of the hill—a toilsome, time-consuming task. As early as 1882, an inspector observed that the cemetery's trees and shrubs required a great deal of water during the dry summer months. "Some arrangement should be made to obtain the necessary water," he advised. "The hill from the well to the Cemetery is too steep to haul water up."[60] Although nothing seems to have been done at that time, the army later installed two water hydrants in the cemetery. One stood at the eastern tip of the triangle formed by the carriageway divide; the other stood a few yards west of the triangle's north corner. A water line entered the cemetery at the main gate and then followed the carriageway up the hill, providing water to the hydrants.[61] By 1914, just one hydrant was in operation, and it was old and in disrepair. Superintendent Robinson ordered a new hydrant, but it broke during a cold snap in February 1917. Workers got it to function, however, and it remained in operation until 1928, when the army removed it for lack of sufficient water pressure.[62]

Water also played a key role in fire safety. The loss of life and property by fire was an ongoing concern at the cemetery. One of Superintendent Fitchett's most potent arguments for construction of a brick maintenance building in the 1880s was that the existing log building might catch fire and spread flames to the adjoining stone lodge.[63] Fire was also on inspector W. H. Owen's mind a few years later. In discussing improvements to the well pump, Owen recommended purchasing a one-hundred-foot-long hose with a nozzle as protection against fire.[64] Over the years, the government bought a hose and other fire safety equipment for Fredericksburg National Cemetery. In 1920, Superintendent Robinson wrote that the cemetery owned four "galvanized water buckets, an extension ladder," and a fire ax. By then, the lodge had public water. If a fire sprang up inside the house, workers could extinguish it by hooking up a hose to the kitchen spigot. If they needed water outside the building, they could tap into a spigot located near the corner of the building.[65] Fortunately, neither method was needed. Throughout the cemetery's history, there has never been a fire.

### Sewage

Although Fredericksburg National Cemetery had public water by 1897, it did not acquire a sewage system until a quarter century later. Prior to that time, the superintendent and his family had to share a privy with cemetery workers and visitors. The privy, consisting of a wooden seat perched atop a bucket, occupied a small room in the northeast corner of the brick maintenance building behind the lodge. Lack of a proper sewage system galled Superintendent Robinson, and he frequently complained about it to his superiors in Washington, D.C.

> That you understand the necessity for this much needed improvement at the Cemetery, the present mode of disposing of excreta is here given, to wit: Droppings are deposited in buckets, wheeled across the Cemetery by laborers and dumped over the [back] wall into hole prepared to receive same. This has to be done 2 or 3 times each week and is a very unpleasant duty imposed on laborers, and for which, I have to pay extra from my own personal fund as former Superintendent[s] have done. While the Govt is supposed to own a narrow strip of land on which this dump is made, yet it must be unsightly and unpleasant to people passing that way.

To remedy the situation, Robinson urged the government to tap into the city sewer line, just one block away, and construct two toilets: one inside the lodge for the private use of the superintendent and his family, and one at the location of the existing privy for use by employees and the public. The cost for such work was $500.[66]

At first Robinson's plea fell on unsympathetic ears. "Four years ago," he complained, the quartermaster clerk "informed me that as former Superintendents had lived here under existing conditions I must get along without sewage in the Lodge and instructed me to leave the matter of sewer connection with Lodge out of estimates to be submitted in future." Robinson refused to be silent, however, and continued his crusade for a proper sewage system. His persistence paid off with the construction of a sewer pipe into the cemetery in July 1921.[67]

## *Electricity*

The last modern convenience to reach the national cemetery was electricity. As early as 1915, Superintendent Robinson recommended installation of a lighting system to replace the kerosene oil lamps then in use. Although the nearest hookup was just one block away, the lodge did not receive electricity until May 1924. Even then, just three of the four downstairs roomed were wired. Due to an oversight, the east room—the one used by most superintendents as a living room—did not receive power for three more years.[68]

## *Telephone Service*

Superintendent Robinson believed in progress. In September 1914, one year before starting his quest for indoor plumbing, he petitioned the Quartermaster Department for permission to install telephone service in the lodge. His superiors granted his request on the condition that he pay for the service himself. Robinson agreed, and telephone service was in place by 1921. The U.S. government took over payment of the cemetery's telephone service around 1930.[69]

Improvements to the superintendent's lodge in the late nineteenth and early twentieth centuries mirrored improvements taking place in the cemetery itself. Like the lodge, the grounds were austere at first, having been built with an eye toward function rather than beauty. But once the immediate task of burying the dead was complete, the army set about the task of making Fredericksburg and other national cemeteries not just places of interment but appealing places that people would want to visit.

# 7. ✤ Refinements

National cemeteries had been constructed in the 1860s to fill an immediate and pressing need: the burial of 300,000 Union dead, whose remains lay scattered throughout the South. They were thrown up quickly and with as little expense as possible. Every element served a practical purpose: the walls kept animals out of the cemetery; the headstones identified the dead; the buildings sheltered employees and equipment; and the driveways and avenues provided access. But cemeteries are not purely functional places; they are places of reflection and remembrance. That was especially true in the decades following the Civil War. Recognizing this, the U.S. government began incorporating features into the cemeteries that would give them a parklike setting. Some of these elements date to the cemeteries' earliest years while others came later, but each of them contributed to the cemeteries' dignity and beauty.

## The Flagstaff

For forty years a flagstaff stood at the center of Fredericksburg National Cemetery in the location now occupied by the Humphreys Monument. The first flagstaff rested on a small earthen mound that was six to eight feet tall and fifteen feet wide and had nearly vertical sides. A stairway with seven steps ran up the eastern face of the mound, which was surmounted by an octagonal picket fence, approximately three feet in height. The fence was white except for the top rail, which was of a darker hue. The flagstaff itself rose 125 feet above the Willis Hill plateau. It consisted of a main mast and a shorter topmast held together by a brace, known in nautical circles as a trestle tree, which was shaped like the letter *H* and supported by four guy wires. Erected by October 1867, the pole blew down in an 1873 storm, damaging the mound as it fell.[1]

To replace it, Superintendent Charles Fitchett proposed erecting a 120-foot-tall flagstaff. The pole would have two parts: an 80-foot-tall mainmast, 10 feet of which would be below the ground surface; and a 40-foot-tall topmast. The mainmast would be twelve inches wide at the bottom, tapering to six inches at the top, where there would be an ornamental ball. Fitchett proposed making the new mound seven feet tall. It would have a fifteen-foot-wide base, narrowing to ten feet at the top. The mound would have two sets of stairs, a railing around the top, and benches. Counting the height of the mound, the flagstaff would stand 117 feet above the Willis Hill plateau.[2]

The flagstaff, as actually constructed, differed significantly from Fitchett's proposal. Rather than having two masts that together measured 120 feet in height, it consisted of a single pole measuring approximately 90 feet, 10 of which were below the ground surface. The whitewashed staff had alternating pegs on either side, and it did not have an ornamental ball on top.[3]

Cemetery after the army erected the second flagstaff but before it replaced the wooden headboards, circa 1874. *National Archives, Washington, D.C.*

The Quartermaster Department hired Jonathan C. Comfort to erect the pole and repair the damaged mound. Comfort was the same contractor whom the government had hired to renovate the cemetery lodge. His work on the lodge was going badly, and it did not appear that his work on the flagstaff was going to be any better. When Comfort arrived at the cemetery with a tree for the new pole, Superintendent Fitchett noted that the wood was unsound, being "badly worm eaten . . . and . . . more sap than heart." He recommended the Quartermaster Department cancel its contract with Comfort and get someone else to finish the job.[4]

Inspector G. D. Chenoweth judged the pole to be satisfactory, but he criticized Comfort's work on the mound. According to the terms of the contract, Comfort was obliged to trim the height of the mound from six feet to four feet, reduce its width on the top from fifteen feet to ten feet, and decrease the angle of the slope so as to render it more stable. He had done none of those things. Moreover, Chenoweth complained that Comfort had not seated the pole far enough into the ground, that he had done a slipshod job in setting the cleats, and that he had installed an inferior halyard sheave.[5]

Although Comfort eventually addressed most of Chenoweth's concerns, he did so with his usual ill grace. In a letter to Quartermaster General Montgomery C. Meigs, he complained that Chenoweth's confusing verbal instructions had cost him a great deal of money and insisted that thenceforth he would take orders from Meigs alone. The quartermaster general supported Chenoweth in his dispute with Comfort, but he may have urged the zealous inspector to be more lenient with the contractor. When Chenoweth inspected the flagpole and mound again on February 18, 1874, he accepted them without complaint.[6]

Comfort's flagstaff lasted just forty months. On June 8, 1877, a storm swept through Fredericksburg, snapping it in two. Superintendent Fitchett must have derived secret satisfaction from the incident. From the beginning he had warned the department that the pole was faulty.[7] The government next contracted with Wallace Stetson to replace the pole for $100. The new pole was made of pine and stood approximately forty-five feet above the ground. Thicker and considerably shorter than its predecessor, it had a decidedly "stumpy" appearance. Moreover, the pole was out of plumb and featured wooden pegs rather than cleats. The mound itself was not changed. As before, it stood about four feet high, was about ten feet across at the top, and featured gently sloping sides.[8]

Although Stetson promised to complete the pole by Decoration Day 1878, he did not have the flagstaff in the ground until summer.[9] In the tradition of unscrupulous contractors everywhere, Stetson then tried to squeeze an extra

$22.40 out of the Quartermaster Department, claiming that the job had cost him more than he had anticipated. His efforts met with a sharp rebuke from Assistant Quartermaster J. M. Marshall. "The fact that the cost exceeded your estimate does not entitle you to any additional compensation," Marshall lectured the contractor. But even if it did, he felt that Stetson's addition charges were "exorbitant in the extreme." In submitting his bill, Stetson claimed that he had had to purchase extra equipment and hire additional men to complete the job. Marshall knew that was a lie. "I am informed by the Superintendent at Fredericksburg that you *did not* use 'Extra tackle &c,' [and] that *you did not use* any extra force . . . excepting men employed in the Cemetery; for which you paid nothing," he wrote pointedly. Needless to say, Stetson did not get the extra money.[10]

Stetson was dishonest and slow, but he did good work. His flagstaff stood until October 1905, when the government removed it in favor of a seventy-five-foot-tall, single-masted steel flagpole with ornamental balls.[11] The new flagstaff—the cemetery's fourth—stood just west of the carriageway, at the point where it crested the hill. It has remained there ever since. The Quartermaster Department probably moved the flagpole in order to make it more visible to train passengers and to people in the town.[12]

The government flew two types of flags at Fredericksburg: a storm flag and a much larger post flag that the superintendent raised on national holidays.[13] By the mid-1920s, just the storm flag was used. Under normal conditions, the flags lasted about three months. When a flag became too tattered to use, the superintendent mailed it back to the Quartermaster Depot and got a new one in return.[14]

## Gun Monuments and Cannonball Stands

Since the cemetery's earliest years, four upright Columbiad cannon tubes have adorned the flagstaff mound. The army shipped the black "gun monuments," as they were called, to Fredericksburg National Cemetery in the fall of 1868. They must have been erected soon after, because they needed a new coat of paint by the summer of 1871.[15] The cannon tubes were set out in the shape of a square and stood about thirty feet from the northeast, southeast, northwest, and southwest corners of the flagstaff mound. They have never been moved.

In 1874, the Quartermaster Department affixed a bronze plaque in the shape of a shield to the southeast cannon monument. It bears the following inscription:

UNITED STATES
NATIONAL MILITARY CEMETERY
FREDERICKSBURG.
ESTABLISHED JULY 15TH 1865.
INTERMENTS 15243.
KNOWN 2473.
UNKNOWN 12770.[16]

In addition to the gun monuments, the flagstaff area featured four stands of twenty-four-pounder cannonballs. Each stand had a white wooden base and was four tiers high. Installed in the late nineteenth century, the cannonballs stood on the northeast, southeast, northwest, and southwest edges of the flagstaff mound, mirroring the cannon monuments. A driveway circled the mound. The gun monuments stood on the outside of the circle; the cannonballs stood inside of it. The cemetery received eighty-four projectiles in all.[17]

The cannonball stands remained in place until the twentieth century, at which point things began to change. A photograph taken early in the century seems to show the stand of cannonballs in the northeast corner reduced to just two tiers.[18] On top of the pyramid is a twenty-four-pound ball, while the three balls underneath it appear to be from a twelve-pounder gun. A photograph taken about the same time shows no cannonballs at all.[19] The army may have transferred the missing projectiles to the Fifth Corps Monument. Erected in 1901, the monument was flanked by four stands of twenty-four-pounder round shot, each three tiers high. They remain there to this day.[20]

In 1905, officials moved the flagpole from the center of the cemetery to its present location at the brow of the hill. They removed the center mound and the cannonball stands that surrounded it, erecting two stands of twelve-pounder round shot at the base of the new flagstaff.

## Lawn Seats

Benches, or lawn seats, were another early feature of Fredericksburg National Cemetery. Wooden pew-like seats appear in early photographs of the flagstaff mound that were taken in the early 1870s. Within ten years, the cemetery received a set of benches featuring delicate cast-iron frames with wooden slats. They appear in many of the old photographs, often in an avenue, near a monument, or arrayed along the brow of the hill. At one time there may have been as many as a dozen lawn seats, but over the years the number diminished.

In the 1990s the National Park Service took the four remaining benches from the cemetery and moved them to Chatham, an eighteenth-century house alongside the Rappahannock River.[21]

## Signs

Fredericksburg National Cemetery has always had signs. Some carried practical messages; others featured poetry. Early photographs of the cemetery entrance show three signs: a small one affixed to a post situated on the terraces to the left of the carriageway; a somewhat larger sign nailed to a small tree near the brow of the hill, inside the triangular plot created by the carriageway fork; and a huge sign, with a rounded top, that stood inside the triangle at the point where the carriageway divided. Although none of the signs is legible, it is likely that the large sign contained the cemetery regulations and that another contained verbiage from section 3 of the 1867 act that established and protected national cemeteries.[22]

Some of the earliest signs in the cemetery featured stanzas from George Meitike's 1861 patriotic poem "The Stripes and the Stars." Measuring perhaps three feet wide by two feet high, one placard read:

> Invincible Banner! the Flag of the Free!
> O, where treads the foot that would falter for thee?
> Or the hands that would be folded 'till triumph is won,
> And the eagle looks proud, as of old, to the sun!
> Give tears for the parting, a murmur of prayer,
> Then forward, the fame of our standard to share!
> With a welcome to wounding and combat and scars,
> And the glory of death for the stripes and stars.[23]

A second sign bore a different stanza:

> Oh! wrap him in that banner proud,
> To keep whose honor bright he died,
> None other fit for soldier's shroud,
> Than our flag of stars—our nation's pride.
> And lay his sword down by his side,
> His work is well and nobly done,
> Our flag to day floats high with pride,
> The glorious battles dearly won.[24]

These signs stood at the northwest and southwest corners of the square opening that now surrounds the Humphreys Monument. Interestingly, they stood among the graves rather than in the adjacent avenue. Just as surprising, both signs appear to be angled inward toward the mound rather than facing due west like the headboards around them.[25]

Sharing the cemetery with "The Stripes and the Stars" were signs containing the words of John Kells Ingram's poem "The Memory of the Dead." The author, a twenty-year-old student at Trinity College in Dublin, wrote the lines in 1843 to honor Irish freedom fighters of 1798. U.S. government employees altered the words and combined portions of two different stanzas to make the poem applicable to the fallen soldiers of the Union.[26] A placard that stood approximately fifty yards south of the flagstaff bore the following words from Ingram's verse:

> They rose in dark and evil days
> To right their native land
> Then kindled here a living blaze
> That nothing shall withstand;
>
> Then here's their memory, may it be
> For us a guiding light
> To cheer our strife for liberty
> And teach us to unite![27]

Although we can positively identify just two Meitike signs and one bearing lines from Ingram's poem, there undoubtedly were more. Early photographs of the cemetery show placards adjacent to each of the four cannon monuments and one on the west side of the avenue that divided section CA from section CB.[28]

In the 1880s, cemetery officials replaced Meitike's and Ingram's poems with cast-iron signs featuring stanzas from Theodore O'Hara's poem "The Bivouac of the Dead." O'Hara had written the verse in 1850 to honor soldiers of the Second Kentucky Regiment who had died fighting in the Mexican War battle of Buena Vista. Eight years later, he published it in his newspaper, the *Mobile Register*. An instant hit, the poem soon appeared in newspapers throughout the country.

O'Hara had been a U.S. Army officer in the Mexican War, but during the Civil War his allegiances took him in a different direction. In 1861 he offered his services to the Confederacy, serving on the staffs of Generals Albert Sidney Johnston and John C. Breckinridge.[29] Ignoring the loyalties of the poem's author, Northerners began posting "The Bivouac of the Dead" stanzas in national cemeteries throughout the country.[30] In 1881–82, the War Department formalized the practice, ordering the Rock Island Arsenal, in Illinois, to fabricate cast-iron tablets of the poem "to take the place of notices, verses, &c., on painted signboards which had become unsightly and were too costly to renew as frequently as required." As a result of this order, "The Bivouac of the Dead" became the official poem of national cemeteries throughout the country.[31]

Signs bearing stanzas from O'Hara's poem appeared in Fredericksburg National Cemetery shortly after that. A photograph taken late in the nineteenth century shows two such signs, apparently without bases, resting on either side of the carriageway, just above the future location of the Fifth Corps Monument. A different photograph, taken about the same time, shows another tablet of this type on the plateau, affixed to a short, stocky signpost. In all, Fredericksburg National Cemetery had no fewer than ten such placards, embracing seven different stanzas of the poem; six of those signs adorn the cemetery yet.[32]

At one time there were as many as twenty-two signs in the cemetery, but by 1909 that number had dropped to fifteen. In addition to the ten "Bivouac of the Dead" tablets already mentioned, one sign contained the text of General Orders No. 80, and four signs quoted excerpts from section 3 of the 1867 act for creating and maintaining national cemeteries.[33] General Orders No. 80, published in 1875, restricted access to the cemetery to daylight hours, prohibited picnicking within the cemetery enclosure, and confined the speed limit for vehicles to a walk. Section 3 of the 1867 act cited the penalties for vandalizing cemetery property, destroying trees and shrubs, or desecrating graves, and it authorized cemetery superintendents to arrest and bring charges against anyone suspected of such a crime. Although the signs featuring General Orders No. 80 and the 1867 act have disappeared, identical versions of them are on display thirty miles away at Culpeper National Cemetery, Virginia.

A 1906 photograph shows the location of several signs. The tablet featuring General Orders No. 80 stood at the point of the grassy triangle, where visitors could not help but see it. The sign bearing section 3 of the 1867 act stood on the north side of the main carriageway at a point just below the maintenance road. Two "Bivouac of the Dead" signs are visible in the image, one on each branch of the main carriageway, perhaps ten yards uphill from the General Orders No. 80 tablet.[34]

A smaller, less substantial sign stood at the base of a decorative urn, near the point where the lodge walkway left the pedestrian walkway. It read, "Visitors are invited to enter the Office in the Superintendent's lodge where a register is kept and where information concerning this cemetery will be cheerfully given." Inside the office were framed copies of three additional signs: a copy of the national cemetery regulations, a blueprint of the Fredericksburg National Cemetery grounds, and a copy of Lincoln's Gettysburg Address.[35] The text of the Gettysburg Address likewise appeared on a bronze tablet affixed to the cemetery lodge's south wall, next to the porch. The Rock Island Arsenal shipped the tablet to Fredericksburg in July 1909, and Superintendent Jefferys affixed it to the lodge wall on December 17 of that year. It has never been moved.[36]

## Monuments

Just five months after General Robert E. Lee surrendered his army at Appomattox Court House, a group of Union "officers and soldiers, loyal citizens and refugees" met in Fredericksburg to discuss plans for erecting "a suitable Monument on the plain, in rear of town, to commemorate the heroic deeds of our officers and soldiers who have fallen on this historic ground in defence of their country." Joseph Williams was the interim president of the organization, and Charles W. Tankersly was its secretary. The group invited the public—particularly Union veterans who had fought at Fredericksburg—to attend a mass meeting in Fredericksburg in October for the purpose of organizing a monument association. Three Unionist citizens joined Major Henry Terwilliger and Lieutenant Henry Ryan of the First Mounted Rifles on the Committee of Arrangements.[37]

The group did its job well. On October 12, 1865, several hundred soldiers and loyal citizens assembled on the plain below Marye's Heights and organized themselves into the Soldiers Monument Association. To ensure that local citizens opposed to the monument would not stir up trouble, two companies of infantry and one company of cavalry monitored the event.[38] Tankersly and Brigadier General Thomas M. Harris addressed the crowd from a speaker's stand erected for the occasion. The association's purpose, they explained, was to collect the remains of the Union dead at Fredericksburg, deposit them in the Wallace icehouse on the plain west of town, and construct a stone column over the site. After Tankersly and Harris had finished speaking, the association took a collection for the monument and elected officers. The crowd chose General Harris as president, Colonel C. Moffit and Joseph Williams as vice presidents, Tankersly as secretary, and John R. Elvans of Washington, D.C., as treasurer. Secretary of War Edwin M. Stanton, Secretary of the Interior

James Harlan, and Generals Ambrose E. Burnside, Joseph Hooker, and Daniel Sickles served on the board of directors.[39]

Despite the large gathering and the impressive list of backers, the project came to naught. Within six months, the federal government announced its intention of creating a national cemetery at Fredericksburg, relieving the Monument Association of the responsibility for reburying the dead. The government established the cemetery on Willis Hill and constructed a circular mound at the southern end of the cemetery as a base for the soldiers' monument, but it was never used. Vexed that the army had built the cemetery on Willis Hill rather than on the plain below, the Monument Association withdrew its support from the project and disbanded.[40]

## Moesch Monument

A quarter century passed before Fredericksburg National Cemetery got its first monument. On September 24, 1890, veterans of the Eighty-Third New York Volunteers traveled to the town to dedicate a monument over the grave of their former commander, Colonel Joseph A. Moesch, who had died in the May 5, 1864, fighting in the Wilderness. Moesch's body had been buried in an unmarked grave at James Horace Lacy's plantation, Ellwood, and remained there until October 1887, when Superintendent Andrew J. Birdsall and two members of the Eighty-Third exhumed the body and reburied it in the national cemetery. Three years later, members of the regiment traveled to Fredericksburg and dedicated a monument over the remains.[41]

## Fifth Corps Monument

The cemetery's first monument was erected by many to honor one; the second monument was erected by one to honor many. On May 25–26, 1900, the Society of the Army of the Potomac held its thirty-first reunion at Fredericksburg—the first such meeting to be held in the South. On the first day of the reunion, Union veterans gathered at the national cemetery to lay the cornerstone for a monument honoring the Fifth Corps, whose soldiers had attacked Marye's Heights in 1862. The monument stood south of the carriageway, just inside the front gate.

General Daniel Butterfield, who had commanded the Fifth Corps at Fredericksburg, privately funded the monument. Unfortunately, the general's failing health prevented him from attending the ceremony. In his absence, Lieutenant Colonel Edward Hill of the Sixteenth Michigan and Secretary of War Elihu Root committed the monument to the care of the Fredericksburg

Fifth Corps Monument, funded by its former commander, General Daniel Butterfield. He did not live to see its completion. *Fredericksburg and Spotsylvania County
National Military Park.*

and Adjacent Battlefields National Park Association. Union veterans formally dedicated the monument in 1901.[42]

### 127th Pennsylvania Monument

The Fifth Corps Monument was the first of four cemetery monuments dedicated to military units. The second one came five years later with the dedication of the 127th Pennsylvania Monument. A nine-month regiment, the 127th Pennsylvania participated in just two battles, both at Fredericksburg. Veterans of the regiment and their guests—220 people in all—traveled to the town in June 1906 to watch Governor Samuel W. Pennypacker of Pennsylvania convey title of the monument to General Ezra A. Carmen, representing the U.S. government.[43]

### Humphreys Monument

Two years later, in 1908, veterans dedicated another monument to Pennsylvania troops: General Andrew A. Humphreys's division of the Fifth Corps. Humphreys had commanded eight regiments at Fredericksburg, each hailing from the Keystone State. To honor these men, the Pennsylvania legislature appropriated $23,500 for a monument and hired sculptor Herbert Adams to craft it. In a fit of largesse, it even offered to pay the transportation costs of any honorably discharged veteran of the division who wished to attend the dedication. As a result of the legislature's generosity, three thousand people attended the November 11 unveiling. The monument stands at the center of the plateau in the location previously occupied by the cemetery flagstaff. Arguably the finest memorial in Fredericksburg and Spotsylvania County National Military Park, the Humphreys Monument has become not only the cemetery's centerpiece but also its symbol.[44]

### Parker's Battery Memorial

The most recent monument erected in Fredericksburg National Cemetery was dedicated in 1973. It honors the men of Captain William W. Parker's Virginia battery, which defended Marye's Heights during the Second Battle of Fredericksburg. The monument has several distinctions: it is the only Confederate monument in Fredericksburg National Cemetery; it is the only monument in Fredericksburg and Spotsylvania County National Military Park dedicated to a Virginia military unit; and it is the only monument connected to the Second Battle of Fredericksburg. Thomas Brown McCune, a descendant of a battery

Humphreys Monument, constructed in the center of the cemetery, on the spot previously occupied by the flagstaff. It is the cemetery's most recognized feature. *Fredericksburg and Spotsylvania County National Military Park.*

officer, funded the small marker. He dedicated it on May 3, 1973, 110 years to the day after Parker's men lost two guns defending the Heights.[45]

## The Rostrum

Fredericksburg National Cemetery originally had two mounds: a small one for the flagstaff, located in the center of the cemetery, and a larger one meant to support a soldiers' monument. The second mound stood adjacent to the south wall, near the current site of the Parker's Battery Memorial. When plans for the soldiers' monument fell through, the army removed the mound and planted a small copse of trees in its place.[46]

Meanwhile, Memorial Day was growing in popularity. To provide its speakers with a proper venue, the government in 1888 constructed a rostrum near the southern brow of the hill. Octagonal in shape, the rostrum was covered with vines and had steps on the southeast side. Although it was standing as late as 1927, no pictures of it have yet come to light.[47] However, the rostrum at Poplar Grove National Cemetery, which still stands, provides evidence of how it may have looked.

## The Decorative Urn

Among the final elements to be added to the cemetery was a decorative urn that stood on the east side of the walkway that ran between the carriageway and the lodge. The urn first appears in a photograph of the lodge taken in 1906, but as Superintendent Jefferys mentioned painting the urn in 1907, it was probably in place prior to that time. The clearest image of the urn, taken in 1939, shows a two-foot-wide bowl with two elaborately curved handles resting on a stone pedestal. It last appears in a photograph taken around the 1950s.[48]

## Hitching Posts

Prior to the advent of the automobile, most people came to the cemetery on a horse or in a horse-drawn carriage. A metal hitching post featuring a horse's head stood next to the Sunken Road, a few feet north of the pedestrian gate. It is still there today. An identical post stood inside the cemetery, at the point where the maintenance road left the main carriageway. That post has disappeared. Both hitching posts had a large rectangular stone block at their base to assist visitors alighting from their carriages. Superintendent Jefferys installed the posts in May 1907.[49]

# Trees, Shrubs, and Flowers

*Trees*

Fredericksburg National Cemetery had few trees or shrubs when the army began burying soldiers there in 1866. Whatever trees had existed prior to the Civil War vanished when Confederates occupied the area in the winter of 1862–63.[50] Fredericksburg was not alone in that regard; most other national cemeteries throughout the country lacked greenery too. Congress addressed the situation in 1870, appropriating $20,000 to landscape national cemeteries. At Fredericksburg, the Quartermaster Department used the money to plant hundreds of trees and bushes.[51]

Growing trees on Willis Hill during Virginia's hot, dry summers was a challenge. Many withered and died. Although the army tried to replace them, it could not keep up. By 1876, inspector James Gall Jr. found Fredericksburg National Cemetery "exceedingly bare of trees." Gall petitioned his superiors in the Quartermaster Department for funds to purchase three hundred new ones, offering to personally supervise their planting. Just two years later, the army had to move several of the trees because they interfered with the lawn mowers.[52]

The army planted additional trees in the late 1870s and early 1880s. About half the trees were deciduous; the rest were evergreens. The deciduous trees included elms, maples, silver poplars, chestnuts, and ashes, while the evergreens consisted mostly of hemlocks, pines, cedars, and spruces. Once they took root, the trees thrived and grew, aided by liberal applications of manure and compost. The cemetery staff pruned the trees and inspected them regularly for harmful insects, such as worms and bores.[53]

In all, the army planted more than one thousand trees in Fredericksburg National Cemetery. It followed a predetermined design but not very rigidly. For instance, evergreens ran along the inside of the enclosing wall, but only on the southern and western sides. Along the north wall, deciduous trees mixed with the evergreens, and trees alternated with shrubs. Lines of trees marked the boundaries of each section. Inside each parcel was a smattering of trees and shrubs—mostly pines or cedars but occasionally leafy trees as well.[54]

The trees on the terraces likewise followed a distinctive pattern. Evergreens bordered the stairways; otherwise, evergreens and deciduous trees alternated—one and then the other—in vertical rows that started at the top terrace and ran down the eastern hill slope with military uniformity. On the southern terraces alone there were no fewer than twenty-five rows of trees, not counting four rows that bordered the steps.[55]

The greatest concentration of plant life was in the triangle formed by the fork in the carriageway and at the southeast corner of the plateau, the area later occupied by the rostrum. The army had purposely left those areas free of graves, and cemetery personnel later filled the voids with trees and shrubs. Unfortunately, nature killed the trees as fast as the army planted them. Snow, sleet, and ice destroyed trees in the winter, while windstorms claimed victims year-round. The elms and the chestnuts fell to disease, and fires from lightning strikes scorched the cedars. The cumulative impact of these hazards was devastating. By 1934, just 197 trees remained—fewer than 20 percent of the number that had been present just forty years earlier.[56]

## Hedges

The earliest and most visible plant in Fredericksburg National Cemetery was the Osage orange hedge. Planted in 1871 on the inside of the picket fence that circled the grounds, the hedge acted as barrier to keep out dogs, pigs, and other animals that might root up the graves.[57] The hedge became superfluous two years later when the Quartermaster Department erected a brick wall around the premises. At that time contractors removed the hedge, leaving only the part that ran inside the east wall.[58]

The surviving portion of the hedge extended on both sides of the carriageway. North of the carriageway, it ran between the east wall and the maintenance building. Across from it, on the west side of the maintenance building, was an arbor vitae hedge. Five feet wide, the arbor vitae hedge ran along the base of the bottom terrace in a line with both the terrace and the building. It was still living as of 1937.[59] Despite an inspector's recommendation in 1888 that it be torn out, the Osage orange hedge continued to thrive for many years. As late as 1907, Superintendent Jefferys noted that it was still growing along the wall in rear of the maintenance building. The government finally removed it sometime before 1942.[60]

Boxwood hedges also grew in the cemetery. A 1906 photograph shows a twelve-foot-tall hedge running along the length of the porch, on its east side, screening the superintendent and his family from vehicles in the roads below. That same photograph shows a three-foot-tall hedge running from the maintenance road entrance to the lodge walkway, then turning northward to a point opposite the decorative urn. On the other side of the lodge walkway, a line of small boxwoods ran from the urn south to the pedestrian walkway and then down the slope to the carriageway entrance. The purpose of these bushes was to create a hedge east of the lodge walkway that mirrored the one west of it. Although it took nearly half a century, the hedge finally grew in.[61]

## Vines

Most national cemeteries had hedges running along the inside of the enclosing wall. At Fredericksburg, rows of trees replaced the hedges. However, it took several years for the young trees to mature. In the meantime, the Quartermaster Corps softened the visual impact of the wall by planting vines along the wall's inner face. This was done around 1882. Later, Superintendents Andrew Birdsall and M. M. Jefferys planted vines around the rostrum too.[62]

## Rosebushes

In addition to its trees, hedges, and vines, Fredericksburg National Cemetery featured a variety of shrubs. Although they were scattered throughout the cemetery, the shrubs seem to have abounded in the triangle that stood between the carriageway forks and in the area immediately south of the rostrum. Most of the shrubs appear to have been either roses or oleanders. A shrub resembling a rosebush climbs an entrance gate pillar in an 1873 photograph, and early twentieth-century photographs show flowering shrubs that may be rosebushes on the south side of the carriageway and on the flagstaff mound.[63] Superintendent Birdsall recorded planting several rosebushes in 1890 and 1891, and Superintendent Jefferys planted a rosebush at the grave of Lieutenant Colonel Thomas E. Morris in 1908. A photograph taken about that same time shows rose vines growing on the southern and eastern walls of the lodge and overhanging the porch. The vines had been trained to resemble garlands. Fredericksburg National Cemetery continued receiving new rosebushes from the Quartermaster Department into the 1930s. Unfortunately, none have survived.[64]

## Flowers

Colorful flowerbeds greeted visitors to Fredericksburg National Cemetery. Each spring, usually in May, the Quartermaster Department forwarded a large shipment of flowers to Fredericksburg from its greenhouses at Arlington National Cemetery.[65] In 1921, it sent Fredericksburg five different types of flowers—165 plants in all. Superintendents potted the flowers and planted them in beds outside the lodge and in the triangle created by the carriageway fork.

At one time or another, zinnias, geraniums, dahlias, hyacinths, and tulips all blossomed within the cemetery walls.[66]

Some national cemeteries created flowerbeds with fanciful geometrical shapes, often corresponding to the corps insignias of soldiers who were buried there. Fredericksburg may have done the same. The earliest map of the cemetery shows beds shaped like hearts, six-pointed stars, and Maltese crosses inside the triangle created by the carriageway fork. Another flowerbed stood just inside the cemetery gate, to the left of the carriageway, where the army later placed the Fifth Corps Monument.[67] By the 1920s, the cemetery had just two flower-beds: a heart-shaped bed located on the slope beneath the 127th Pennsylvania Monument and a circular bed in front of the lodge. Both were planted in tulips. In addition, two floral borders stood somewhere near the lodge.[68]

The army's annual shipment of flowers to Fredericksburg ceased when the National Park Service took over administration of the cemetery in 1933. Shortly thereafter, work on the flowerbeds ceased.

### Greenhouse and Hotbed

To raise the plants needed to adorn the cemetery, the army constructed a greenhouse on the property in 1873.[69] The structure was eighteen feet wide and twenty-four feet long with a four-foot-high, thirteen-inch-thick brick base supporting the white frame and glass superstructure. At its peak, the building stood approximately twelve feet high.[70]

Greenhouse, built by the army in 1873, adjacent to the lodge. Deemed an eyesore, it was removed within six years. *National Cemetery Administration, Washington, D.C.*

Local businessman George Wroten built the greenhouse for $792.16, beginning work in the early fall of 1873.[71] Wroten planned to subcontract construction of the structure's wooden frames to a Baltimore firm, but when the company quoted him a price higher than expected, he decided to make the frames himself. Gathering the necessary material and finding laborers capable of making the frames proved difficult in a small town like Fredericksburg, however, and he did not complete the job until November.[72]

Rather than build the greenhouse behind the toolhouse, in the northeast corner of the cemetery, the army chose to put it just inside the gate, between the carriageway and the lodge. It could not have picked a worse location. The building dominated the entrance, detracted from the beauty of the lodge, and blocked the ornamental triangle located above the carriageway fork. Nevertheless, the army cultivated flowers inside the building for four years. It discontinued the practice in 1877 and removed the greenhouse a year or two later.[73]

In its place it built a hotbed adjacent to the cemetery's north wall, a few feet west of the side gate.[74] The purpose of the hotbed was to keep bulbs alive throughout the winter months.[75] Like the greenhouse, it had a brick base supporting a wooden frame. By 1917, the wooden members had rotted and the glass panes had disappeared. Superintendent Robinson considered the hotbed "unsightly, impracticable and not needed." Rather than fixing it, he recommended that it be torn down.[76] Robinson could not make this decision himself. Like all national cemetery superintendents, he operated under the distant but watchful eye of his superiors in the Quartermaster Department.

# 8. ❊ Cemetery Employees

Fredericksburg National Cemetery initially belonged to the Third Quartermaster District, Department of the East. Starting at the top, the chain of command was as follows:

Secretary of War (Washington, D.C.)
Quartermaster General (Washington, D.C.)
Chief Quartermaster, Department of the East (New York)
Chief Quartermaster, Third Quartermaster District (Philadelphia)
Assistant Quartermaster, Third Quartermaster District (Fort Monroe, Va.)
Superintendent, Fredericksburg National Cemetery (Fredericksburg, Va.)

This arrangement changed over time. In the 1920s, Fredericksburg's superintendents reported to the quartermaster supply officer, Washington General Intermediate Depot, at Twentieth and "C" Streets, N.W., Washington, D.C. Ten years later, jurisdiction over the cemetery passed to the commanding general, Third Corps area, at 311 St. Paul Street, Baltimore.[1]

Quartermaster Department officers kept a tight rein on the cemeteries within their districts. Superintendents could not take any unusual action or make the simplest purchase without first obtaining approval from higher quarters. Inspectors acted as the department's eyes and ears. Made up of field officers (majors or lieutenant colonels) or civil engineers working under contract with the government, the inspectors made unannounced visits to Fredericksburg National Cemetery at least once a year. After examining the grounds and meeting with the superintendent, they submitted succinct but comprehensive reports describing the condition of the cemetery and making recommendations for its improvement. Their influence on the development of the cemeteries cannot be overstated.

## Superintendents

Day-to-day administration of Fredericksburg National Cemetery fell to its superintendent. In 1872, Congress directed the secretary of war "to select the superintendents of the national cemeteries from meritorious and trustworthy soldiers, either commissioned officers or enlisted men of the volunteer or regular Army, who have been honourably mustered out or discharged from the service of the United States." Applicants were selected based on a variety of factors, not least of which was neat handwriting and sobriety, with disabled soldiers receiving first consideration.[2]

Before becoming a superintendent, applicants underwent apprenticeship at a national cemetery. Fredericksburg served as the training ground for at least three future superintendents: a man named Brown in 1878, Oscar Wright in 1908–9, and W. H. Kiger in 1914. For six months, these "assistant superintendents" worked alongside the maintenance crew cutting grass, raking leaves, straightening headstones, and doing other chores. At the same time, they learned the administrative side of the business from the superintendent. When they had successfully completed six months of training, the Quartermaster Department assigned them a cemetery of their own.

Superintendents in the nineteenth century received a salary of between sixty and seventy-five dollars per month "according to the extent and importance of the cemeteries to which they may be respectively assigned." Fredericksburg, being one of the largest national cemeteries in the nation, had "First Class" status and rated the full seventy-five dollars.[3] In addition to their salary, superintendents received free lodging and fuel. However, they were on duty seven days a week and got little in the way of time off. If they wished to leave town, they had to apply to the Quartermaster Department for permission to do so and supply a caretaker to watch over the cemetery in their absence at no expense to the government. Not until the 1920s were they granted annual leave.[4]

The superintendent was the cemetery's overseer and manager. He supervised the work of employees; solicited bids from contractors; ordered and purchased supplies; directed visitors to gravesites; and maintained records on disbursements, burials, and official correspondence. In addition, the army required him to submit a wide range of reports. He turned in quarterly property returns, estimates of supplies, and condition reports; monthly interment reports; and biweekly time sheets. In addition, he submitted an annual budget, made periodic reports on the government roadway, and did odd jobs around the cemetery. His most important job, however, was to safeguard the cemetery and its property. A superintendent had to live at the cemetery and could not leave the premises unattended at any time, even to go to church. Because of these stringent requirements, he had to coordinate his activities with those of his family and employees to ensure that someone was always on the grounds.[5] Superintendents were not just watchdogs but also law enforcement officials. Congress granted them authority to arrest anyone caught willfully committing vandalism inside the cemetery and to bring them to justice. Fortunately, at Fredericksburg they never had to exercise that responsibility.[6]

Superintendents sometimes transferred between cemeteries, commonly staying at one place from six to twelve years before moving on. Promotions were based on efficiency ratings. Superintendents usually began their career at a Third Class cemetery and then worked their way up the ladder to administer a First Class cemetery like Fredericksburg. Like National Park Service superintendents today, they could lobby for a particular assignment, but there was no guarantee they would get it.[7] Being Union veterans, many of the early superintendents preferred to serve at cemeteries in the North. Gettysburg National Cemetery, in particular, was considered a plum assignment.[8]

The quartermaster general issued transfer orders to several superintendents at once. The first superintendent on the list relieved the second, the second superintendent relieved the third, and so on until the rotation was complete.[9] Of course, such an orderly transfer of authority was not always possible. Deaths, resignations, and other circumstances often forced a superintendent to leave a cemetery before his replacement arrived. In such instances, the Quartermaster Department appointed a temporary superintendent to act in his stead. Normally, officials selected a long-term cemetery laborer for the job, but in at least one instance they chose the superintendent's son. The acting superintendent received the pay and benefits of the full-time superintendent during the period that he served. Fredericksburg had at least seven acting superintendents who held the office from a few days up to five months.[10]

Leaving Fredericksburg was not always easy. Some superintendents, like Charles Fitchett, Andrew Birdsall, and M. M. Jefferys, became active members of the community and made many friends there. When they departed, the residents genuinely missed them. "Fredericksburg has so far been fortunate in the selection of the Superintendents of her beautiful National Cemetery," wrote the editor of the *Fredericksburg Free Lance* in 1892. "They have been gentlemen who have easily assimilated with the people, and between them quickly grew a feeling of kindness and attachment."[11]

## Fredericksburg National Cemetery's Superintendents

Between 1867 and 1940, Fredericksburg National Cemetery had fourteen superintendents. Most appear to have been conscientious men, attentive to their duties.[12] The list below gives the years that each man served as superintendent at Fredericksburg; his name, rank, and regiment; and the nature of his disabling wound, if known, and the battle where he sustained it.

1867–70    Edward H. McMahon, first lieutenant, Eightieth New York. Wounded in the left thigh at Battle of Second Manassas resulting in the amputation of his left leg.[13]

1870–83    Charles L. Fitchett, private, Eleventh Pennsylvania Cavalry. Shot in the right arm at Battle of Reams's Station.[14]

1883–92    Andrew J. Birdsall, corporal, Second New York Heavy Artillery. Wounded at Second Deep Bottom.[15]

1892–95    Thomas D. McAlpine, second lieutenant, Company 13, Second Battalion Veterans Reserve Corps. Shot in the heel at Battle of Antietam while serving as a private in the Second Massachusetts.[16]

1895–1901  Richard B. Hill, private, Second Ohio Heavy Artillery. No information on the location or nature of his wound.[17]

1901–3     William Dillon, private, Second New Hampshire. Wounded at Gettysburg.[18]

1903–4     Harrison C. Magoon, corporal, Second Company, Minnesota Sharpshooters. Captured at Reams's Station and imprisoned at Salisbury, North Carolina, where he suffered from debilitation.[19]

1904–14    Melker Jefferson Martin Jefferys, private, Fifteenth West Virginia. Shot in the right hand at Battle of Lynchburg necessitating removal of his lower arm.[20]

1914–22    Thomas B. Robinson, corporal, Tenth Illinois Cavalry. No information on the place or nature of his wound, although he is reported to have worn a double truss later in life.[21]

1922–25    Frederick E. Wagner, private, Fourth Pennsylvania Artillery. Did not serve in the Civil War. Retired from military service in 1912 due to an unspecified disability.[22]

1925–30    James W. McCall, private, Second Battalion Engineers. Served in the Philippine Insurrection and in Cuba. No record of disability.[23]

1930–31    William K. Sump. No information.[24]

1932–40    George Nelson, first lieutenant, Texas Coast Artillery. No record of disability.[25]

1940–45    Emmet H. Sacrey. Served in Army Medical Corps in World War I. No record of disability.[26] Worked for the National Park Service from 1945 until his death in 1963.

Thomas McAlpine, Frederick Wagner, and George Nelson died while serving at Fredericksburg. Wagner and Nelson are buried in the cemetery, as are three earlier superintendents: Andrew Birdsall, Richard Hill, and Thomas Robinson. McAlpine's family buried his remains in Arlington National Cemetery.[27]

## Other Employees

In addition to its superintendent, Fredericksburg National Cemetery had a staff of as many as three seasonal laborers. Most cemetery laborers worked six days a week, Monday through Saturday.[28] Often at least one employee had to come in on Sundays and holidays too, if only to raise and lower the flag and to feed the cemetery's horse or mule.

Workers' duties varied with the season and the circumstances. During the growing season, between April and October, they would plant flowers, trim shrubbery, cut and rake grass, trim around headstones, prune trees and vines, maintain buildings and signs, make repairs to National Boulevard, and other such work. Once it got cooler they would cut down trees, haul dirt and sand, grade the grounds, fill sunken graves, saw wood, straighten headstones, and spread manure on the grounds. These were their official duties. In addition, they did a number of unofficial chores for the superintendent and his family. For instance, they would watch over the cemetery in the superintendent's absence, help him hitch up the horse and carriage, and run private errands for him if, for instance, there was any prospect of lifting or the like. In short, they helped their disabled chief do things that he could not do for himself.[29]

All the employees appear to have been white, and at least three were Confederate veterans. William H. Hogan and Thomas F. Proctor had both served in the Thirtieth Virginia Infantry during the Civil War, and Robert

C. Hart had been a member of the Twenty-Fourth Virginia Cavalry. Hogan, Proctor, and Hart were among Fredericksburg's last surviving veterans, dying respectively in 1921, 1933, and 1934. Although each man worked at the national cemetery for several years—in Hogan's case upward of twenty—not one of their obituaries noted the connection.[30]

## Animals and Equipment

Maintaining the grounds at Fredericksburg National Cemetery required a great deal of equipment. Workers needed lawn mowers to cut grass, sickles and scythes to trim around headstones, rakes and baskets to collect leaves, saws to cut dead limbs from trees, wheelbarrows to haul dirt and manure, shovels to dig graves, and rollers to smooth the ground. When equipment became unserviceable, it might be shipped back to the quartermaster supply officer in Washington, D.C., and replaced by new equipment, sold at public auction, or destroyed.[31]

A horse or mule was indispensable for cutting grass and hauling heavy loads. Initially the government had no place to stable a public animal and had to rent one locally. The construction of the brick maintenance building in 1881 solved that problem, however, and within a year the Quartermaster Department purchased a mule. Inspector James Gall Jr. predicted that the animal would be a great boon to the superintendent and his staff. "The mule recently furnished to the Cemetery is a fine animal and will be of great use on the place," he wrote. "All the hauling of soil, manure, and other materials, and the operating of the lawn mower, will now be done by the Govt. animal instead of by one hired at considerable expense and not always obtainable when most needed."[32]

A horse named Bill replaced the mule around the turn of the century. It consumed approximately four thousand pounds of hay, four thousand pounds of oats, and twelve hundred pounds of straw each year. Like its predecessor, the new animal hauled sod, sand, gravel, and other heavy loads in the government cart and pulled the large mower used to cut grass on the cemetery plateau. Cemetery superintendents also used the horse to take carriage rides into town. Bill worked faithfully until 1914, when his health deteriorated and he had to be sent away. For a while cemetery workers hired an animal to take his place, but in 1920 they disposed of the horse mower altogether and adopted seventeen-inch-wide, gas-powered push mowers to cut the grass. At one time they had as many as six such mowers, although just two of them worked. They received a riding lawn mower in 1928. For trimming around headstones, workers still relied on sickles and scythes.[33]

## National Boulevard

Planting flowers, cutting grass, trimming headstones, raking leaves: these were fundamental tasks of cemetery employees throughout the country regardless of where they served. However, the men at Fredericksburg had an additional responsibility that most of their colleagues did not share—one that extended beyond the confines of Willis Hill into the town itself—for they had to maintain not only a cemetery but also a road.

Prior to the Civil War, travelers heading south from Fredericksburg had to use either the Bowling Green Road, which ran along the Rappahannock River, or the Telegraph Road, farther west. The Telegraph Road left Fredericksburg at Hanover Street and angled west, then south, along what are now Kirkland Street, the Sunken Road, and Lafayette Boulevard. Many wagons coming north into town along the Telegraph Road turned east after crossing Hazel Run and headed across country to the train depot or to the city dock. Over time this shortcut became known as the Telegraph Road Cutoff.[34]

In 1856 developers started selling lots for Mercer Square, a subdivision situated at the foot of Marye's Heights. To provide direct access into Fredericksburg from Mercer Square, they planned to extend Frederick Street westward across the Narrow Gauge Railroad to the Telegraph Road, thus making the Telegraph Road Cutoff an actual street. Buyers for the Mercer Square lots were scarce, however, and by 1861 only two buildings—the Hall and Jennings houses—stood along the western end of Frederick Street, which itself remained unpaved. Although the road is clearly visible in an 1863 photograph of the Fredericksburg Battlefield, it does not appear on any Civil War–era maps, and few soldiers took notice of it.[35]

When the Civil War ended, interest in the Mercer Square development revived. A plan devised by Carter M. Braxton in 1867 shows Frederick Street running between the town and the subdivision, as it had a decade before.[36] In 1891 the federal government took possession of that portion of Frederick Street north of the Narrow Gauge Railroad to provide direct access to Fredericksburg National Cemetery from the train depot. Rather than linking it to Frederick Street, south of the railroad, engineers angled the road—which they called National Boulevard—slightly northward, connecting it to Prussia Street, on the northern side of the tracks. Mr. James Snyder of Sharpsburg,

Maryland, actually built the road.[37] When Germany fell into disfavor during World War I, the city fathers changed the name of Prussia Street to Lafayette Street. National Boulevard was simply an extension of Lafayette Street, and before long people began referring to it as Lafayette Boulevard.[38]

Altogether National Boulevard ran for a distance of 3,500 feet. It began at Princess Anne Street, on the east, and ran to the national cemetery, on the west. Some 3,105 feet of roadway fell within the Fredericksburg city limits; the remaining 395 feet were in Spotsylvania County.[39] Although the public did not appreciate the difference, the segment of Lafayette Boulevard between Princess Anne Street and the national cemetery remained a separate entity until the mid-1920s. Up to that time, the federal government owned the road and was responsible for maintaining it. As the government's local representative, Fredericksburg National Cemetery's superintendent exercised direct oversight over the road. Cemetery workers made minor repairs, as necessary, and the superintendent solicited bids from local contractors to do work that was beyond his crew's abilities.[40] Along the roadside, from Willis Street to the Court House Road, formerly the Telegraph Road, the government planted twelve Norway maple trees.[41]

The federal government paved the road in 1896 at a cost of $2,000. Made of crushed limestone, the macadamized surface was 25 feet wide. Cobblestone gutters bordered the road. In 1909 authorities added a concrete sidewalk on the road's north side, and in 1915 it replaced the cobblestone gutters with ones made of concrete. In 1916, the government resurfaced the road again, widening that part that was within city limits to 60 feet. Three years later, it widened the 395 feet of road on the Spotsylvania side of the line and laid water, sewer, and gas lines along it.[42]

By then, National Boulevard had become part of Route 1, the main highway on the Eastern Seaboard. Local traffic, lumber trucks, and travelers heading up and down the coast quickly wore potholes into its surface. The Virginia State Highway Commission re-graveled National Boulevard in 1920 with the permission of army officials, but the potholes returned within two years.[43]

That the federal government owned and maintained a half-mile stretch of busy highway struck Superintendent Thomas Robinson as absurd. In 1920, he recommended the government convey its ownership of National Boulevard to the state of Virginia. The Virginia State Highway Commission felt the same way, and in 1922 it requested that the federal government relinquish the macadamized road so that the state could pave it in concrete. Although the U.S. government was not yet ready to give up its rights to the road, it did grant the commission permission to pave and maintain it. The Highway Commission completed the work in August 1924.[44]

Meanwhile, the judge advocate general's office examined the army's title to the road and concluded that the "United States does not hold a title in fee to any part of the roadway" and "held it doubtful [that] the United States had any legal interest in the roadway." On July 25, 1925, the Quartermaster Department notified Robinson's successor, Frederick Wagner, that cemetery superintendents no longer had responsibility for the road's management. And so, after thirty-four years of federal management, National Boulevard quietly transferred to the state of Virginia. In 1933, city officials formally renamed the road Lafayette Boulevard.[45]

## Life in the National Cemetery

Among the documents in Fredericksburg and Spotsylvania County National Military Park's manuscript collection is the diary of Superintendent Andrew J. Birdsall, which covers the period from April 1890 through December 1891. The diary provides an interesting look at the day-to-day tasks and responsibilities of a superintendent and his crew. At that time Birdsall had one full-time worker, William Hogan, and two part-time workers, Robert C. Hart and E. P. Carneal, who labored from April to September. The crew worked six days a week with Sundays off, the time of year dictating their duties. Spring was the season for planting. In 1890, Birdsall planted a number of rosebushes in the cemetery. His crew likewise planted vines around the rostrum, thinned out an arbor vitae on the east side of the toolhouse, repotted plants, spread grass seed on bare spots, and planted flower bulbs in spaded beds.[46]

In the summer, Birdsall's men cut weeds, scraped moss off of the trees, raked the terraces, and repaired their equipment. However, they spent most of their time cutting grass. It took Birdsall's crew five days to mow the cemetery, and it had to be done three times a month. To keep the grass down, the men used a horse mower (or "pony mower," as it was sometimes called), a hand mower, and scythes. Workers used the horse mower for cutting grass on top of the hill, although at least one entry refers to it being used on the terrace slopes. They used the hand mowers to cut the terraces, the yard around the lodge, and the borders of the cemetery, reserving the scythes for trimming around headstones. Birdsall proudly noted that on an average day each of his men could trim nine hundred graves.[47]

Cemetery employee at work. Cemetery workers used a horse mower, hand mowers, and scythes. *Historic Fredericksburg Foundation, Inc.*

In addition to maintaining the grass, cemetery workers had to care for hundreds of trees and bushes. They removed dead trees, trimmed and pruned living ones, and picked worms off of those suffering from infestation. During periods of drought, the workers had to irrigate the shrubs and small trees with water from a pump. "It is quite a job to do all the watering of plants that need moisture," Birdsall complained.[48]

In October, once the grass stopped growing and leaves began to fall, mowing grass gave way to raking leaves. As winter set in, Birdsall and Hogan cleaned the lodge's gutters, chopped kindling for the wood-burning stove, and placed brush around the rosebushes to protect them from frost. Winter was also the season for repairing sunken graves. Hogan would "chop in" the sunken graves—that is, remove the sod from them—fill the depressions with dirt and mulch, tamp them down, and then replace the sod. As the years passed and the soil settled, workers had to do the task less frequently.[49]

Some tasks knew no season. As time allowed, Birdsall and his men re-pointed the cemetery walls, cleaned the open brick gutters at the foot of the terrace, repaired the gravel driveway, worked on the sidewalk, painted the house, whitewashed the kitchen, constructed platforms for stands of cannonballs, replaced broken slats on benches, and made repairs to the various buildings. In the winter of 1890–91, they added concrete floors to the tool room and to the stable. While doing so, they killed twenty-one rats that had made a nest under the oat bin.[50]

As superintendent, Birdsall set his employees' schedules and supervised their work. He performed administrative duties as well. He had to make out monthly and quarterly reports, order equipment and supplies, send unserviceable equipment back to the Quartermaster Depot in Washington, and prepare an annual estimate of funds needed for the coming year. Birdsall did his job well. After visiting the cemetery in 1888, a Northern visitor wrote, "Through the good management of Major Birdsall, this Marye's cemetery is each year becoming more attractive. It is largely patronized by the town people as an attractive resort, and many walk out to its agreeable shades in pleasant weather."[51]

Like other superintendents, it was Birdsall's duty to recover and inter the skeletons of any Union soldiers that turned up in the area. In June 1887, E. L. Landram plowed up the remains of several Union soldiers buried on his farm near the Bloody Angle. He reported the discovery to Birdsall, who reputedly told him "that it is not his business to look after them . . . and he would not do so." This account is either false or Birdsall was reprimanded for his response, for just four years later he interred the remains of a Union soldier unearthed in Fredericksburg.[52]

As cemetery superintendent, Birdsall greeted out-of-town visitors and helped them locate the graves of friends and family members. For the visitors this was an emotional experience. Miss M. E. Andrews traveled from Massachusetts to Fredericksburg in September 1892 to find the grave of her brother, Major William C. Morgan. Like most first-time visitors to the cemetery, she stopped at the superintendent's office to register her name and to get directions to the grave. An employee found Morgan's name in the cemetery register and led the woman to his grave, which rested under a beautiful japonica tree. As Miss Andrews stared down at the granite slab that bore her brother's name, her eyes welled up with tears. "I was pretty well overcome," she confessed to her sister, "and the tears dropped fast. I felt and know that he was beside me. I knelt down on the grave and sobbed." As she did so, an apple from the japonica tree fell into her lap. The worker picked it up and gave it to her, suggesting that somehow it was a sign from her brother. Before leaving the site, he cut three shoots from the tree and, wrapping them in some grass and dirt taken from the grave, gave them to her as a memento of her visit. The man suggested that the family might wish to buy a rosebush for the grave and offered to plant the shrub himself. Miss Andrews returned to Massachusetts "perfectly satisfied" with her brother's gravesite. "It is the most bea[u]tiful spot I have seen," she insisted. "I shall go there again if I am spared."[53]

Not surprisingly, visitors often turned to cemetery workers for information about the local battles. Unfortunately, the superintendent and his employees were not historians, and they frequently provided erroneous information. In one instance, an employee insisted that the Twenty-Sixth New Jersey had fought on the very ground where the cemetery stood, even though the visitors—veterans of the regiment—knew that it had fought more than a mile to the south. "He also informed us that the Color Sergeant of the 26th was buried in the cemetery and his head-stone marked," one disgusted veteran wrote, "but the name is wrong, for the Sergeant lived to come home, and resided in Newark a number of years after."[54]

In contrast to Birdsall's diaries, which cover a period of just twenty months, M. M. Jefferys diaries span more than a decade. A disabled veteran, Jefferys was fifty-nine years old when he took over management of Fredericksburg National Cemetery in 1904. Although he occasionally assisted his workers with simple tasks, like painting, the loss of his right arm during the war prevented him from doing much in the way of physical labor.

The government assigned superintendencies to Jefferys and other disabled veterans as a reward for their sacrifice and to provide them with gainful employment. Although it would be wrong to label them sinecures, the jobs were hardly taxing. Jefferys had enough free time to travel into Fredericksburg once or twice a day. Occasionally he went into town on cemetery business, but more often than not his trips were of a personal nature: to get a shave, to take his wife shopping, or to stop at the post office. On Sundays, he attended worship services at the Methodist Evangelical Church, often going to both morning and evening services. His wife, Addie, attended meetings of the Foreign Missionary Association and the Anti-saloon League. For recreation, the superintendent and his family went on picnics, took river excursions, and attended local fairs. Sometimes they took a ride into town on the carriage, stopping for ice cream at the local drugstore. It was a lifestyle enjoyed by millions of Americans who lived in small towns at that time.[55]

Like National Park Service superintendents today, national cemetery superintendents were a small, close-knit group. They regularly exchanged

M. M. Jefferys, who served as superintendent at Fredericksburg from 1904 to 1914. His diary entries are an excellent source of information about the day-to-day life of a cemetery superintendent. *Courtesy of Sarah L. Thayer.*

correspondence and paid social calls on one another when they happened to be in town. Jefferys was typical. He wrote to at least half a dozen other superintendents and hosted many of them at his home. At other times he played host to friends or relatives, who often stayed with him at the cemetery for days or weeks at a time.[56]

Thomas B. Robinson replaced Jefferys as superintendent in 1914. Although Robinson did not leave a diary, we know a great deal about him and his successors from synopses of his letters that appear in the cemetery's official correspondence log. Started in 1913, during Jefferys's final months as superintendent, the log spans twenty-seven years and contains abstracts of every official letter sent during that time. More than any other source, the log illuminates the daily workings of the cemetery. It also provides insight into the personalities of the superintendents. Robinson, for instance, comes across as an embattled superintendent, constantly at odds with his superiors in the Quartermaster Department.

Not long after Robinson came on duty at Fredericksburg, the department appointed William H. Kiger to be his assistant. Kiger was a superintendent in training, assigned to Fredericksburg for six months to learn the ropes. During that time, the department reduced Robinson's workforce from three employees to two. When Robinson requested authority to hire an additional man, his letter drew a sharp rebuke from Lieutenant Colonel J. B. Hauser, his superior in Washington. Why did Robinson need a third laborer? Hauser demanded. He already had two laborers, not counting Kiger. Wasn't that enough? What did Robinson and Kiger do, anyway? he pointedly asked. Robinson took offense at Hauser's tone and shot back an angry reply.[57]

Robinson kept his superiors apprised of Kiger's progress, reporting that his assistant was "attentive and interested in his duties and labors at the cemetery during all working hours of the day." On October 24, 1914, Kiger successfully completed his training. Robinson affirmed that Kiger's "conduct, industrious habits, and abilities are such that it is my opinion he is qualified to perform the duties of a Superintendent of a National Cemetery." The following week the Quartermaster Department promoted Kiger to a full superintendent and ordered him to report to Hampton National Cemetery, Virginia. With his departure, the Quartermaster Department restored Robinson's third laborer.[58]

The row over laborers was just one of several altercations Robinson had with Lieutenant Colonel Hauser. His problems started with his initial trip to Fredericksburg. Robinson came to Virginia by train, but at one point he missed his connection. As a result of this mishap, his journey took an extra day. He charged the additional meals and lodging expenses to the government. When Hauser questioned the expenses, Robinson took offense.[59]

Hauser likewise questioned the superintendent's request for a new horse to replace the sickly animal then in use. He had somehow learned that Robinson had purchased a surrey from Jefferys, and he suspected the new superintendent of wanting the new animal for racing through town, an accusation Robinson vigorously denied. "My notion has been to be able to have the grass cut properly," he protested. "To be sure I bo't the old surrey of Mr Jefferys to help him out as he couldnt sell before leaving thinking I might drive to church on Sunday and to town on errands at such times as the animal was not needed for work," but that is not why he had requested the horse. "I think my record will bear out the Statement that in this Service my first interest and effort has been for the Cemetery Where I have been in charge and it is so here."[60]

Relations between Robinson and his superior continued to deteriorate. In May 1914 Hauser chided Robinson for sending official communications on plain paper rather than on the official letterhead stationery supplied by the department. Robinson replied sharply that he had found just a few sheets of letterhead in the office when he took charge. Although he had requested additional paper from Hauser's office, none had been sent.[61]

Matters reached a head one year later, when Robinson requested a twenty-day leave of absence. Hauser replied that it was not customary to grant superintendents extended leaves of absence during the growing season but that he would grant Robinson leave for fifteen days if the superintendent could find a responsible person to stay at the lodge and safeguard the cemetery in his absence. Cemetery employees could not be used, Hauser added. When Robinson read Hauser's letter, he indignantly explained that his wife, Clara, had been visiting a daughter in Texas. She had fallen ill there, and he had to go there to bring her back to Virginia. The cemetery was in excellent shape, he argued, and not much could go wrong in just twenty days. As for getting a substitute to watch the cemetery, Robinson insisted that it was absurd for him to pay a stranger twenty-five to thirty dollars out of his own pocket when he had workers who would do it for free. He concluded by requesting that he be allowed to place in charge a man who had worked at the cemetery for more than twenty years—probably a reference to William Hogan. Robinson reminded Hauser that he was entrusting the substitute not only with the care of government property but also with the care of his own property. In the end, Hauser allowed Robinson to leave the employee in charge of the cemetery, but he held firm in his demand that Robinson return within fifteen days.[62]

Robinson's ongoing battles with Hauser took their toll, and in March 1916 he requested a transfer. Before the department took any action on his request, however, Clara died. Robinson reported the sad intelligence to his superiors, noting that he had buried his wife in grave #6665, reserving the adjacent plot for himself. As required by regulations, he submitted for approval a sketch of the private tombstone that he wished to erect over their graves. Tears fell from his cheeks onto the page, smearing his handwriting, as he copied the letter into the correspondence log.[63] After Clara's death, Robinson ceased his efforts to leave Fredericksburg. Unwilling to leave the cemetery where he had buried his wife, he remained at Fredericksburg for the rest of his career. When he finally tendered his resignation in August 1922, he was seventy-eight years old and in failing health. He died the following month and is buried next to Clara in grave #6666.

# 9.  ✜  Interments

ork on Fredericksburg National Cemetery began in May 1866. For two years the Burial Corps scoured the countryside within a thirty-mile radius of Fredericksburg gathering up the remains of every Union soldier it could find. The crews ranged as far north as Manassas, as far south as the North Anna River, as far east as Warsaw, Virginia, and as far west as Mine Run. Their work took them to six battlefields—Fredericksburg, Chancellorsville, Wilderness, Spotsylvania Court House, Mine Run, and North Anna River, as well as to Northern campgrounds in Stafford County.[1] Soldier remains were placed in "coffin boxes" made of pine and placed in the ground so that the head of the deceased lay to the west and his feet to the east.[2]

Within two and a half years the interment process was largely complete. A survey conducted on October 21, 1868, found a total of 15,128 interments at Fredericksburg. Of those, 133 were white officers, 14,985 were white enlisted men, 4 were white sailors, 4 were black soldiers, and 2 were cemetery employees. The Burial Corps was able to identify just 16 percent of those they buried.[3]

In 1870, the federal government began publishing the *Roll of Honor*, listing individual burials at national cemeteries throughout the country. Superintendent Charles Fitchett did not put much faith in the new report's accuracy. Writing to his superior in the Quartermaster Department, he asserted, "I would state that the 'Roll of Honor,' Vol. No. 25, contains numerous errors and omissions, and the same can not be relied on for reference."[4] Since then, several attempts have been made to tally the number of soldiers buried at Fredericksburg. Each tabulation used different categories and came up with different figures. The discrepancies resulted in some measure from the addition or transfer of remains, but for the most part they were simply the result of faulty counting.

## Identifying the Dead

Identifying the dead was a daunting task. Few Civil War soldiers wore dog tags, and many had been buried in mass graves or had not been buried at all.

Some soldiers were fortunate enough to have marked graves, but in many cases residents burned the wooden headboards for fuel before the bodies could be collected. Consequently, 84 percent of the Union soldiers buried at Fredericksburg are unidentified. Information on the remaining 16 percent is, in many cases, incomplete or in error.[5]

In 1874, granite headstones replaced the original wooden headboards. Before ordering the headstones, Superintendent Fitchett attempted to identify soldiers about whom he had incomplete information. He compiled lists of incomplete names and sent them to adjutants general throughout the Northern states in the hope that by comparing the information on the list against information on the states' regimental rosters, the adjutant generals might be able to identify some of the soldiers. In most cases, they could not.[6] Rather than bury those soldiers in unknown graves, Fitchett placed what little information he had on the headstones and buried the soldiers in individual graves. As a result, many headstones contain just a soldier's initials or portions of his first or last name. Even in cases where an entire name appears on the headstone, the information may be incorrect. When errors are detected, it has been the National Park Service's policy to correct the information in the cemetery register but to leave erroneous headstones in place. As former chief historian Robert K. Krick explained, the headstones "have developed an historicity of their own . . . ; they match one another; and they benefit from the tremendous cachet of having been placed by fellow veterans immediately after the war."[7]

In instances where descendants request the correction of a stone, the park's policy has been to leave the original headstone in place but to place a stone containing the proper information directly in front of it. This solution has worked well, satisfying the descendants while maintaining the cemetery's historical and visual integrity. At present, Fredericksburg National Cemetery has set replacement stones at eight graves. As the cemetery records improve, this number will certainly increase. The graves that currently have replacement stones are as follows:

| Original Name | Corrected Name | Grave |
| --- | --- | --- |
| Avrin Faust | Arvin Faust | 578 |
| J. May | John Moy | 318 |
| —— War—r | John Warner | 4913 |
| J. S. Hamesson | Jno. S. Hamilton | 6082 |
| J. Monroe | James N. Morang | 3135 |
| Wm. Hartnug | William Hartung | 4725 |
| Geo. Simons | George Seamans | 249 |

Jack Butler (grave #6698) too received a replacement headstone, but it clarified his military unit rather than corrected his name.

Every so often someone will contact the park wishing to erect a private headstone in honor of a relative who died in the area but whose body was never identified. Such requests run contrary to National Park Service regulations and are denied. As an alternative, park officials recommend that the individual erect the memorial stone in the soldier's hometown.[8]

## Burial of Unidentified Soldiers

Five out of every six men brought to Fredericksburg could not be identified. Rather than furnish individual graves for these soldiers, the army decided to bury the unknown dead in mass graves. Interring more than one soldier in a grave had its advantages: it took less time, saved the army money in coffins and headboards, and conserved space. By 1870, there were 6,574 graves at Fredericksburg National Cemetery—less than one grave for every two soldiers buried there. If every soldier had received his own grave, a twenty-eight-acre plot of ground would have been needed to hold them all.[9]

Unidentified soldiers share a coffin with others exhumed from the same location. Their bones did not mix with those of soldiers who had died on a different farm or lot, much less with those who died on a different battlefield. The sole exception to this rule is grave #4084, which includes the remains of two soldiers originally buried in the Wilderness, one buried on the Mine Run Battlefield, and one buried in Stafford County. Each of the men belonged to the First U.S. Sharpshooters.

The number of unknown soldiers placed in a single grave depended in large measure on where they perished. Unknown soldiers found on the Chancellorsville Battlefield, for instance, were almost always buried in groups of five. Coffins brought in from Marlborough Point in Stafford County and from the Beverly, Sanford, McCoull, and Dabney farms at Spotsylvania usually held four skeletons apiece; those coming from Chatham, in Stafford County, and from the Fredericksburg Agricultural Fair Grounds in front of Marye's Heights had three; while deceased soldiers culled from the Alsop farm at Spotsylvania received individual graves. Even when the number of bodies per coffin varied, there was a distinct pattern. For instance, of the 103 unknown soldiers exhumed from Wilderness National Cemetery No. 2, 93 were buried together in groupings of three, while the remaining 10 soldiers were divided equally between two coffins.[10]

## Multiple Burials of Identified Soldiers

While burying unknown soldiers together was commonplace, burying *known* soldiers together was not. There are just twelve instances of identified soldiers being buried together in a single grave. In seven of those instances, the soldiers belonged to the same regiment and may have shared a battlefield grave.[11] In three of the remaining five cases, the soldiers came from different regiments but were originally buried at the same location. They too may have shared a common grave on the battlefield.[12]

The individuals buried in grave #6742 had a different connection. Admol L. Jett and Admol G. Jett were father and son. The elder Jett served in the U.S. Marine Corps from September 18, 1917, to June 3, 1919. When he died on November 29, 1940, his family buried him at Fredericksburg National Cemetery. Corporal Admol Glorial Jett followed his father into the Marine Corps. On March 1, 1945, he was shot by a Japanese sniper at Iwo Jima while deliberately exposing himself in an effort to draw the enemy's fire. Despite his wound, he called back the location of the enemy's position to his comrades, who were then able to eliminate it. Jett died later that day. The U.S. government later flew his body back to Fredericksburg, where it was buried on May 22, 1949, in the same plot as his father. Jett has the distinction of being the last soldier to be interred at Fredericksburg National Cemetery.[13]

Grave #152 is the last plot containing the remains of more than one identified soldier. The occupants are "known" only insofar as the Burial Corps found their initials: J. M. M. and J. B. We know nothing more about them, and given the accuracy of the cemetery's early records, we cannot even be certain that the initials are correct.

## Later Interments of Civil War Soldiers

Although most Civil War soldiers were interred by 1868, skeletons continued to turn up for decades thereafter. When farmers discovered a grave on their property, they would contact the superintendent, who then made arrangements to collect and bury the remains. Local residents found the skeletons of at least two dozen soldiers after 1870 and reburied them at Fredericksburg. Undoubtedly there were more. The single greatest number of interments in the twentieth century took place on Armistice Day 1934. On that date, the remains of six Union soldiers were interred in grave #6716. Civilian Conservation Corps employees had unearthed the graves earlier in the year while working in the park. The American Legion conducted the burial ceremony assisted by a detachment of U.S. Marines and the Quantico Marine Band. Among the speakers was Harry Belgrano, the American Legion's national commander.[14]

After the Civil War, Congress expanded the pool of those eligible for burial in national cemeteries to include honorably discharged veterans, spouses of soldiers, and their dependent children. As a result of this legislation, several Union veterans were buried at Fredericksburg in later years. The last of these was Private Evander Willis, Eighth Vermont, who died in October 1935. Willis, an owner of the Ellwood plantation, is buried with his wife, Lucy Sprague Willis, in grave #1869A. Like all Union veterans who died in the twentieth century, Willis received a Civil War–style headstone.[15]

## Transfer of Remains to and from Other Cemeteries

At the conclusion of the initial burial process in October 1868, the Quarter-master Corps counted 15,128 interments at Fredericksburg. A tabulation made just two years later, in 1870, showed just 15,068 burials—60 fewer than before.[16]

Evander Willis, the last Civil War veteran buried at Fredericksburg National Cemetery, and his wife, Lucy, one of twenty women buried there. *Courtesy of Carolyn Elstner.*

The decrease may reflect the transfer of soldier remains from Fredericksburg to cemeteries in the North. In 1866 alone, the Quartermaster Department's Washington Depot answered five thousand letters requesting information about deceased soldiers and issued four thousand permits for the removal of bodies.[17]

Among those whose remains were sent north were Colonels John W. Patterson of the 102nd Pennsylvania, John Coons of the Fourteenth Indiana, and Henry O. Ryerson of the Tenth New Jersey; Lieutenant Colonels Charles Wiebecke of the Second New Jersey, Moses N. Collins of the Eleventh New Hampshire, and Theodore Hesser of the Seventy-Second Pennsylvania; and Major Henry P. Truefitt of the 119th Pennsylvania. The name of each of these officers appears on a list of soldiers interred by burial crews combing the Wilderness and Spotsylvania Battlefields in June 1865, yet none is buried at Fredericksburg today. Patterson's relatives recovered his bones prior to their interment at Fredericksburg. In Wiebecke's case, family members retrieved the remains only after the lieutenant colonel's name appeared in the *Roll of Honor*.[18]

We have evidence of just one soldier being transferred from Fredericksburg in the twentieth century. That occurred in December 1958, when the widow of Corporal Louis Morris Lyons (Lifschitz) requested that her husband's remains be moved to nearby Oakwood Cemetery.[19]

## Tomb of the Unknown Soldier

Nestled among a row of twentieth-century graves is a headstone like those used to mark the graves of known Civil War soldiers in the 1860s. It bears the number 286 and has three distinctions. First, it is the only slab-style headstone occupying that particular row. Second, it is the only headstone of that type in the entire cemetery that has no inscription except for the plot number. And third, the plot number on the top of the stone is the same as that of another grave in the cemetery. The latter grave marks the burial plot of Fanning Merritt and his wife, Sarah. Merritt, a corporal in the Thirty-Sixth Massachusetts, died in the May 12, 1864, fighting at Spotsylvania Court House. The army brought his remains to Fredericksburg and probably erected a slab-style headstone over his grave in the late 1860s, as it did for other identified soldiers.[20] But today a Civil War–style headstone stands over Merritt's grave. On the back of the stone is an inscription to his wife, who shares his grave. Sarah T. Merritt died in 1917 and is the only woman buried in the cemetery whose spouse died during the Civil War. The current headstone was probably erected over the Merritts' grave at the time of Sarah's death.

But that does not explain why a slab-style headstone with the number 286 appears in a row of twentieth-century graves in a different part of the cemetery. Is anyone buried there? If so, who? Fanning? Sarah? Or someone else entirely? If someone is buried there, why is there no inscription? And if the stone marks an empty grave, why is it there at all? Might it have been a joke—a parody on Arlington's Tomb of the Unknown Soldier? The only thing we can say with assurance is that the stone was erected just before America's entry into World War II. The soldier on one side of this mysterious stone died in 1939; the soldier on the other side died in 1940. Cemetery workers presumably erected the blank marker in one of those two years. That is about all we can say with any confidence, however. For now, the grave remains a mystery.

## Officers Row

On the ninth terrace, just behind the Fifth Corps Monument, lie the graves of seven officers and four of their wives. This is known as the Officers' Section or Officers Row. The first man to be buried there was Lieutenant Colonel Edward Hill of the Sixteenth Michigan, a Civil War veteran who died in 1900. Hill resided in St. Louis, Wisconsin, but had spent several winters in Fredericksburg. Five months before he died, Hill spoke at the laying of the Fifth Corps Monument's cornerstone, and he may have requested to be buried at Fredericksburg at that time.[21]

Lieutenant Colonel Thomas E. Morris of the Fifteenth Michigan died in 1908 and was interred beside Hill by order of the quartermaster general.[22] When Hill and Morris were first buried, they apparently had numbered plots like all the others; Hill was allotted grave #6640 and Morris grave #6655. Over time, however, the row gained an identity all its own. It became known as Officers Row, and the graves there acquired their own peculiar numbers. Morris's grave, on the northern end of the row, was redesignated Officers Row #1 with the ten graves to his left being given the numbers 2 through 11.

For thirteen years, Hill and Morris had the terrace to themselves. But on July 23, 1921, First Lieutenant Urbane Bass's remains were brought back from France and buried a few yards away. A black surgeon, Bass had volunteered to serve his country in World War I even though he was above the age of enlistment. He died in 1918 while working at an aid station in France. After his death, the army recognized Bass's patriotism by awarding him the Distinguished Service Cross. Hill, too, had been a war hero, and cemetery personnel may have thought it fitting to bury them in the same row. Possibly because

Bass was black, cemetery workers chose to place his grave some twenty feet from Hill and Morris. During World War II they filled the intervening space with the remains of other white officers and their spouses. For some reason, the workers did not utilize that portion of the terrace south of Bass's grave.[23]

The last notable burial in Officers Row is First Lieutenant George Nelson, who became Fredericksburg National Cemetery's superintendent in 1931 and held that position until his death in 1940.[24]

## Closed to New Burials

The orderly interment of soldier remains at Fredericksburg ended in 1868 with the burial of a single unidentified soldier's remains in grave #6604. In following years, approximately two hundred more people were interred in the cemetery. No longer were they buried in orderly rows of graves bearing sequential numbers, however. From that point on, cemetery personnel buried them randomly in whatever plots remained open.

In 1909, the quartermaster general asked superintendents to report how many additional interments their cemeteries could hold. Superintendent M. M. Jefferys estimated that Fredericksburg could accept approximately 250 additional burials: 100 on south terrace #9, south of Officers Row; 110 in the triangular plot formed by the fork in the main carriageway; 30 in the vicinity of the rostrum; and 10 along the southwest wall. In addition, he suggested that the army could place graves in some of the cemetery avenues. Jefferys's superiors adopted the latter proposal, turning three of the original avenues into burial space: the long avenue that separated sections CB, BB, and BD from sections CA, BA, and BC; and two shorter avenues that separated section CD from section CE, and section CE from section CF.[25] Following World War I, still more plots were needed. Jefferys's successor, Superintendent Thomas B. Robinson, suggested that he could scrape together 200 "vacant sites"—40 in Officers Row and 160 elsewhere—"without material interference with original designs" of the cemetery. If the War Department needed more than that, he was willing to create additional plots by consolidating the graves of unknown soldiers. Fortunately, the War Department did not act on his proposal.[26]

The last soldier to receive a separate grave at Fredericksburg National Cemetery was Harry Bankard in 1945; he occupies grave #6765. Since then, ten people have been buried at Fredericksburg, each of them the wife of a soldier who is also buried there. Four of the women share a grave with their husbands; the other six lie in adjacent plots. Berta Watt Whitehouse (Officers Row #6) was the last person, man or woman, to receive a separate grave. She died in 1992. Iva C. Boggs was the cemetery's last interment of any sort. She died on April 19, 1994, two years after Whitehouse and more than half a century after her husband, Francis C. Boggs. She and her husband are buried together in grave #6754.[27] Iva Boggs, Berta Watt Whitehouse, and the other women were granted the right to be buried in Fredericksburg National Cemetery because they had reserved a space for themselves there at the time of their husbands' deaths. Five other women reserved plots for themselves but never used them.[28]

# 10. ❈  Special Populations

Fredericksburg began as a homogeneous cemetery. Prior to 1898, nearly everyone interred there was a young white male who had fought in the Civil War, few holding rank above that of a captain. There were exceptions, of course—early burial records list a small number of field grade officers, four black soldiers, a Native American, and perhaps even a Confederate—but by and large the cemetery's phalanx of young white men remained undented throughout its first thirty years. In the twentieth century, that began to change. There were three reasons for this. First, Congress passed legislation allowing spouses and minor children of soldiers to be buried in national cemeteries. Second, starting in World War I women began serving in the military, thus earning the privilege to be buried in national cemeteries in their own right. And, finally, the twentieth century saw African Americans serving their country in ever greater numbers.

As a result of these changes, Fredericksburg National Cemetery's population became more diverse over time. However, there is no diversity in the headstones. Except for the Medal of Honor recipients and those with privately funded markers, every person in the cemetery has a standard, government-issued headstone, irrespective of their rank, race, religion, or sex. Nor, as a rule, is there any difference as to where they are interred. Colonels are buried beside privates, black soldiers are next to white soldiers, and women are next to men. There is no difference between them.[1]

## Field-Grade Officers

Fredericksburg is the domain of common soldiers. No general officers and just eight known field-grade officers are buried there, altogether representing just three-tenths of 1 percent of the known dead. The field officers include two colonels, four lieutenant colonels, and two majors. James Crowther (grave #2897) is the highest-ranking officer in the cemetery. Crowther became colonel of the 110th Pennsylvania on March 18, 1863, and died in the May

3, 1863, fighting at Chancellorsville.[2] First Lieutenant Francis Cassidy was with Crowther when he died. The Union troops on either side of the 110th had given way, allowing Confederate troops to turn both of the regiment's flanks. Crowther had just given the order to retreat, remembered Cassidy, when the fatal bullet struck him just below the right breast. "Stay with me Lieutenant," he admonished. Cassidy took his commander by the arm in an effort to help him reach the rear, but after just a couple of steps Crowther crumpled to the ground. "I saw in a moment all was over," the subordinate wrote. With the advancing Confederate line less than a hundred yards away, Cassidy abandoned his charge and disappeared into the woods. After the battle Confederate soldiers buried Crowther, carefully marking his grave with a board taken from a cracker box. Soldiers in the 110th Pennsylvania found his grave during the Battle of the Wilderness one year later, but there was no time to retrieve his remains. Crowther's bones would remain on the battlefield until the war ended.[3]

Next in rank is Joseph A. Moesch (#6618). Born in Eiken, Switzerland, on August 13, 1829, the future officer immigrated to the United States around 1854, settling in New York City, where he found employment as a clerk. When the Civil War commenced, Moesch enlisted in Company B of the Ninth New York State Militia (Eighty-Third New York Volunteers), nicknamed the "Swiss Rifles." He became its captain on October 10, 1861, and rose to become a full colonel by the spring of 1864. "He was a good soldier," remembered one of the men in his command, "brave, almost to rashness; a quality that endeared him to the men in the ranks."[4] Moesch met his end on May 6, 1864, leading his regiment into action in the Wilderness. His corpse was taken to the division hospital, placed in a rough coffin, and buried in a secluded corner of the Lacy family cemetery at Ellwood plantation. Chaplain Alfred C. Roe of the Ninth Regiment supervised the burial. He purposely left the gravesite unmarked for fear that Southerners would desecrate Moesch's remains.[5]

Following the war, Captain George A. Hussey and Superintendent Andrew Birdsall of Fredericksburg National Cemetery attempted to locate Moesch's body. With the help of Chaplain Roe, they succeeded in doing so. Hussey later described what they found: "The pine box had entirely decomposed, save a portion of the bottom. Fragments of the poncho tent cloth, wrapped around the body, were found, but crumbled on exposure to air. An entire human skeleton was exhumed, together with pieces of clothing, buttons, denoting state and rank, belt buckle, etc., and upon the bottom of the coffin lay a leaden bullet, Confederate, the missile guilty of that deed of death."[6] Birdsall placed

Moesch's remains in a wagon and carried them back to Fredericksburg National Cemetery. On October 10, 1887, he buried them in grave #6618.[7]

Thomas Morris, Fifteenth Michigan Infantry; Edwin Burt, Third Maine Infantry; H. H. Pearson, Sixth New Hampshire Infantry; and Edward Hill, Sixteenth Michigan Infantry are the four lieutenant colonels buried at Fredericksburg. Burt (#3953) died on May 6, 1864, and Pearson (#1129) on May 26, 1864. Hill (#6640) and Morris (#6655) survived the war and were buried in 1900 and 1908, respectively. Fellow Michiganders, they lie side by side in Officers Row. The two majors interred on Marye's Heights are Frank A. Rolfe of the First Massachusetts Heavy Artillery (#1169) and William C. Morgan of the Third Maine Infantry (#3615). Like many men in his regiment, Rolfe died on May 19, 1864, in fighting at the Harris farm, near Spotsylvania Court House. Morgan died just four days later, in fighting along the North Anna River.[8]

## Medal of Honor Recipients

Fredericksburg National Cemetery contains the graves of two Medal of Honor recipients: Lieutenant Colonel Edward Hill (#6640) of the Sixteenth Michigan and Sergeant William Jones (#2248) of the Seventy-Third New York. Hill earned the Medal of Honor for his actions on June 1, 1864, at Cold Harbor, where he led skirmishers in a dawn assault on an entrenched Confederate position. He captured the works and despite being severely wounded remained on the field until evening brought an end to the fighting. After the war, Hill briefly became a Fredericksburg resident. On May 25, 1900, he spoke to a gathering of the Society of the Army of the Potomac at the dedication of the Fifth Corps Monument. When he died later that year in Green Bay, Wisconsin, the army transported his body back to Fredericksburg and buried it at the foot of the monument. The date of Hill's interment was December 13, 1900, the thirty-eighth anniversary of the Battle of Fredericksburg, a battle in which he had taken part. It was the first grave in what would later be known as the Officers' Section or Officers Row.[9]

First Sergeant William Jones was a twenty-six-year-old Irish immigrant. Although he had a wife and two small children, the former stevedore and mariner enlisted in the Seventy-Third New York on May 21, 1861, for a period of two years. When his enlistment expired, he reenlisted as a veteran. He died on May 12, 1864, at Spotsylvania Court House while capturing a Confederate flag near the Bloody Angle and was buried on the McCoull farm, where he fell. Jones was awarded the Medal of Honor posthumously on December

1, 1864. Ironically, the regiment whose flag he captured—the Sixty-Fifth Virginia—did not exist.[10]

Hill and Jones both have unique headstones. Hill's grave features a bronze plaque that lies flush to the ground, while a shield insignia painted in gold leaf adorns Jones's grave. Both stones are later additions. The War Department did not introduce flat headstones until 1936, and gold-leaf insignias identifying Medal of Honor recipients did not appear until 1976.[11]

## African Americans

Among Fredericksburg's 15,300 burials are at least twenty African Americans. They include five men who fought in United States Colored Troops (USCT) regiments during the Civil War and the spouses of three World War I veterans.

William Branch, Moses Humphrey, and Peter Wilson each died during the Civil War. Branch succumbed to typhoid fever on May 11, 1865, and was originally buried at Mannsfield, a large plantation south of Fredericksburg, while Wilson died at the hands of Confederate guerrillas on June 16, 1864, in Richmond County, Virginia.[12] Moses Humphrey is an enigma. The *Roll*

Graves of two Medal of Honor recipients: William Jones (*left*) and Edward Hill (*above*). *Fredericksburg and Spotsylvania County National Military Park.*

*of Honor* indicates that he served in the 135th USCT and that he died in May 1864 in Spotsylvania County. However, the "Soldiers and Sailors" database shows no one by his name in that or any other USCT regiment. Even if it did, it would not solve the mystery, for the 135th USCT was active only in 1865 and served exclusively in North Carolina.[13]

Charles Henry Sprow (or Sprout) and Thomas Hill likewise fought in the Civil War. Sprow began his life as a slave at Chatham, the Fredericksburg-area home of Major James Horace Lacy, who also owned Ellwood. During the war, Sprow escaped to freedom and at the age of twenty-one took up arms for the Union, serving in the First Cavalry, USCT. He mustered out of service in Texas in 1866 and returned to Fredericksburg, where he lived until his death in 1926.[14]

There may be one additional black Civil War soldier buried at Fredericksburg. Both the 1868 and 1871 inspection reports list four black interments: two known and two unknown. Cemetery inspectors visiting Fredericksburg in 1874 and 1875 likewise found four African American graves, three of which belonged to identified soldiers, presumably Branch, Humphrey, and Wilson. They did not give the grave number of the unidentified soldier. By 1882, the unknown soldier had disappeared from the records. Because his identity was unknown, it is unlikely that anyone claimed his remains. Thus he is probably still buried at Fredericksburg, although the location of his grave is as uncertain as his identity.[15]

Private Luther M. Ellet fought for the U.S. Army in the Philippines, where he died of a fever. He was interred at Fredericksburg on March 16, 1900.[16] Several of the black soldiers buried at Fredericksburg fought in World War I; Corporal Grant Wright is a case in point. He served in Company G, 368th Infantry, Ninety-Second Division, during World War I. Wright fought in France, where he was exposed to poisonous gas; he died on November 8, 1922, in Amelia, Pennsylvania, as a result of that exposure. A brother brought his body back to Fredericksburg by train. Following a funeral service at Shiloh Baptist Church (New Site), the army buried Wright's remains in grave #6679.[17]

First Lieutenant Urbane F. Bass is the by far the most noteworthy African American soldier buried in Fredericksburg National Cemetery. Born in 1880 in Richmond, Virginia, he graduated from Leonard Medical School of Shaw University in Raleigh, North Carolina, in 1906. Three years later he moved to Fredericksburg, opening a medical practice and pharmacy on what is now William Street. Bass was Fredericksburg's first black physician and, in fact, the only black doctor practicing medicine between Washington, D.C., and Richmond, Virginia, at that time.[18]

Although he was then thirty-eight years old, had a wife and four children, and was well past the age of compulsory service, Bass nonetheless volunteered his services to the government when the United States entered World War I. He made his reasons for that decision clear in an April 6, 1917, letter that he wrote to the secretary of war. "Realizing that patriotism and loyalty should be paramount in the breast of all American citizens at this time," it read,

First Lieutenant Urbane F. Bass, the cemetery's only black officer. He was awarded the Distinguished Service Cross after losing his life in France during World War I. *Fredericksburg and Spotsylvania County National Military Park.*

"and feeling (although a negro) that loyalty for my country and the desire to serve her in this critical period, I am herewith offering my services for the Army Medical Corps should there be a need for a negro physician for that branch of service."[19] The secretary accepted Bass's offer and assigned him to the 372nd Infantry, one of four segregated regiments belonging to the Ninety-Third Division. These regiments were parceled out among depleted French divisions. They received French rations and equipment, including the distinctive French helmet.

Bass died on October 7, 1918, when an enemy shell exploded over his aid station near Monthois, France, severing both his legs. Despite his wounds, he remained cool, directing subordinates who attempted to help him. But the loss of blood was too great. The gallant doctor succumbed to his injuries before he could be taken to the field hospital. As a result of his courage and patriotism, the army posthumously awarded Bass the Distinguished Service Cross and set aside a plot for him in Officers Row. He was interred there on July 23, 1921, the only black commissioned officer to be buried in Fredericksburg National Cemetery.[20] About the same time, friends in town erected a stained-glass window to his memory at Shiloh Baptist Church (New Site), where he had been an active member.[21]

Next to Bass is the grave of his wife, Maude, who was just thirty-two when her husband died. She never remarried. Maude had studied music at both Howard University and Shaw University. She remained in Fredericksburg until her husband's burial and then moved with her family to Raleigh, where for thirty years she taught music at the North Carolina School for the Blind. When she died in 1982 at the age of one hundred, she was interred next to her long-departed husband. She is one of just three African American woman buried in the cemetery.[22]

## Native Americans

To date, just one Native American has been identified as being buried at Fredericksburg National Cemetery. Private Ira Bucktooth, a member of the Seneca tribe, died of disease while serving in the Fifty-Seventh Pennsylvania and is now buried in grave #1957. The *Roll of Honor* indicates that he died on April 13, 1863, and was buried initially on the Harris farm. Historian Samuel Bates agreed that Bucktooth died in April 1863, but he does not identify his original burial location. As the Harris farm was well behind Confederate lines at that time, either the date or the location of Bucktooth's death must be in error.[23]

# Women

Buried in the cemetery are twenty women, two of whom were veterans and the rest wives of veterans. One of the female veterans interred at Fredericksburg National Cemetery, Annie Florence Lockhart (#6715), was born in Canada in 1882. She immigrated to America in 1902 and was living in Lexington, Kentucky, on April 6, 1918, when, at the age of thirty-six, she became a U.S. Army Corps nurse. When the country had entered World War I, one year earlier, there were just 403 nurses on active duty with the army. By the time the war ended, two years later, some 22,000 women had served. Lockhart reported for duty at Camp Meade, Maryland, and served briefly on the Meuse-Argonne front in France. She was honorably discharged at the end of the war and returned to Lexington, where she became a civilian nurse at Good Samaritan Hospital.

Over the next decade, Lockhart rose in her profession. She served as an instructor at a hospital in Sayre, Pennsylvania, and later accepted the position of superintendent at Riverside Hospital in Paducah, Kentucky. She left Kentucky in 1931 to become superintendent of Mary Washington Hospital in Fredericksburg. During her four years in Fredericksburg, she became a member of the Bowen-Franklin-Knox Post of the American Legion and president of the Business and Professional Women's Club. Sadly, pneumonia cut short her life. She died at Mary Washington Hospital on New Year's Day 1935 and two days later was buried with military honors at Fredericksburg National Cemetery. The town's veterans, businessmen, and medical community turned out en masse for the funeral, which featured six active pallbearers and thirty-four honorary pallbearers. Among the latter were eighteen doctors.[24]

The other female veteran buried at Fredericksburg, Edith Rose Tench, was born in August 1890. She lived with her parents and four siblings at 507 Main (now Caroline) Street in Fredericksburg. Edith married thirty-six-year-old Samuel B. Tench of Petersburg, Virginia, on February 20, 1917, in Washington, D.C., only to divorce a short time later.

When World War I began, Tench joined the U.S. Naval Reserve Force (USNRF) as a yeoman, third class. The USNRF had been created in 1916 to meet a shortage in clerical personnel. The enlistment of women began the following year, just before the United States entered the war. It was the first large-scale employment of women by the navy. By the time the conflict ended, more than eleven thousand women had served in the USNRF. Popularly referred to as "Yeomanettes" (a name they detested), the women

Edith Rose Tench, one of just two servicewomen buried at Fredericksburg. *Courtesy of Bill Sielski.*

performed a variety tasks, including clerical duties, designing camouflage for battleships, and acting as translators, draftsmen, fingerprint experts, and recruiting agents. They did not serve as officers. Although a few went overseas, most Yeomanettes served in the continental United States. That seems to have been the case with Tench, who worked at the Norfolk Navy Yard. She was probably the only local woman to actively serve in the military in World War I. (Lockhart did not move to Fredericksburg until after the war.) After World War I, the navy released the Yeomanettes from active duty. With the exception of nurses, women would not serve as uniformed personnel in the navy again until 1942.

Tench returned to Fredericksburg in 1920 and worked as a clerk in a dry goods store. When she was not working, she attended Fredericksburg Methodist Church, served as adjutant of the Bowen-Franklin-Knox Post of the American Legion, and studied nursing at Mary Washington Hospital. Tench graduated from the hospital's school in 1928, but she did not live long enough to put her new skills to use. On November 29, 1929, she died of Bright's disease, an inflammation of the kidneys. At the time of her death, she was living with her family at their home at 1309 Princess Anne Street. Her comrades in the American Legion buried her with military honors in grave #2915A.[25]

The remaining women buried at Fredericksburg were married to veterans. Four were wives of cemetery superintendents and four were spouses of soldiers buried in Officers Row. Nine of the women share a grave with their husband, while the remaining nine occupy an adjacent plot. Clara Robinson (#6665) shares a common headstone with her husband but technically occupies a separate plot.

## Children

In his 1882 inspection report of the cemetery, Major Richard Arnold included "Civilians and Children" as a category of burials. He listed two people in that category. That same year a different inspector listed the same two individuals under the heading "Women & Children."[26] Interestingly, neither individual appears in the 1889 or 1904 cemetery tabulations. One of the individuals was probably Marian Mabelle Fitchett, the infant daughter of Superintendent Charles Fitchett. Marian died on August 15, 1877, before reaching her second birthday and may have been buried by her parents in Fredericksburg National Cemetery. When Charles Fitchett transferred to Natchez National Cemetery in 1883, he probably took his daughter's remains with him. This would explain why she is not listed in later reports. The other individual is unknown.[27]

Some twenty-three years later, Arthur Hill was buried at Fredericksburg National Cemetery. The young boy died on August 7, 1891, after living just three months and twelve days. His father, Richard Hill, was then superintendent of Poplar Grove National Cemetery, near Petersburg. Hill, a veteran, buried his son at Poplar Grove in a plot that he had set aside for himself. That was perfectly legal, inasmuch as cemetery regulations permitted the burial of minors with their parents. Later, Hill transferred to Fredericksburg, where he lost his wife, Mary Ann to pneumonia. Rather than transport her remains to Poplar Grove, Hill interred his wife in grave #6636 at Fredericksburg National Cemetery. On January 22, 1900, he buried Arthur beside her and placed over them the tombstone that had marked Arthur's grave in Petersburg.[28]

Arthur Hill is the only minor buried in the cemetery, but he is not the only child buried there. Admol G. Jett and Roy Butler likewise have parents interred in the cemetery, although both Jett and Butler were adults when they died. Jett is buried with his father in grave #6742, while Butler had his ashes sprinkled over his father, Jack Butler, who is buried in grave #6698.

## Confederate Soldiers

In their reports to the War Department, superintendents insisted that Fredericksburg National Cemetery contained the remains of no Confederate soldiers; however, a recent discovery suggests they may have been wrong. In grave #3867 are the remains of a soldier identified as Private A. J. Grant of Company G, Fifty-Eighth Pennsylvania. According to the burial register, Grant died in the Battle of Spotsylvania Court House and was originally buried on the McCoull farm. However, the Fifty-Eighth Pennsylvania did not serve in the Fredericksburg area. Moreover, no soldier with the last name of Grant who came from a Pennsylvania unit or who served in the Fifty-Eighth Regiment fought at the McCoull farm. The Fifty-Eighth Virginia, however, did fight there, and in its ranks was a private named Andrew J. Grant. Grant served in Company G and perished on May 12 at Spotsylvania. It is not only possible but probable that Grant is the soldier buried in grave #3867. When the fighting ended, Union and Confederate dead lay side by side on the battlefield. Grant had probably donned a Union coat captured in the Wilderness a few days earlier and was mistaken as a Union soldier by a later burial party.[29]

## Foreign Soldiers

Sergeant Jack Butler is a unique figure at Fredericksburg National Cemetery. Of the 15,300 soldiers buried in the cemetery, he is the only one who was not a citizen of the United States. Butler served instead in the Second Squadron of the Royal Air Force.

Born in Southsea, England, in 1893, Butler immigrated to America in 1907 at the age of thirteen. His father, Alfred W. Butler, worked in the coal industry and died of tuberculosis in 1906. One year later, Jack's mother married Alfred's brother, Elkanah E. Butler. At that time, it was illegal for a man to marry his deceased brother's wife, a fact that undoubtedly prompted the family's move to America. After a brief sojourn in Richmond, Virginia, the Butlers settled down near Fredericksburg. They lived, by turn, in Falmouth; at "Lewisana," near New Post; and finally at 104 Main (now Caroline) Street in Fredericksburg.[30]

When England entered World War I in 1914, Jack—then twenty years old—decided to return to England and fight for his native land. The details of his wartime service are rather muddy. Some sources insist that he was a pilot or observer in the Royal Flying Corps, based in France, but his service record indicates that he spent most of the war in Ireland as a mechanic with the Twenty-Fourth Training Squadron. In any case, he joined the Royal Air Force in 1918 and by war's end was serving as a sergeant mechanic in England.[31]

By then, he was the husband of Doris Tucker, his wartime bride who would bear him four sons and one daughter. Butler received an honorable discharge in 1920 and returned to Fredericksburg with his family. Putting his wartime skills to use, he went to work as a mechanic for the James Motor Company before opening his own garage in the mid-1920s. Called Jack's Garage, the business stood at 1010 Princess Anne Street, across from Fredericksburg Baptist Church. His lived nearby at 706 Lewis Street. In 1928, while working in his garage, a small sliver of steel lodged in Butler's left eye, permanently blinding him on that side. Two years later, at the age of thirty-five, he died from acute appendicitis.[32]

At the time of his death, Butler was an active member of the American Legion and had applied for U.S. citizenship. Although the application was still pending at the time of his death, he was buried with full military honors and received a plot in Fredericksburg National Cemetery. A color guard provided by the American Legion led the cortège from Fredericksburg Presbyterian Church to the cemetery, and seventy-five members of the post took part in

Jack Butler and his son, Roy. Family members scattered Roy's ashes over his father's grave. *Courtesy of Brad Butler.*

the ceremony. According to Butler's daughter, the War Department granted her father special permission to be buried at Fredericksburg National Cemetery because he had applied for American citizenship before his death. He is buried in grave #6698.[33]

Butler's son, Roy, followed in his father's footsteps, serving as a corporal in the U.S. Air Force in Italy during World War II. After the war, he became a noted archaeologist in Fredericksburg. When he died on November 2, 1986, family members wished to bury him at Fredericksburg, but by then the cemetery was closed to new burials, the only exceptions being the spouses of soldiers who were already there. Thwarted in their efforts to have Roy and Jack buried together, the family did the next best thing: they had Roy cremated and scattered his ashes over his father's grave.[34]

# 11. ❀ Stories

Each of the 6,794 headstones in Fredericksburg National Cemetery represents approximately two people, each of whom had his or her own personality and own story. Sadly, most of those stories will never be known; like the people themselves, they have been lost to time. However, a small number remain, either captured in family lore or written down in the form of soldier letters, reminiscences, newspaper articles, or regimental histories. They remind us of those who fought here—their courage, their sacrifice, but most of all their individuality.

## "I Die Like a Man"

Samuel and Sarah Rice cannot have been surprised when their son, Samuel Jr., announced to them in the summer of 1862 that he wanted to join the army. Even as a child he had wished to be a soldier. As a boy he had formed his playmates into a military company with himself as their captain. Years later, with civil war looming, he enlisted in the Kentish Guards, a local militia unit, and despite being just sixteen years old, he was given the rank of sergeant. Two years later, when hostilities began, many men in his community signed up to fight. Rice longed to join them, but his friends, with difficulty, persuaded him that he was too young. A year later, however, when the Seventh Rhode Island was created, Rice decided he had waited long enough. To his parents' distress, he determined to go to war. He was their only son.

He met his end on May 18, 1864, at Spotsylvania Court House. Ordered to silence a Confederate battery, the Seventh Rhode Island quickly found itself pinned down by the very guns it was sent to attack, unable to advance or to retreat. Solid shot plowed up the ground around the regiment, while bursting shells filled the air overhead with fragments of deadly iron. Rice was among the first hit when a shell exploded among his company, killing or wounding six men. The shell must have been very close to the young corporal when it went off, for it shattered his left leg below the knee, tore off his right arm, and inflicted injuries to both his side and his right leg. He nevertheless continued to cheer his comrades on, telling them as they passed, "Boys go in! I can't be with you any more!"[1]

Rice remained conscious for several hours, apparently free of pain. Comrades carried him to a field hospital in the rear, where he died at five o'clock that afternoon. His last words were, "Tell them all at home I die like a man." He now lies in grave #1161.[2]

## Family Breadwinner

The death of every soldier had repercussions that spread far beyond the battlefield. John Warner is a case in point. Warner was the son of German immigrants, and German appears to have been his first language. In fact, in his letters home he signed himself "Johann." His father, a shoemaker by trade, was sixty-one years old when John went off to war. Deaf, nearly blind, tremulous, and suffering from rheumatism, the older man had ceased to support his family many years before, compelling John to labor on nearby farms in order to put food on the family table. His mother, also infirm, gathered rags off the streets and resold them to earn a few dollars more.

Warner was twenty-one when he joined the army as a private on April 30, 1861, at his home in Syracuse, New York. Promotion followed, and Warner was wearing a corporal's chevrons on December 14, 1862, when he died of a wound received in the Battle of Fredericksburg. Comrades buried him in front of the Cunningham house, in Stafford County, where he remained until the Burial Corps moved his remains to grave #4913 in Fredericksburg National Cemetery.

Warner had been the sole support of his parents and three younger siblings when he left home in 1861. Money that he earned as a corporal had kept his family alive for the next year and a half, but with his death that modest flow of revenue came to an abrupt end, leaving his family destitute. His mother applied for a pension in 1870, but the eight dollars a month that she received in compensation for her son's death was hardly enough to keep the family alive.[3] How did they survive between 1862 and 1870? Did his parents have to sell their house? Did John's brothers have to leave school in order to earn a living? Did his sister, Magdalina, have to marry a man she did not love so as not to be a burden to her family? We will probably never know.

# Death of a Zouave

Second Lieutenant Peter D. Froeligh led a charmed life, or so it seemed. Although his regiment fought at Bull Run, Antietam, Fredericksburg, Chancellorsville, and several other battles, the brown-haired, blue-eyed soldier who stood five foot seven had always emerged from the battles unscathed. That was unusual under any circumstances, but what made it even more remarkable was the fact that Froeligh belonged to the Fifth New York Volunteers, a Zouave regiment. Zouaves modeled their uniforms after French army regiments serving in North Africa. In place of the standard navy blue worn by most Union soldiers, they donned flamboyant outfits straight out of *Tales from the Arabian Nights*. Froeligh's Fifth New York, for instance, wore blue jackets and vests trimmed in red, and red pants and sashes trimmed in blue. On their heads they sported red bucket-shaped hats, known as fezzes, swathed in a white turban and dangling a yellow tassel. The colorful uniforms made quite an impression on the ladies, but, as Froeligh and his comrades learned to their grief, they also attracted the attention of enemy riflemen.

After two years the Fifth New York mustered out of service, and Froeligh was transferred to another Zouave regiment, the 146th New York. More battles ensued—Gettysburg, Bristoe Station, Mine Run—but still his luck held. Then came the Wilderness. In the opening engagement of that battle, the 146th New York charged across a clearing known as Saunders Field and grappled with the Confederates in brutal hand-to-hand combat. Froeligh, now a second lieutenant, died in the fighting. Apparently he had foreseen his fate, for on the eve of the battle he had asked a comrade to cut his hair, explaining that "he expected to be shot in the head in the next battle and wanted the surgeon to be able to see the wound clearly."[4]

The twenty-four-year-old officer was interred on the battlefield, possibly by Confederate soldiers. For a year, his grave remained unmarked. Finally, in June 1865, a Union burial party came to the Wilderness and placed a headboard over his grave. It read simply, "Officer of the 146th New York Vols., Killed May, 1864." Government workers eventually dug up Froeligh's remains, brought them to Fredericksburg National Cemetery, and buried them in grave #3834. But still no name appeared on his headstone. The government did not issue dog tags at that time, and the only thing cemetery officials knew about Froeligh was what they could deduce from the location of his original grave and the tattered remnants of his uniform, that is, that he had been a second lieutenant of the 146th New York and had died in the Wilderness. As it turned out, that was enough. Froeligh was the only soldier to match that description. In later years, cemetery officials replaced his anonymous headstone with the current marker that bears his name. Because the new headstone came at a later date, it has a slightly different appearance from the ones around it. But Froeligh would not have minded, for it kept him from being consigned to a nameless grave.[5]

## From the Mines to the Battlefields

Wisconisco differed little from dozens of other small coal towns in Pennsylvania. Each day men like Jacob Workman left their modest homes and trudged wearily through man-made tunnels to labor in the inky blackness of the mines. Come evening, they would return soiled and weary to their homes, eat dinner, enjoy a brief hour or two with their families, and then go to bed in preparation for another day in the dangerous, soot-filled shafts in which they spent their lives. Life was hard and short in such towns, and so it was for Jacob Workman, who died in 1857, leaving behind a wife, Mary, and eight children with another on the way. Jacob's death left his family in dire straits. It had lost not only a husband and father but also its sole provider.

To support the family, Workman's two oldest sons took his place in the mine. The youngest, Josiah, was probably no more than eleven or twelve at the time, but his four-dollar weekly salary, added to that of his older brother, David, kept the family alive. The two boys might have worked in the mines their entire lives had it not been for the Civil War. Both brothers enlisted in the Union army following the attack on Fort Sumter—not just to preserve the Union but to escape the mines. David enlisted in the 127th Pennsylvania and survived the war. Because he was just sixteen at the time, Josiah had to lie about his age. He enlisted in the Ninety-Sixth Pennsylvania in September 1861, earning thirteen dollars a month, ten of which he sent home to his mother. Serving beside him in the same company were two other brothers named Workman, Levi and Joseph—possibly his cousins. The former received a medical discharge in March 1863.[6]

Josiah matured quickly in the army. In a single week in the summer of 1862, he participated in no fewer than three battles, all of which he survived. He was not so lucky at Crampton's Gap, Maryland; one year into his enlistment, he fell in battle there. The wound was not serious, however, and indeed may have preserved his life by keeping him out of the fighting at Antietam and Fredericksburg, two far bloodier battles fought a short time later. Josiah returned to his regiment in December 1862 and in the coming year fought again at Salem Church, Gettysburg, and Rappahannock Station. Each time he emerged unscathed. His luck, it seemed, was improving.

In February 1864, Josiah left the army on furlough to visit his family. When he returned, he brought with him a new recruit: his young brother Frank. Although he could not have been much older than fifteen, Frank was eager to share his brother's adventures, and, like Josiah, he had no compunctions about lying about his age to do so. Both brothers received substantial bounties—Frank for enlisting and Josiah for re-enlisting—money that must have been of infinite value to their cash-strapped mother and younger siblings.[7]

They would pay dearly for that money, however. In May 1864, the Army of the Potomac engaged the Confederate army in the Battle in the Wilderness and then pushed on to Spotsylvania Court House. On May 10, 1864, Colonel Emory Upton assaulted the Confederate lines at Spotsylvania with five thousand men in a column three regiments wide and four regiments deep. The Ninety-Sixth Pennsylvania held a position in the center of Upton's first line. To reach the entrenched Confederate position, it had to cross 250 yards of open ground, tear aside a barrier of felled trees, and scramble over a line of heavy logworks—all the while exposed to the fire of hostile infantry and artillery.

None of the Workmans made it. Before reaching the Confederate works, Frank fell with a round of canister in his chest. A few yards away, Josiah crumpled to the ground, struck in the side—possibly by another ball from the same cannon blast. Joseph, too, fell in the charge. In all, twenty-eight men of the Ninety-Sixth Pennsylvania died in the attack, while thirty others were reported as missing. Survivors buried Josiah and Frank with two other soldiers in a single grave close to the earthworks. "We buried them in one trench," wrote Corporal Henry Kaiser, "first placing a blanket underneath and one on top, placing a board of a cracker box at the head of each, with name, Company and Regiment." Joseph was taken prisoner and later died of his wounds in Richmond.[8]

Josiah and Frank's deaths dealt a crushing blow to their mother both emotionally and financially. She had relied on her sons' wages to pay the mortgage on her house and to support her and the younger children. She would no longer receive those wages. In May 1868, the government compensated her for her loss by granting her an eight-dollar-a-month pension, but it must have seemed a paltry sum for such a great loss.[9]

Around the time Mary was granted her pension, burial crews moved Josiah and Frank's remains to Fredericksburg National Cemetery. They buried the two brothers just yards apart, Frank in grave #3231 and Josiah in grave #3256.[10] Mary may never have known about the graves, for the army originally misidentified her sons as "Frank Woodman" and "J. Wulkman."[11] By the time it erected permanent headstones over the graves in the 1870s, the army had corrected the spelling of the boys' last name, but apparently confusion lingered as to their first names. To this day, the inscription on Josiah's grave erroneously bears the moniker of his relative Joseph.[12]

## The Death of Two Brothers

Except for the Workmans, the Forsythes are the only set of brothers definitely known to be buried in Fredericksburg National Cemetery. Private Leighton G. Forsythe, age twenty-seven, and Private Jesse H. Forsythe, age twenty-two, served together in the Fourth U.S. Volunteer Infantry during the Spanish-American War. Their unit camped at Gunnery Springs, just outside Fredericksburg. For reasons never explained, Jesse had enlisted under the name of Charles Dunn. It may have been because Jesse and Leighton wished to stay together, and military policy following the Civil War forbade brothers from serving in the same regiment.

A train struck the brothers on August 7, 1898, near Potomac Run, six miles north of Fredericksburg. Although the circumstances surrounding their deaths in unclear, it is believed that they were walking along the tracks toward Brooke, Virginia, with the intention of catching a train to Washington, D.C., and fell asleep on the tracks.

The Forsythes had worked as painters in Washington prior to their enlistment three months earlier. Their mangled bodies were brought to Fredericksburg and buried in the national cemetery with military honors the day following their deaths. They lay side by side in graves #6631 and #6632.[13]

## A Tragic Accident

Not all soldiers died by disease or enemy bullets; a small number died as a result of accidents in camp. Such was the case of Private Heinrich Kullman of the 140th New York. The German native had survived the horrific fighting in the Wilderness and at Laurel Hill and was eating breakfast with other members of his regiment on May 17, 1864, when the rifle of a nearby soldier accidentally discharged, killing Private Daniel Cooper and wounding Kullman in the leg. The thirty-one-year-old Kullman was carried to a field hospital at the Gayle house, where he expired later that night. He is buried in grave #240 under a headstone that misidentifies him as "Henry Coleman."[14]

## A Mother's Sacrifice

Many mothers lost a son in the Civil War; some lost two. Agnes Allison lost four. When the Civil War began, Allison was a widow with six sons, four of whom left their home in the coal-mining town of Port Carbon, Pennsylvania, to become soldiers. Alexander, age twenty-three, became a second lieutenant in the Ninety-Sixth Pennsylvania Infantry. His older brothers, James and George, both of whom worked as boatmen on the Schuylkill Canal, enlisted the First Pennsylvania Cavalry and Fifty-Sixth Pennsylvania Infantry, respectively. A third brother, nineteen-year-old John, served under his brother Alexander as a corporal in the Ninety-Sixth Pennsylvania.

On May 3, 1863, the Ninety-Sixth Pennsylvania received orders to charge the Confederate line at Salem Church, four miles west of Fredericksburg. Alexander was shot through the stomach and transported by comrades to a hospital back at Aquia Landing. The journey was too much for him, however, and he died on May 5, just hours after his arrival there. His brother John died in the same action, but unlike Alexander his body was not recovered. After the war Alexander was buried in grave #6145A in Fredericksburg National Cemetery. John presumably lies near his brother in an unknown grave.

George led a charmed life. As a sergeant in the Fifty-Sixth Pennsylvania, he survived more than half a dozen bloody conflicts with nary a scratch. But his luck ran out at Spotsylvania Court House. On May 12, 1864, the Fifty-Sixth Pennsylvania was pulled from its position on the Union right to reinforce troops fighting at the Bloody Angle. In the ensuing struggle, George was shot in the hip. Carried to the rear, he was placed aboard a ship at Aquia Landing and sent to a general hospital in Washington, D.C. He died there on May 23.

In some ways, James's story is the most tragic of all. He served in the First Pennsylvania Cavalry until November 1862, when he was thrown against the pommel of his horse. So severe were his injuries that he received a discharge and returned home, where he remained until early 1864. Wishing perhaps to avenge the deaths of his brothers Alexander and John, he reentered the service, this time as a private in the Forty-Eighth Pennsylvania. He survived the vicious fighting in the Wilderness and at Spotsylvania Court House only to fall in combat just weeks later near Bethesda Church, outside of Richmond.

Agnes Allison—already a widow—had sacrificed four sons on the altar of liberty, perhaps more than any other mother in the North. (The oft-told story of Lydia Bixby losing five sons is not true; she lost but two.) To compensate for her loss, Allison received a fifteen-dollar-per-month pension from the federal government and the gratitude of her community. Union veterans named the local Grand Army of the Republic post after her sons, and when she died in 1887 they organized an impressive funeral for her. Some twenty-one years later, the citizens of Port Carbon unveiled a monument to Mrs. Allison and her sons in the town's Presbyterian Cemetery. It was a fitting tribute to a family that had sacrificed so much.[15]

## Finding a Body in the Cemetery

While working at the cemetery in October 1873, laborers discovered the remains of a soldier buried just inside the wall near the northwest corner of division C, section D. The body, which had its head to the north and its feet to the south, lay one foot below the surface of the ground and was dressed in Union clothing. It had no coffin. Superintendent Charles Fitchett surmised that the soldier had died on May 3, 1863, during the Second Battle of Fredericksburg. He exhumed the remains, placed them in a "rough coffin box," and reburied them just feet from where his men found them. The soldier's identity is unknown.[16]

## Comrades in Life and Death

Fred Wildt and James E. Clark were childhood chums. Both had grown up in Ann Arbor, Michigan, and when the Civil War began they enlisted together in Company D of the Fourth Michigan. Wildt was then twenty-two; Clark, who had moved to the United States from England as a child, was nineteen. Although he was the younger of the two, Clark enlisted as a corporal while his friend joined the ranks as a private. Over the course of the next sixteen months, Clark moved up through the ranks, first to sergeant major and then to lieutenant. By the end of 1862 he was the regiment's acting adjutant. Sadly, both young men yielded up their lives at Fredericksburg. Major John Randolph remembered that just moments before his death, Clark walked along the firing line and, halting over his friends in Company D, who were lying prone on the ground, urged them to keep their front rank filled. "One of the boys told him to keep down, or he would be hit," Randolph wrote. "The words were hardly out of his mouth when a musket ball struck poor Jimmy on the third button of his overcoat, glanced to the left and went directly through him!'"[17]

Wildt too died instantly. "And what shall I say of Fred. Wildt?" Randolph asked. "He was the First Corporal in company D, and one of the best and neatest soldiers in the regiment, ever ready to do his duty, which was always done cheerfully and willingly; and one who kept the neatest and cleanest equipments in the company. Brave boy! He, too, has yielded up his young life upon his country's altar. He, too, was carried to the rear; and to-day Fred Wildt and James Clark lie side by side in Fredericksburg." Captain J. W. Hall and Chaplain John Seage buried them "on a pretty little knoll, in separate coffins, marking the graves with a carved head board, in order to find them again if necessary."[18] The knoll stood on a parcel of land known as Genther's lot, located in what is now the neighborhood of Mayfield. In 1866 or shortly thereafter, a burial crew discovered the young men's remains and reinterred them side by side in graves #2863 and #2864 of Fredericksburg National Cemetery.

## No Greater Love

On May 7, 1864, the 140th New York held a position on the south side of the Orange Turnpike in the Wilderness. There was little fighting that day, and Private Morris Ritter volunteered to slip out in front of the lines to do some scouting. While there, he encountered a Confederate on a similar errand. Ritter brought him back as a prisoner. That night the Union army started for Spotsylvania Court House. Two miles shy of the town, it encountered Confederate troops entrenched at Laurel Hill. The 140th New York attacked the enemy line but had to retreat, leaving its leader, Colonel George Ryan, mortally wounded between the lines. Five men of the regiment volunteered to go out and bring him in. All five were killed in the attempt, including Ritter, who had made it to Ryan's side and was attempting to carry him back when he was killed. He is buried in grave #5079.[19]

If possible, Lieutenant Frank Lombard's story is worthy of even greater praise. A former employee with the Smith and Wesson factory in Springfield, Massachusetts, Lombard enlisted in the First Massachusetts Cavalry, a regiment armed with single-shot carbines. During the war, the regiment traded in these weapons for Spencer seven-shot repeating rifles. Because of his expertise in firearms, Lombard received the first Spencer rifle in the regiment.

It is bravery rather than his marksmanship that makes Lombard noteworthy, however. On November 27, 1863, the First Massachusetts Cavalry and the First New Jersey Cavalry regiments battled Confederates at New Hope Church, a sanctuary situated on the Orange Plank Road just east of Mine Run. A soldier in the First New Jersey had been badly wounded, and as Union troops fell back, the men in his regiment abandoned him to his fate. Lombard and Private John Doran refused to let that happen. Although they did not know the man, they went back at the risk of their lives and tried to bring him off. Lombard paid for his bravery with his life. As he was carrying the wounded man to the rear in his arms, a Confederate bullet struck him in the head, killing him instantly. He is now buried in grave #4100.[20]

## One Vacant Chair

Like so many other Northern soldiers, David W. Stevens (#3205A) sacrificed his comfort, happiness, and ultimately his life for the Union. Although he had a wife and five young children, the thirty-five-year-old farmer left his home in south-central Pennsylvania in March 1862 to enlist as a corporal in the Forty-First Pennsylvania Infantry. He was later promoted to sergeant. David's younger brother Frank served with him in the Forty-First Pennsylvania, while a second brother, William, became chaplain of the 148th regiment. Like many men who wore the blue, David wished to preserve the Union intact for his children. Unfortunately, one of them would not live to enjoy that blessing. His four-year-old daughter Lucinda died in 1863 while he was away in the army. David would follow her to the grave one year later.[21]

On May 8, 1864, the Army of the Potomac engaged Robert E. Lee's Confederates at Spotsylvania Court House. The Forty-First Pennsylvania went into the battle at sunset near Laurel Hill. In the fighting that ensued, David Stevens and some of his comrades captured a Confederate soldier. As they brought him to the rear, the prisoner snatched a loaded weapon from the ground and shot David through the body, inflicting a mortal wound. Stevens's enraged friends wrenched the weapon from the man's hands and battered him to death with it. Some soldiers of the 100th Pennsylvania, who witnessed the incident, carried David to the rear and laid him beneath a pine tree, where he soon breathed his last.[22]

Frank Stevens found his brother's corpse the next day. Major General John Sedgwick's headquarters were just a hundred yards away, and Frank requested that the general provide a detail of men to help him bury the body. Sedgwick kindly agreed. It was one of the last things he ever did. Before the soldiers had completed the grave, Sedgwick was dead, the victim of a Confederate sharpshooter. Frank was too consumed by his own personal grief to pay more than passing notice to the general's demise. "It was the saddest day that had ever come to my young life," he later wrote of David's death, "when on the morrow after the battle I wrapped his mangled body in his blanket and placed it in its narrow grave." Having completed that mournful office, he then performed an even more sorrowful task: he wrote to David's wife "telling her that she was a widow, and that her four little children were fatherless."[23]

Two days later, on May 11, Frank conducted his brother William to David's grave. They found the area under heavy bombardment. "The shot was falling so heavily about the grave that we were compelled to leave our horses in shelter and creep to it," William recalled. Although the artillery fire was then too intense to examine the grave closely, William made it to the site a short time later and found that a Confederate shell had torn up the ground around it. Fortunately, the grave was deep enough that the body was not disturbed.[24]

David's death deeply affected not only his wife and children but also his brothers. "Others may sing 'When Johnny comes marching home again,'" Frank reflected, "but I will join with the sad hearts singing, 'We shall meet but we shall miss him; There will be one vacant chair.'"[25]

Sergeant David Stevens. *Courtesy of Roy S. Stevens.*

# Cut Down in Their Youth

Far more soldiers died of germs than of bullets. One of these was Private Tilghman Jacoby (#5830). The son of a German shoemaker, Jacoby's blue eyes and blond hair bore evidence to his Teutonic heritage. In the summer of 1862, when just eighteen, he left his uncle's farm near Harrisburg and enlisted in the 128th Pennsylvania. Remaining behind was a wife named Catherine, whom Jacoby had married just a few weeks earlier. Although he did not know it at the time, she was pregnant.

Jacoby escaped the horrific Battle of Antietam unharmed only to contract dysentery a few days later while camped on Maryland Heights, just outside of Harpers Ferry. Despite his illness, he remained with the army when it pursued General Robert E. Lee's Confederates back into Virginia. Defeated at Fredericksburg in December, the Army of the Potomac settled into winter quarters in Stafford County. As snow and frigid temperatures gripped the countryside, Jacoby's health took a turn for the worse: his dysentery turned into typhoid fever. In early February he entered a hospital, but he never improved. Just after midnight, February 20, 1863, he breathed his last.

A guard consisting of a lieutenant, a corporal, and two privates transported Jacoby's corpse in an ambulance to the Army of the Potomac's supply base at Aquia Landing. There, they procured a coffin in order to send Jacoby's body back to Pennsylvania. Something interfered with that plan, however, and they ended up burying him at the landing. Tilghman's friends informed Catherine of what they had done with her husband's remains in case she wanted to send for them. She never did. She had given birth to a son just days earlier, and as a young widow with a child to support, she simply could not afford it. Catherine received a pension of just eight dollars a month after her husband's death, but she had to forfeit even that modest sum when she remarried in September 1866. Her new husband was Milton Jacoby, Tilghman's brother.[26]

Ira M. Whittaker also died of disease during the harsh winter encampment that followed the Battle of Fredericksburg. What made Whittaker's death so poignant was his extreme youth. Jacoby had been eighteen when he died; Whittaker was just sixteen. Whittaker, a soldier in the Thirteenth New Hampshire, was the first soldier in his company to perish. That, together with his tender age, led to an outpouring of grief among his comrades. As one remarked, "The simple burial of a private soldier is one of the saddest scenes on earth at any time, but here departs a mere boy."[27] Sympathetic friends fashioned a crude coffin for the lad out of three cracker boxes placed end to end and nailed together with a couple of saplings. His company then formed ranks and marched to the burial site to the beat of a muffled drum with arms reversed, a fifer or two playing a dirge.

Cursory as Whittaker's ceremony may seem, it was better than many soldiers received. Those who died on the field of battle often had no burial at all. Whittaker also had one other advantage that most other soldiers did not enjoy: his friends took the precaution of placing in the grave a corked bottle containing his name, regiment, and home address, so that family members could identify his remains after the war even if the wooden headboard had disappeared. It is probably due to that bit of foresight that Whittaker today occupies a grave that bears his name (#2086). Five out of every six men buried in Fredericksburg National Cemetery are not so fortunate.[28]

# First to the Slaughter

It was 1864. Spring had finally arrived and with it a new campaign, one that both sides felt might decide the war. Around Culpeper, Virginia, soldiers of the Army of the Potomac packed their winter belongings and sent them to the rear, and after dark on May 3, 1864, they started south toward the Rapidan River. Six weeks of incessant fighting and more than fifty thousand Union casualties lay ahead. Among the first of those casualties was Sergeant Joseph M. Sieger of the 140th New York (#3778). Sieger and his regiment crossed the Rapidan on May 4, camping that night in the Wilderness. The next morning, as they were breaking camp, word arrived that Southern troops were approaching in force along the Orange Turnpike. Wrongly believing that the force constituted just a small portion of the Confederate army, army commander George G. Meade determined to attack the Confederates and destroy them. The 140th led the opening assault.

The Confederates had taken a position along the western edge of Saunders Field. The men of the 140th advanced to the opposite side of the field and lay down. Finally, after what seemed an interminable delay, they received the order to advance. With a shout the regiment started forward, led by its colonel, George Ryan. Bullets thinned the blue ranks as they crossed the field, but the New Yorkers resolutely continued forward, finally coming to grips with the enemy in the woods beyond. Ryan's men lacked support on both ends of the line, however, and the 140th quickly found itself not only outflanked but nearly surrounded. Finding themselves under fire from all directions, Ryan's men broke for the rear, suffering even greater casualties in their retreat than they had in their advance. "The regiment melted away like snow. Men disappeared as if the earth had swallowed them," remembered one officer. In all, 268 New Yorkers fell in the attack.[29]

Three bullets plowed through the body of Joseph Sieger: one entered his right hip, a second pierced his stomach, and a third shattered his left arm. One of Sieger's men, Private John McGraw, found him lying on the field and helped him to the rear. Sieger had looked after McGraw when he had first joined the regiment, and McGraw had not forgotten his kindness. As he looked at his wounded friend, tears flowed from his eyes. He gently helped Sieger to his feet and helped him walk three-quarters of a mile to the rear, where he procured a stretcher for his friend. At a field hospital later that day, a surgeon examined Sieger's wounds and told him that he could not live. "Doctor, do not tell me that!" the sergeant exclaimed. But it was true. He died later that day, among the first to give his life in what was to be the bloodiest campaign of the Civil War.[30]

## A Patriotic Family

Interred in grave #1840 is Liberty Richards, a private in the Thirteenth New Hampshire. Richards, who was forty-seven years old at the time of his enlistment, was not drafted; in fact, he had to lie about his age in order to get into the army, telling enlistment officers that he was just forty-three. His sixteen-year-old son, Silas, enlisted with him. According to family tradition, Silas too lied about his age, but in his case he had to add a couple of years. In addition to Silas, Liberty Richards had three other sons who fought for the Union, and two of Liberty's brothers likewise served in Northern regiments. When Liberty marched off to war, he left behind a wife, Abigail, three daughters, and two young sons. Abigail was then pregnant with a fourth daughter.

Fredericksburg was Liberty Richards's first and last battle. Exposed to cold weather both before and after the fighting, he succumbed to heart disease on December 26, 1862, while being treated at a field hospital in Stafford County. It was his forty-eighth birthday. Fortunately, each of his sons survived the war.[31]

## Three Brothers

During the Civil War it was not unusual for members of the same family to serve together in the same regiment. Such was the case with the Hitchcock brothers. Stanbury, Eli, and Chauncey (better known as "Chant") left their home in Millville, Wisconsin, in 1861 and enlisted in the Badger State Guards, an organization that later became Company H of the Seventh Wisconsin, a regiment in the famous Iron Brigade. Two of the boys never made it back. In the spring of 1862, Eli fell ill and was taken to a hospital on Potomac Creek, approximately eight miles east of Fredericksburg. Placed on a "good straw bed," he was cared for by soldiers detailed as nurses, some of whom, his brother Stanbury claimed, were so hard-hearted that they "dont care whether a man lives or dies." Perhaps for that very reason Chant remained with Eli throughout his illness, acting as his brother's personal attendant. It did no good. Despite Chant's constant attentions, Eli died on May 16.[32]

Stanbury was the next to go. Although severely wounded in the ankle at South Mountain, Maryland, in September 1862, he was able to return to duty after a few months. However, death continued to dog him. On May 10, 1864, during the fighting at Laurel Hill, a gentle ridge two miles northwest of Spotsylvania Court House, a shell fragment struck Stanbury, killing him instantly. Comrades recovered his body and interred it on the Sanford farm. Chant was not available to help bury his brother, having been seriously wounded himself in the Wilderness just a few days earlier. Fortunately, he survived his wound and returned home in 1865. Not so Eli and Stanbury, the former who now occupies grave #3028.[33] Stanbury too is probably buried at Fredericksburg National Cemetery but, like so many, occupies an unknown grave.

## Death at the Bloody Angle

Each year thousands of people visit the infamous "Bloody Angle" on Spotsylvania Battlefield. Today it is a quiet, peaceful spot, but in May 1864 it was a scene of unspeakable horror, what one soldier described as "a seething, bubbling, roaring hell of hate and murder."[34] For twenty-two hours, Union and Confederate soldiers struggled with one another over a short stretch of earth and log breastworks, their bodies piling up like cordwood on the rain-soaked ground. "The trenches are filled with them," wrote a soldier who later examined the site, "4 and 5 on top of each other, and sometimes the lowest on the bottom are wounded and alive, yet were covered with mud and smothered. Trees of 1 and 2 feet thick are shot off by musket bullets, and the wounded and dead bodies which had fallen in the first charge at the commencement of the battle were shot to pieces. . . . God, have mercy on those who started this cruel war."[35]

Since 1909 a stone sentinel has stood guard over the site, its cold, soulless eyes staring south across the scene of carnage. The figure is carved into the face

of a monument dedicated to the Fifteenth New Jersey, a regiment composed
of troops from the northwestern quadrant of the state. The regiment charged
into battle around 10 a.m., more than five hours after fighting at the Angle
first erupted. Because the Fifteenth held a position on the extreme right of the
attacking Union line, it received fire not only in its front but from unengaged
Confederate troops on its flank. Despite taking heavy casualties, the regiment
swept across an open field and engaged the enemy in a hand-to-hand fight
over the works, capturing one hundred prisoners and a Georgia battle flag. But
without support on its right, it could not hold its position. After thirty minutes,
the Fifteenth New Jersey relinquished its hold on the Confederate works and
fell back across the field, leaving 151 dead and wounded men its wake.[36]

Among the slain were Lieutenant George C. Justice (#3351), Corporal
John L. Young (#2966), and Sergeant Paul Kuhl (#3077). Young, an eighteen-
year-old member of the regimental color guard, appears to have fallen early in
the charge. Despite his wound, he managed to drag himself to safety in the
rear. He was later found lying behind a log, dead, his hands clasped in prayer
over his breast. By contrast, Kuhl was shot in the leg in front of the works. In
an effort to stanch the bleeding, he fashioned a tourniquet for himself using
a handkerchief and a bayonet tightened above his wound. The retreat of his
regiment, however, left the young sergeant stranded between the lines and
exposed to fire from both sides. By the end of the day, dozens of bullets had
perforated his body, leaving it a mass of lifeless flesh.[37] George Justice was the
only one of the three to reach the Confederate works. When the Fifteenth
New Jersey struck the Confederate line, the thirty-six-year-old father of seven
mounted the enemy works with sword in hand urging his men forward. An
instant later, he toppled from the parapet, shot in the back by a Confederate
soldier who had surrendered and then rejoined the fight. In retribution, one
of Justice's men pinned the killer to the ground with his bayonet.[38]

On the night of May 12–13, the Confederates fell back, leaving the Union
army master of the field. In the brief lull that followed, soldiers of the Fifteenth New Jersey fanned across the now-bloody ground searching for their
missing friends. Justice, Kuhl, Young, and eight others were buried together in
shallow, muddy graves close to where they fell, their identities hastily carved
on boards taken from abandoned hardtack boxes. The regiment's remaining
dead—about forty in all—had to be buried in a single unmarked grave when
the regiment was suddenly ordered to a new position. While all of these men
now presumably lie in Fredericksburg National Cemetery, most of them
occupy unknown graves.[39]

Lieutenant George Justice (*left*) and Sergeant Paul Kuhl (*right*), Fifteenth New Jersey Volunteers. Both lost their lives at Spotsylvania's Bloody Angle. *Courtesy of Bilby, Three Rousing Cheers, and John Kuhl.*

## Friends to the End

Living in Lawrence County, Pennsylvania, at the time of the war were two teenage boys, Sam Wilson and Dave Hutchison. Sam and Davy were as close as brothers, the neighbors often remarking that "if Davy gets his feet wet, Sam's sure to take a cold!" When Brigadier General John H. Morgan's Confederate cavalry invaded Ohio in 1863, the two boys enlisted in an emergency regiment to resist his advance. Morgan's Raiders were captured before the boys saw any combat, and the regiment disbanded. But Sam and Davy were unwilling to quit the war without having seen action, and they re-enlisted in the 100th Pennsylvania. Although their parents cried at their parting, they permitted the boys to go, believing "that since there were so many who had had to give up their sons 'they should do their share.'" Neither boy returned home. Sam died at Spotsylvania on May 12, 1864, in an attack against a portion of the Confederate line known as Heth's Salient. His comrades buried him where he fell. He is now interred in grave #1177. Davy was captured at Spotsylvania and died from starvation in a Southern prison camp.[40]

# A Horrible Discovery

On October 20, 1896, Fredericksburg National Cemetery was the scene of a tragedy. At 5:00 p.m., employee E. P. Carneal heard a shot. Fifteen minutes later, when he climbed Willis Hill to lower the cemetery flag, he discovered a man fifty-five to sixty years of age with blond hair, moustache, and chin whiskers, seated on a cemetery bench. The man was dead, shot through the right temple. In his hand he held a .32-caliber pistol with an empty chamber. Carneal rushed back down the hill to the cemetery lodge and returned with Superintendent Richard Hill. Taking in the situation, Hill summoned the police and local coroner. An inquest held on the spot concluded that the man had died by his own hand.

Documents found in his pockets identified the victim as William T. Rambusch of Juneau, Wisconsin, a veteran of the Fifty-First New York. Born in 1839, the Denmark native had graduated from the University of Copenhagen in 1859 and immigrated to the United States in 1860. A few months later, he enlisted in the Union army. Rambusch received his discharge in January 1863, following the Battle of Fredericksburg, and moved to Minnesota; he lived there until 1874, when he relocated to Juneau, where he soon took his place as one of the town's leading men. Over a period of twenty years, Rambusch became a bank president, co-owner of an investment company, and the chairman of the Dodge County Republican Party. He also became a thief. During his sojourn in Juneau, he defrauded clients out of an estimated half-million dollars by altering his ledger books.

Rambusch's crimes came to light in October 1896, when a client discovered that he had changed the mortgage figure on his property title from $2,500 to $500. Realizing that he was about to be exposed, Rambusch fled to Philadelphia. Once there, he wrote his wife a letter in which he admitted his guilt and told her of his intention to commit suicide. He wished to be buried in Fredericksburg National Cemetery, he said, rather than in Wisconsin. Traveling by train to Fredericksburg, Rambusch checked in at the Exchange Hotel under the name of C. A. Anderson. For several days he remained there undetected. On the day of his death, however, he discovered an article in the *New York Herald* chronicling his misdeeds, including a woodcut bearing his likeness. Realizing that detection was now but a matter of time, the fugitive resolved to put his terrible plan into action. After writing a few last letters, he left the hotel, walked across town to the cemetery, and ended his life. Despite his wishes, Rambusch was not buried in Fredericksburg. Believing that his uncle's malfeasance disqualified him from an honorable burial in a national cemetery, a nephew sent the body back to Wisconsin.[41]

## Lasting Friendship

Soldiers form strong and lasting bonds of friendship with one another. So it was with Privates Hiram Lare and John B. Cooke. Prior to the war, Lare had worked as a boatman on one of the rivers near Philadelphia, but in September 1861 he left his job and joined the Ninety-Fifth Pennsylvania. While in the service he met Cooke, and the two became fast friends. Lare looked out for Cooke, who was only a teenager at the time and rather frail. Cooke remembered the many times that Lare gave him his last piece of hardtack from his haversack and the last drop of water from his canteen. And during the long march to Gettysburg, Lare insisted on carrying his friend's rifle and knapsack so he could keep up with the regiment.

On May 12, 1864, Lare died at Spotsylvania's "Bloody Angle," a battle in which Cooke was wounded in the leg. Because of his injury, Cooke could not dig a grave for his friend, so he asked others to do it for him. While they excavated a grave with their bayonets, Cooke scratched Lare's name and unit on a cartridge box lid that would act as a headboard. When the job was finished, Cooke thanked the strangers, tears of emotion choking his young voice.

In coming years, he often wondered what had become of his friend's remains. Were they still buried where he had left him, or had authorities discovered his remains and reburied them in a national cemetery? The answer to that question came in 1931 when Major Arthur E. Wilbourn, responding to an inquiry by Cooke, found Lare's name in the cemetery register. He wrote to Cooke informing him that his friend occupied grave #3247. Cooke replied with a letter thanking Wilbourn for his efforts. "For sixty-seven years I have wondered and worried if his body had a soldiers' [*sic*] resting place—not the bloody spot I saw it last. I wish it was possible for me to lay a rose on his grave on May 30"—Memorial Day—"as a token of love and gratitude for him that has never died." Because the ninety-year-old veteran was not able to come to Fredericksburg to perform that deed himself, Wilbourn had it done in his absence. At the Memorial Day program later that month, he had the daughter of a Union veteran place a single rose at Lare's grave on Cooke's behalf.[42]

## Once Lost, Now Found, Never Forgotten

Sergeant Jerome Peirce of Orange, Massachusetts, enlisted in the Thirty-Sixth Massachusetts on August 4, 1862. When the thirty-one-year-old mechanic died on May 12, 1864, at Spotsylvania Court House, he left behind a twenty-nine-year-old widow named Albinia (nicknamed Allie) and a four-year-old daughter named Lucy. After the war, Allie learned that her husband occupied a plot in Fredericksburg National Cemetery (#540). She sent Superintendent Andrew J. Birdsall a check for one hundred dollars with a note requesting that he decorate her husband's grave regularly. Birdsall did so, opening an account at Farmers and Merchants Bank from which he drew money each Memorial Day to decorate the grave with flowers.

When the Quartermaster Department transferred Birdsall to a different cemetery in 1892, his grown daughters, who remained in town, took over the task. One granddaughter, Mrs. Alice Heflin Abernathy, continued the tradition until her own death in the 1990s. "He was always just Jerome to us," she once told a reporter. "We never really knew anything about him except that his family sent my grandfather $100 and asked us to take care of his grave. It was our duty, so that's what we've done." Since Mrs. Abernathy's death, her nieces have taken over that responsibility—the fourth generation to do so. Each year, just before Memorial Day, they place flowers on Jerome Peirce's grave with a card that reads, "Once lost, now found, never forgotten."[43]

Albinia Peirce (*top left*), who arranged for Superintendent Andrew Birdsall (*left*) to place Memorial Day flowers on the grave of her husband, Jerome (*above*). Birdsall's descendants carry on the tradition to this day. *Courtesy of Patricia M. Mason.*

# 12. ❀ Memorial Day Commemorations

Allie Peirce's desire to decorate her husband's grave with flowers was not unique. As soon as the Civil War ended, citizens began making pilgrimages to military cemeteries throughout the country to adorn the graves of their fallen soldiers. Fredericksburg was no exception. On May 3, 1866, Elizabeth French of "Sunny Side" farm in Spotsylvania County noted in her diary that "Lizzie and I adorned the Soldiers graves with flowers this afternoon." She was referring, of course, to Confederate graves.[1] The impulse to honor the fallen was just as great in the North. On May 5, 1868, Major General John A. Logan, commander of the Grand Army of the Republic (GAR), issued General Orders No. 11, formally instituting the decoration of Union graves. In the order he declared, "The 30th day of May, 1868, is designated for the purpose of strewing with flowers or otherwise decorating the graves of comrades who died in defense of their country during the late rebellion. . . . In this observance no form of ceremony is presented, but posts and comrades will in their own way arrange such fitting services and testimonials of respect as circumstances will permit."[2] With that, Decoration Day—better known as Memorial Day—was born.

## An Unfortunate Incident, 1871

In Fredericksburg, Logan's proclamation had little effect—at least among the area's white populace—because so few had supported the Union. African Americans, however, took the general's proclamation to heart. Wishing to honor those who had died for their freedom, black citizens began coming to Fredericksburg in 1868 from Washington, D.C., and Richmond, Virginia, to formally pay homage to their fallen liberators. Their arrival on June 13, 1871, created quite a stir. Charles Fitchett had just become cemetery superintendent the year before, and he had no knowledge of the former slaves' annual pilgrimage to Fredericksburg. Understandably, he became quite alarmed when he looked out his door one day and saw a throng of black excursionists pouring through the cemetery gates. By the time he got outside, a brass band was playing on

164

the grounds. It was Fitchett's job to maintain order in the cemetery, and the group's noisy, unannounced arrival threw him into a tizzy. Charging into the crowd, he located the party's leader and demanded that the band stop playing.[3]

At that, some people in the crowd became unruly. Two men began to scuffle with one another just inside the gate, prompting Fitchett to order them off the grounds. One obeyed; the other refused to go. The embattled superintendent forcibly evicted the man, despite threats by his friends that they would kill Fitchett if he did not let him go. With each passing minute the crowd grew more turbulent. Fights erupted. With matters fast deteriorating, Fitchett demanded that the party leave the cemetery at once. The group reluctantly complied and started back to the depot. On the way, additional fights broke out. Several men and one woman were injured. By now, crowds of Fredericksburg citizens appeared, adding fuel to an already volatile situation. Some people in the throng threw stones, and at one point someone drew a pistol. The situation had all the makings of a riot. Fortunately, authorities were able to restore order, and the excursionists left town without further incident.[4]

The following day, Fitchett shot off a letter to his superiors in the Quartermaster Department describing the incident. He recommended that in the future no large group of any kind be allowed in the cemetery except on Memorial Day. Fitchett's immediate superior endorsed his proposal, but Acting Quartermaster General Judson D. Bingham did not. In reply to Fitchett's letter, Bingham wrote that "national cemeteries should always be open to all orderly visitors, whether single or in parties or processions. The only exclusion," he stressed, "should be of those who are disorderly or rioters."[5]

## Fredericksburg's First Multiracial Ceremony, 1871

Two weeks before this unfortunate incident took place, Fredericksburg citizens held their first Memorial Day program in the national cemetery. Organizing the program was a group of "Northern settlers" led by William Hays and postmaster M. J. Griffith. The group set a date and time for the exercises and appointed a committee to find "a competent orator of national reputation" to speak at the event. Present at the organizational meeting were men and women, white and black—"the first thing of the kind we remember ever to have seen in this quarter," wrote the editor of the *Virginia Herald* with evident disapproval.[6]

At the invitation of Fredericksburg's organizing committee, the John A. Rawlins Post No. 1 of the GAR, out of Washington, D.C., took charge of the Memorial Day exercises. It selected Brevet Brigadier General William

S. Truex to be marshal for the event and Brevet Brigadier General Reuben D. Mussey to give the keynote address.[7] Members of the Rawlins Post traveled to Aquia Landing aboard the steamship *Ironsides* and then by train to Fredericksburg. At the station they were met by a committee representing the Laboring Mechanics' Union, a black organization called the Good Samaritan Temperance Division, and the town's Unionist citizens. Under the supervision of General Truex, the crowd formed an orderly procession and slowly made its way through town to the cemetery. The men of the Rawlins Post led the way with music provided by St. Cecilia's Band of Georgetown, D.C., and Scott's Brass Band of Fredericksburg, the latter an all-black ensemble.

Advertisement for an 1871 Memorial Day excursion to Fredericksburg. *Courtesy of Robert K. Krick.*

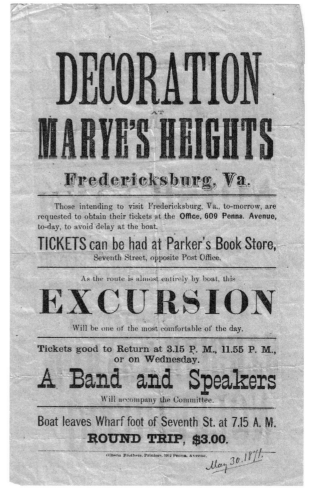

# DECORATION

### AT

# MARYE'S HEIGHTS

## Fredericksburg, Va.

Those intending to visit Fredericksburg, Va., to-morrow, are requested to obtain their tickets at the **Office, 609 Penna. Avenue**, to-day, to avoid delay at the boat.

## TICKETS can be had at Parker's Book Store,
Seventh Street, opposite Post Office.

As the route is almost entirely by boat, this

# EXCURSION

Will be one of the most comfortable of the day.

Tickets good to Return at 3.15 P. M., 11.55 P. M., or on Wednesday.

## A Band and Speakers
Will accompany the Committee.

Boat leaves Wharf foot of Seventh St. at 7.15 A. M.
**ROUND TRIP, $3.00.**

Gibson Brothers, Printers, 102 Penna. Avenue.

*May 30. 1871.*

The program attracted a large and diverse audience, including many black residents and nearly every "Northern settler" within twenty miles of the town. In all, as many as fifteen hundred people may have attended. Absent were the area's many Southern loyalists, who predictably shunned the event. At that time, the cemetery did not have a rostrum. Instead, Union veterans formed a hollow square around the flagstaff mound, and the crowd filled in behind them.

Dr. M. J. Griffith opened the ceremony by welcoming the Rawlins Post on behalf of Fredericksburg's organizing committee, to which J. T. Smith, the post commander, made suitable reply. There followed a long succession of musical numbers, orations, poems, and prayers. The highlight of the program came toward the end, when the crowd formed a procession and marched through the cemetery strewing flowers on graves, each of which was decorated by a small American flag. The bands led the way, playing dirges. Having offered its floral tribute, the crowd reassembled around the flagstaff to sing the doxology and hear a benediction.[8]

Not everyone in Fredericksburg supported, or even quietly tolerated, decoration of the Union graves. The editor of the staunchly unreconstructed *Fredericksburg News* groused,

> Who are these "heroes" whose graves you invite this community, white and black, unitedly, to "honor?" Are they not some of them, the men who bombarded and destroyed one half of Fredericksburg? who sacked our houses? who profaned and polluted our homes and firesides and most sacred relics of the past? who robbed us, and even destroyed what they could not steal? who desecrated our alters [*sic*] and our church[e]s, in which we had worshiped since childhood? Did they not overwhelm us at last by more "brute force of numbers," after the Confederates, man for man, had whipped and destroyed them two to one? All these things are *history*, and will not be denied by any but the ignorant or the depraved.

Although the editor of the *Fredericksburg Ledger* dismissed his competitor as a "constitutional fault-finder," a "bomb-proof hero," and a "cross-grained lunatic," it is likely that the latter's comments reflected the views of most white Fredericksburg residents. Certainly members of the GAR thought so. Thirteen years passed before they would again return to Fredericksburg.[9]

## African American Commemorations, 1872–80

Undeterred by the criticism of local whites, African Americans continued to commemorate Memorial Day each summer. In 1872, a largely black audience hosted exercises featuring Scott's Brass Band, a black preacher from New York, and two white U.S. government officials.[10] Two years later, a "Mr. W. L. Ives, Esq.," spoke at the cemetery to an assembly probably consisting of both black and white residents. These are the only Memorial Day gatherings on record at Fredericksburg in which white orators spoke at what were primarily African American events.[11]

After that, Fredericksburg's black residents appear to have commemorated Memorial Day without their white neighbors. Their exercises mirrored those later hosted by the GAR but on a smaller scale. Participants gathered at Fredericksburg's African American Baptist Church and then marched in a procession through the town to the national cemetery, preceded by Scott's Brass Band. Some years they simply placed flowers on the graves and left, but most years they held a small ceremony featuring local dignitaries like the Reverend Albert Ray or black speakers from Washington. Black organizations like the Good Samaritan Society, the International Order of the Good Samaritans, or the Daughters of Samaritans sometimes took part in the exercises, decked out in the full regalia of their orders.[12]

In 1893, a writer for the *Fredericksburg Free Lance* looked back with derision upon these early ceremonies.

> Some twenty years ago . . . a few colored people, a scattering crowd of men, women, and children, headed by a forlorn white man in the person of a postmaster or deputy collector of internal revenue, and preceded by a wheezy band of dilapidated instruments blown by unskilled players, used to straggle out to the National Cemetery and scatter a few faded flowers over the graves. The white people looked on in disgust and contempt, and many refused to give the small darkeys flowers for the ceremony. It was a pitiful sight, an honor sought to be paid by those who scarcely knew what honor meant, to the dead, in a land that regarded them as occupying dishonorable graves.[13]

The white man mentioned in the article was either Fredericksburg's postmaster, Dr. M. J. Griffith, or the U.S. assessor, R. D. Beckley, both of whom took part in Memorial Day services during that period.[14]

## Return of the GAR, 1884

After a long absence, the GAR returned to Fredericksburg in May 1884. By then the war had been over for nearly twenty years. Old wounds had healed; old hatreds had simmered down. Across the nation former enemies embraced one another in a new spirit of fraternalism. In Fredericksburg, veterans of the Blue and the Gray set aside old differences and agreed to jointly honor the Union dead buried in Fredericksburg National Cemetery. Confederate veterans met their Union counterparts at the train depot and marched with them to the cemetery, where the two sides shared the podium. The GAR department commander called the assembly to order and introduced Judge John T. Goolrick, commander of the Maury Camp, Confederate Veterans, who addressed the audience. It was the first of many such appearances Judge Goolrick would make.

Once Goolrick returned to his seat, a Union veteran read a poem called "Reunited," after which a Confederate veteran recited some verses composed by a Fredericksburg lady. A GAR representative then made a few remarks, and the chaplain of the Maury Camp concluded the exercises with a benediction. From beginning to end, brotherhood was the order of the day. Even the floral offering—a large cross adorned with several miniature American flags and two Virginia State flags—oozed reconciliation.[15]

Unity came at a price, however. In return for Southern participation, the GAR had to agree to exclude black residents from the ceremony. The editor of the *Fredericksburg Ledger* had never approved of black citizens taking part in the ceremony, and he chortled at their confusion. "The darkey, left behind by the drifting tide of fast-changing sentiment, will look on in idle amazement" at the grand ceremonies from which he was excluded "as he wonders why this duty was ever left to him, and why he is not now called on to do his part." Although African Americans continued to hold their own ceremonies at the cemetery for several more years, the GAR's betrayal dulled their enthusiasm. By the twentieth century they had stopped meeting at Fredericksburg National Cemetery, choosing instead to honor their own war dead at Shiloh Cemetery, a black graveyard in town.[16]

Most white Fredericksburg citizens approved banning black residents from the Memorial Day programs. Wrote the editor of the *Fredericksburg Star:* "As a Confederate soldier we rejoiced in witnessing the spectacle of the Blue and the Gray jointly engaged in this patriotic labor of love. Heretofore the decoration of these graves has been done by colored men, women and children, and we are sure the absence of these from the ceremonies on Friday last was not only gratifying to the ex-Confederates, but also to the ex-Federal soldiers." The editor expressed the hope that the joint North-South exercises "will be repeated here year after year, until the 'boys' who wore the blue and the gray, shall have stacked their arms on the eternal camping ground." That did not happen—at least not right away. Perhaps because they had other commitments, the GAR did not return to Fredericksburg for another five years. In the meantime, Confederate veterans took it upon themselves to decorate the Union graves.[17]

## Sentiments—Noble and Otherwise, 1888–89

Some people wanted to do more than simply strew flowers on the graves. Newspaperman J. O. Kerbey happened to be visiting Fredericksburg in May 1888 when two men in Confederate gray approached him on the street and asked him to accompany them to their "camp." The two "meant business," Kerbey wrote, so he went along quietly, all the while fearing for his life. The two men led him down a back street and into the town hall, where the Union veteran found himself in the presence of a man whom he described as a "High Mucky Muck who was sitting on a dais, wearing a Confederate officer's uniform from which dangled the Rebel battle-flag badge."[18]

The man turned out to be Captain Daniel M. Lee, the brother of Governor Fitzhugh Lee of Virginia and the nephew of General Robert E. Lee. Captain Lee happened to be commander of the local camp of Confederate veterans. He explained that local Confederates wished to join Union veterans in honoring the soldiers buried on Marye's Heights. As Kerbey was just one of four Union veterans in town, he wanted Kerbey's views on whether Northern veterans would embrace a joint reunion. The only stipulation, Lee added, was that his Southern comrades "preferred not to be associated with the mob of colored people, who had been in the habit of making a picnic out of the day." Kerbey thanked Lee for the offer, which he believed to be "prompted by the noblest of motives of friendship, loyalty and charity." Another Union veteran, cemetery superintendent Andrew J. Birdsall, also happened to be at the meeting. On behalf of the town's Northern veterans, he accepted Lee's offer.[19]

On Memorial Day, members of the Fredericksburg Grays, a military organization made up of the town's young white men, met the four Union veterans and escorted them to the rendezvous point, where they found eighty-one Confederate veterans drawn up in a line to greet them. Instead of rifles, each Confederate carried a bouquet of flowers to place on the Union graves. Captain Lee stepped forward and presented each of the former Union soldiers with a similar bouquet, explaining that the flowers came from the ladies of the Confederate Memorial Association, which had divided its flowers evenly between the Union and Confederate cemeteries.

At Lee's signal, the procession made its way to the national cemetery. Union veterans led the way, accompanied by the Fredericksburg Grays and a local drum corps. In their wake came the Confederate veterans and a brass band. Carriages and civilian spectators brought up the rear. The procession followed the route of the 1862 Union attack at Fredericksburg. It went out Hanover Street as far as the Sunken Road and then turned south to the cemetery. As the column passed the monument honoring Confederate brigadier general Thomas R. R. Cobb, Southern veterans doffed their hats in salute, a gesture imitated by their Northern counterparts.

At the cemetery gate the band stepped aside to play dirges as the crowds entered "the sacred precincts of the dead." As they passed through the gates, the Confederate veterans again removed their hats, a courtesy that Kerbey never forgot: "When I look back upon this picture and listen to the war talk of the croaker or politician, who, to get soldiers' votes, may appeal to his former prejudices, I recall this day and regret that all may not have witnessed it as I did; that it was wholly a sincere and disinterested exhibition of genuine good comradeship, goes without saying. There was no other motive, there could be none other than that prompted by genuine good feeling, as nothing was to be gained." A large crowd of citizens had gathered around the cemetery rostrum. Union and Confederate veterans alike addressed the crowd, after which the old soldiers, assisted by women and children, decorated each grave in the cemetery.[20]

As a Union veteran, Kerbey was ashamed that the Southern citizens showed more interest in decorating the Marye's Heights graves than did citizens in the North. When he returned to Washington, he chided his fellow veterans on their indifference. "Practically and bluntly speaking," he wrote,

> this cemetery is *neglected* by the G.A.R. as an organization. Being in the Department of Virginia, which in the very nature of things is weak in G.A.R. Posts, is no valid excuse for this shameful oversight of years. Undoubtedly the comrades of the Virginia department would gladly accept the tender of assistance from Washington. The three thousand comrades in that district, who, with their families and friends, crowd to

Arlington each recurring year . . . might at least induce their overflow to come to Marye's Heights and put a few flowers on the neglected graves there. It is but an hour and a half ride from Washington and is on this account practically as accessible as is Arlington.[21]

Prodded to action by Kerbey's rebuke, GAR posts in Washington and Richmond banded together the following year to host a program at Fredericksburg. When Captain Lee and the Maury Camp of Confederate Veterans learned of the GAR's intentions, they offered to join the posts, but the Union veterans flatly turned them down. Kerbey burned with indignation. "Was this gracious or manly on the part of the Virginia [Division, GAR] comrades who had previously overlooked Fredericksburg for years?" he asked. "There is no politics in the G.A.R.," he sneered, "of course not, but I sometimes imagine that the ungenerous refusal to permit the Confederates to again co-operate in this service, emanated from the fact that there was probably some personal politics underlying it." Ashamed of their conduct, Union veterans acted more charitably toward their Southern brethren when they returned to Fredericksburg in later years, inviting them to participate in the programs.[22]

## Fraternity and Fellowship: The GAR Years, 1890–95

From 1890 to the end of the century, the Grand Army of the Republic took the lead in decorating Union graves at Marye's Heights. Each Memorial Day, about noon, Northern veterans steamed into Fredericksburg aboard a special train and were greeted at the depot by the town's Confederate veterans. A marshal appointed for the occasion organized the crowd into a procession on Main Street (now Caroline Street) and herded it to the cemetery, usually going by way of Hanover Street to Marye's Heights, and thence along the Sunken Road to the cemetery entrance. Bowering's Band, a local group led by the former bandmaster of the Thirtieth Virginia, often led the way, horns blaring. At the entrance, the band stepped aside to play dirges as the column ascended the hill.

Crowds of people waited at the top. The procession wended its way through the throng, and the speakers took their place at a rostrum located on the southern edge of the property. Once everyone had arrived, the marshal called the assembly to order and a minister offered an opening prayer, sometimes followed by a recitation from the GAR manual. After that, Union and Confederate representatives stood and offered addresses gushing with patriotism and fraternal spirit. Between speeches, Bowering's Band or other musical groups would render "sweet and soul-inspiring" music, and veterans would recite poems written for the occasion. Sometimes groups of local women presented wreaths or flowers. Toward the end of the program, a person of note—usually a GAR luminary—gave the keynote address, after which the minister offered a benediction. Then, if not before, the crowd scattered to place flowers on the graves. (In 1893, Union veterans brought a boxcar full of flowers with them to Fredericksburg. For a full hour, they and their guests decorated each and every grave.) With that, the program ended, and the people made their way to local hotels to "refresh the inner man." At 6:00 p.m., a train arrived to take the Northern guests back home. With hearty handshakes, Northern veterans parted company with their Southern hosts, each expressing the hope that they would meet again the following year.[23]

## Memorial Day under Richard B. Hill, 1896–1900

The nature of Memorial Day programs at Fredericksburg National Cemetery noticeably changed when Richard Hill became superintendent in 1895. Under him, the programs took on a more intimate, local flavor. Gone were the noisy bands with their marches and dirges; gone the grand processions that led from the business district to the cemetery and aging veterans reading rites from the

Memorial Day exercises, 1893. *Courtesy of Jerry and Louise Brent.*

Grand Army of the Republic manual. In their place, Hill introduced programs that featured local schoolchildren, supported by choral groups and soloists. Hill's own children played a prominent part in the exercises. Miss Emily Hill led the Red, White, and Blue Club, a group comprising some two dozen children dressed in patriotic caps and sashes, carrying the national colors. The children performed drills, recited poetry, and led the audience in singing patriotic standards such as "The Star-Spangled Banner," "My Country, 'Tis of Thee," and "America the Beautiful." Three of Hill's younger children were members of the group, as was a granddaughter of former superintendent Andrew Birdsall.

Not that Hill excluded veterans from the program—far from it. Each year at least two former soldiers stepped forward to extol the bravery of their comrades or to plead for unity between North and South. Sometimes GAR dignitaries did the honors; at other times Hill employed local talent. Such was the case in 1898 when Confederate veterans Judge John T. Goolrick and James Horace Lacy addressed the assembly. As a rule, programs of this period had between one and two dozen elements—speeches, poems, recitations, prayers, and the like. A particularly long program in 1897 lasted three hours. As in former years, the programs usually closed with the audience scattering to decorate the Union graves with flowers.

Hill usually remained in the background at such events, but he was forced to take a more active role in 1900, when several speakers canceled at the last minute—probably due to a problem with the trains. On that occasion Hill manfully helped fill the void. He opened the program by calling the assembly to order and later closed it with a benediction.[24]

## Hiatus: The Dillon, Magoon, and Jefferys Years, 1901–14

William Dillon became superintendent at Fredericksburg after Hill's departure in 1901. During the two years that he was in charge of the cemetery, there were no Memorial Day programs or if there were, there is no record of them. Harrison Magoon succeeded Dillon as superintendent in 1903. Magoon was a minimalist. He purged the program of children and pared the Memorial Day ceremony down to just seven elements: a prayer, two hymns, a musical number, two addresses, and decoration of the graves. Judge Goolrick gave one of the addresses; Magoon, the other.[25] He was the third superintendent to speak at the Memorial Day exercises. In addition to Hill's role in the 1900 program, Superintendent Thomas McAlpine had offered a prayer at the 1895 event. Whether Magoon would have continued to take part in the programs is unknown; he left Fredericksburg after just one year.[26]

With his departure, M. M. Jefferys took charge of the cemetery. Jefferys apparently did not care for formal commemorations. In the ten years that he was superintendent, there was just one Memorial Day program at the national cemetery—an affair put on by Spanish-American War veterans in 1910[27]—and even that was not much of a program. The veterans simply marched to the cemetery, placed flowers on the graves of their fallen comrades, and sounded taps. Although Jefferys eschewed formal exercises, he did mark Memorial Day by decorating each grave in the cemetery with a miniature flag and threw open the gates to vehicular traffic. The local newspaper reported that "Major M. M. Jefferys, the obliging superintendent, was at his office greeting all who called."[28]

## Patriotic Resurgence: Thomas Robinson and the First World War, 1917–22

By the time Jefferys left Fredericksburg in 1914, Europe was at war. President Woodrow Wilson did his best to keep America out of the conflict, but by the spring of 1917 that was no longer possible. Congress formally declared war on Germany on April 6.

Throughout the country, patriotism was running high. Jefferys's successor, Thomas Robinson, harnessed the surging nationalist spirit to resurrect Memorial Day exercises at Fredericksburg. An advertisement for the 1917 program proclaimed that the "exercises will be of a patriotic nature intended to be in harmony with the exigency of our country's peril in meeting its demands for maintaining her rights for humanity." It encouraged all Fredericksburg citizens to turn out "to remember our heroic dead who stood in heat of battle to procure, defend and maintain the principles of a free and democratic people and to assure those who may be called to the 'firing line' that they have the assurance that we will stand behind our government, and them, in supporting and maintaining our great principles." Robinson and the organizing committee designed the program to be not only a memorial for America's deceased soldiers but also as a show of support for the living ones.[29]

A Boy Scout bugle corps announced the beginning of the program by playing "Assembly Call," after which Mayor J. P. Rowe stepped forward and welcomed the crowd. Following a prayer by the chaplain of the local Sons of Confederate Veterans organization, Judge Goolrick said a few words on behalf of Confederate veterans. Superintendent Robinson, representing Union veterans, then read a poem called "The Blue and the Gray." The Reverend E. L. Smith delivered the day's keynote speech, after which Robinson recited the Gettysburg Address. A local quartet then rendered two Memorial Day favorites, "America the Beautiful" and "The Star-Spangled Banner," and the Girl Scouts followed by singing "All Hail to Our Flag." Once the Boy Scout bugle corps played taps, the Girl Scouts decorated the graves with flowers.[30]

One year later, when Fredericksburg citizens again met to honor the dead, war fever was at its highest pitch. In what may have been the largest Memorial Day program in Fredericksburg's history, three thousand people gathered to hear local favorite Judge Goolrick deliver "a most interesting, patriotic and enthusiastic address." Superintendent Robinson presided over the program. As it ended, two girls stepped forward and presented Robinson with two rose wreaths on behalf of Fredericksburg's schoolchildren. The superintendent was so moved by the unexpected gesture, wrote a local newspaperman, that "his emotions . . . almost over came him."[31]

In honor of Memorial Day, Robinson had draped a large American flag across the Humphreys Monument. Citizens who had brought flowers for the graves placed their offerings at the base of the monument and piled additional flowers in a "great mound" at a memorial honoring the cemetery's unknown dead. The flag-draped monument, the flowers, and the miniature flags that decorated each of the graves gave the cemetery a resplendent appearance. "The large beautiful 'City of the Dead' never looked more beautiful than it did on this occasion," thought a writer for the *Fredericksburg Free Lance*.[32]

## Patriots and Politicians: The American Legion Years, 1923–33

So long as Thomas Robinson was superintendent, Civil War veterans played a leading role in Fredericksburg's Memorial Day exercises. Professor A. B. Bowering, a former Confederate musician, led a local band that performed at several of the ceremonies; Judge Goolrick, Fredericksburg's perennial Confederate representative, either gave an address or read the president's Memorial Day proclamation to the crowd; and Robinson himself either recited the Gettysburg Address or acted as master of ceremonies. By the 1920s, however, only a few Civil War veterans were living, and they were too feeble to participate in the programs. With Robinson's death in 1922, the American Legion took charge of the Memorial Day exercises.

The American Legion continued most of the traditions started by the Civil War veterans. Civic and patriotic organizations still marched in a procession to the graveyard, the cemetery staff continued to decorate the grounds with miniature flags, buglers played taps to conclude the ceremonies, ministers continued to lead the audience in prayer, and participants still strewed flowers over the graves. As in the past, music played a large role in the programs. The Elks routinely provided a band for the occasion, and the American Legion, the State Teachers College, and the Normal School took turns in sending choral groups to the event. New to the program was the 111th Field Artillery, which, starting in 1924, fired three-gun salutes from its 75-mm guns.

In the absence of Civil War veterans, the American Legion tapped members of its own organization to address the crowds or invited members of Congress to speak. Most stuck to tried-and-true themes such as peace, unity, and sacrifice, although some congressmen used the occasion to expound upon the current political issues, as in 1929 when the Honorable John E. Rankin of Mississippi extolled the virtues of the Kellogg-Briand Treaty.[33] One congressman spoke extemporaneously, although not by choice. The Honorable J. J. McSwain of South Carolina thought that he was to speak at the Confederate cemetery and had prepared a speech praising Generals Lee and Jackson. Only after he reaching the podium did he discover his mistake. Realizing that his prepared remarks would not do, McSwain pocketed his notes and spoke off the cuff. He carried it off beautifully. According to a local journalist, those who heard McSwain speak said "that the speech in his pocket could not have been better than the one he made."[34]

The tradition of honoring soldiers at Fredericksburg National Cemetery on Memorial Day continues to the present. For many years the National Park Service has organized the event, attracting speakers such as Virginia governor Robert F. McDonnell, National Park Service chief historian Edwin C. Bearss, and Marine Corps brigadier general Gordon D. Gayle. Sadly, audiences are not as large as in the past, but those who attend evince the same patriotic spirit as their ancestors in honoring those who, in Abraham Lincoln's words in the Gettysburg Address, "gave the last full measure of devotion."

# Epilogue: Fredericksburg National Cemetery under the National Park Service

On June 10, 1933, sixty-seven years of army oversight of Fredericksburg National Cemetery came to an end when President Franklin D. Roosevelt signed Executive Order 6166 transferring Fredericksburg and ten other national cemeteries to the National Park Service.[1] Under special agreement with the NPS, the Quartermaster Corps would continue to carry out certain responsibilities at the cemeteries for a few years longer. Among the duties it retained were the verification and authorization of burial requests, the approval of private memorials, and the maintenance of interment records. The Quartermaster Corps likewise continued to appoint superintendents to cemetery vacancies.[2]

At an early date, the NPS removed the brick maintenance building and constructed a cinder-block facility on the site of the former structure. It installed a pump for fueling gas-powered lawn mowers in the northeast corner of the property, where the old well used to be, and, when the heating system at the lodge went from a coal-powered furnace to one fueled by oil, it added a subterranean oil tank next to the lodge.

Changes to the cemetery grounds have been less dramatic. In the 1960s, the agency added a Civil War cannon, an audio station, a directional compass, and two interpretive signs to the grounds. Later, it authorized the erection of a small marker to commemorate Parker's Battery, near the site of the former rostrum, and in the 1990s it installed an irrigation system on the terraces. Early in the twenty-first century, it removed the cannon and the audio station as being incompatible with the cemetery setting and replaced them with a small interpretive panel near the Parker's Battery memorial. As a result of these changes, the cemetery today looks much as it did when the agency first received the property. The exception is the vegetation. The number of trees, shrubs, and flowers have declined drastically over the years due to storms, drought, and disease, leaving it much more open than in years gone by.

If the cemetery has changed little in the past century, the same cannot be said of the area around it. Shortly after the war, subdivisions began appearing at the foot of Marye's Heights, a practice that accelerated early in the twentieth century. With the creation of Fredericksburg and Spotsylvania County National Military Park in 1927, the U.S. government preserved a small strip of land along the Sunken Road. It transferred that and other park land, including the cemetery, to the National Park Service in 1933, during the Great Depression. That period of economic gloom, while hard on the country as a whole, proved a boon for the new park, which initiated various public works projects, including the construction of the Fredericksburg Battlefield Visitor Center in 1936 and the reconstruction of a portion of the Sunken Road's famous stone wall in 1939.[3]

In following years, the National Park Service began augmenting its slender holdings along the Sunken Road with the purchase of the Innis House (1969) and the acquisition of the Kirkland Memorial (1987) and with the Central Virginia Battlefields Trust's purchase of the Montfort Academy tract, north of the cemetery (1997). Restoration followed acquisition. In the past forty years, the NPS has rehabilitated the Innis House, closed the Sunken Road to traffic, and restored the thoroughfare to its Civil War appearance. As a result of these changes, the Sunken Road has become the town's most historic and most beautiful street.

Although these changes have improved the visitor experience immeasurably, they have had little or no effect on Fredericksburg National Cemetery itself. Since its completion in 1868, people have been going there to enjoy its quiet beauty and reflect on the high cost of war. Most visit on their own or as part of a ranger-guided tour, but many come in conjunction with one of the park's two Memorial Day weekend events. The first is a traditional program of speeches and wreath-layings that stretches back nearly a century and a half. A small event, it typically draws an audience of fewer than two hundred people. Far better attended is the annual luminaria, in which Boy Scouts and Girl Scouts light some 15,300 candles in the cemetery—approximately one for each soldier buried there. Held each Memorial Day weekend since 1997, the three-hour program attracts upward of four thousand people each year.[4] It is easily Fredericksburg and Spotsylvania County National Military Park's most popular program.

Most of those who attend the luminaria are drawn by its visual splendor. That is understandable. The sight of lights extending across the plateau and

Annual luminaria program, which attracts thousands of people each year. *Fredericksburg and Spotsylvania County National Military Park.*

cascading down the hillside in orderly rows is a breathtaking sight. Often forgotten, however, is the underlying tragedy behind that beauty, for each of those lights represents not only a deceased soldier but also in many cases a grieving mother, a destitute wife, a fatherless child. That fact was not lost on Lieutenant Samuel S. Partridge, who wrote, "How little, very little, we think of the grief produced by wars calamities."[5]

If that was true in Partridge's day, it applies even more today. Nearly one hundred years ago, in 1918, crowds flocked to Fredericksburg National Cemetery on Memorial Day to honor those who had sacrificed their lives for this country and to show their support for living servicemen then fighting in France. There were few cars then, and the local population was a fraction of what it is today. Still, three thousand people came. Today, Fredericksburg and its neighboring counties of Stafford and Spotsylvania number more three hundred thousand people. And yet fewer than two hundred people attend the annual Memorial Day program—just one person for every fifteen hundred who live in the area. Most of us give little thought to the meaning of the day. We are too busy driving to the beach, going to local swimming pools, or preparing for a holiday barbecue.

How little we think of the grief produced by war's calamities! And yet, as Americans, we should think of it. We owe a great debt to those who fought for our country and who continue to fight for it to this very day—too often at the expense of their lives. Fredericksburg National Cemetery stands as a vivid reminder of the debt we owe them. We can never repay it, but we must never forget it.

Appendixes
Notes
Bibliography
Index

# Appendix 1: Key Orders and Legislation in Establishing National Cemeteries

General Orders
No. 33.

War Dept., Adjt. General's Office
*Washington, April 3, 1862.*

. . . II. In order to secure, as far as possible, the decent interment of those who have fallen, or may fall, in battle, it is made the duty of commanding generals to lay off lots of ground in some suitable spot near every battle-field, so soon as it may be in their power, and to cause the remains of those killed to be interred, with headboards to the graves bearing numbers, and, where practicable, the names of the persons buried in them. A register of each burial ground will be preserved, in which will be noted the marks corresponding with the headboards.

L. THOMAS
Adjutant-General.[1]

\*    \*    \*    \*    \*    \*    \*    \*

### An Act to Define the Pay and Emoluments of Certain Officers of the Army and for Other Purposes

. . . Sec. 18. *And be it further enacted,* That the President of the United States shall have power, whenever in his opinion it shall be expedient, to purchase cemetery grounds, and cause them to be securely enclosed, to be used as a national cemetery for the soldiers who shall die in the service of the country.[2]

\*    \*    \*    \*    \*    \*    \*    \*

### A Resolution Respecting the Burial of Soldiers Who Died in the Military Service of the United States during the Rebellion

*Resolved by the Senate and House of Representatives of the United States of America in Congress assembled,* That the Secretary of War be, and he is hereby, authorized and required to take immediate measures to preserve from desecration the graves of the soldiers of the United States who fell in battle or died of disease in the field and in hospital during the war of the rebellion;

to secure suitable burial-places in which they may be properly interred; and to have the grounds enclosed, so that the resting-places of the honored dead may be kept sacred forever.

APPROVED, April 13, 1866.[3]

\* \* \* \* \* \* \* \*

### An Act to Establish and to Protect National Cemeteries

*Be it enacted by the Senate and House of Representatives of the United States of America in Congress assembled,* That in the arrangement of the national cemeteries established for the burial of deceased soldiers and sailors, the Secretary of War is hereby directed to have the same enclosed with a good and substantial stone or iron fence; and to cause each grave to be marked with a small headstone, or block, with the number of the grave inscribed thereon, corresponding with the number opposite to the name of the party, in a register of burials to be kept at each cemetery and the office of the quartermaster-general, which shall set forth the name, rank, company, regiment, and date of death of the officer or soldier; or, if unknown, it shall be so recorded.

Sec. 2. *And be it further enacted,* That the Secretary of War is hereby directed to cause to be erected at the principal entrance of each of the national cemeteries aforesaid, a suitable building to be occupied as a porter's lodge; and it shall be his duty to appoint a meritorious and trustworthy superintendent who shall be selected from enlisted men of the army, disabled in service, and who shall have the pay and allowances of an ordnance sergeant, to reside therein, for the purpose of guarding and protecting the cemetery and giving information to parties visiting the same. The Secretary of War shall detail some officer of the army, not under the rank of major, to visit annually all of said cemeteries, and to inspect and report to him the condition of the same, and the amount of money necessary to protect them, to sod the graves, gravel and grade the walks and avenues, and to keep the grounds in complete order; and the said Secretary shall transmit the said report to Congress at the commencement of each session, together with an estimate of the appropriation necessary for the purpose.

Sec. 3. *And be it further enacted,* That any person who shall wilfully destroy, mutilate, deface, injure, or remove any monument, gravestone, or other structure, or shall wilfully destroy, cut, break, injure, or remove any tree, shrub, or plant, within the limits of any said national cemeteries, shall be deemed guilty of a misdemeanor, and upon conviction thereof before any district or circuit court of the United States within any State or district where any of said national cemeteries are situated, shall be liable to a fine of not less than twenty-five nor more than one hundred dollars, or to imprisonment of not less than fifteen nor more than sixty days, according to the nature and aggravation of the offence. And the superintendent in charge of any national cemetery is hereby authorized to arrest forthwith any person engaged in committing any misdemeanor herein prohibited, and to bring such person before any United States commissioner or judge of any district or circuit court of the United States within any State or district where any of said cemeteries are situated, for the purpose of holding said person to answer for said misdemeanor, and then and there shall make complaint in due form.

Sec. 4. *And be it further enacted,* That it shall be the duty of the Secretary of War to purchase from the owner or owners thereof, at such price as may be mutually agreed upon between the Secretary and such owner or owners, such real estate as in his judgment is suitable and necessary for the purpose of carrying into effect the provisions of this act, and to obtain from said owner or owners title in fee simple for the same. And in case the Secretary of War shall not be able to agree with said owner or owners upon the price to be paid for any real estate needed for the purpose of this act, or to obtain from said owner or owners title in fee simple for the same, the Secretary of War is hereby authorized to enter upon and appropriate any real estate which, in his judgment, is suitable and necessary for the purposes of this act.

Sec. 5. *And be it further enacted,* That the Secretary of War or the owner or owners of any real estate thus entered upon and appropriated are hereby authorized to make application for an appraisement of said real estate thus entered upon and appropriated to any district or circuit court within any State or district where such real estate is situated; and any of said courts is hereby authorized and required upon such application, and in such mode and under such rules and regulations as it may adopt, to make a just and equitable appraisement of the cash value of the several interests of each and every owner of the real estate and improvements thereon entered upon and appropriated for the purposes of this act, and in accordance with its provisions.

Sec. 6. *And be it further enacted,* That the fee simple of all real estate thus entered upon and appropriated for the purposes of this act, and of which appraisement shall have been made under the order and direction of any of said courts, shall, upon payment to the owner or owners, respectively, of the appraised value, or in case said owner or owners refuse or neglect for thirty days after the appraisement of the cash value of the said real estate or improvements by any of said courts to demand the same from the Secretary of War, upon depositing the said appraised value in the said court, making such appraisement to the credit of said owner or owners, respectively, be vested in the United States, and its jurisdiction over said real estate shall be exclusive and the same as its jurisdiction over real estate purchased, ceded, or appropriated for the purposes of navy yards, forts, and arsenals. And the Secretary of War is hereby authorized and required to pay to the several owner or owners, respectively, the appraised value of the several pieces or parcels of real estate, as specified in the appraisement of any of said courts, or to pay into any of said courts by deposit, as hereinbefore provided, the said appraised value; and the sum necessary for such purpose may be taken from any moneys appropriated for the purposes of this act.

Sec. 7. *And be it further enacted,* That the sum of seven hundred and fifty thousand dollars is hereby appropriated to carry out the purposes of this act out of any moneys in the treasury not otherwise appropriated.

Approved, February 22, 1867.[4]

# Appendix 2: "The Bivouac of the Dead"

The muffled drum's sad roll has beat
The soldier's last tattoo;
No more on Life's parade shall meet
That brave and fallen few.
On Fame's eternal camping-ground
Their silent tents are spread,
And Glory guards, with solemn round,
The bivouac of the dead.

No rumor of the foe's advance
Now swells upon the wind;
No troubled thought at midnight haunts
Of loved ones left behind;
No vision of the morrow's strife
The warrior's dream alarms;
No braying horn nor screaming fife
At dawn shall call to arms.

Their shivered swords are red with rust;
Their plumèd heads are bowed;
Their haughty banner, trailed in dust,
Is now their martial shroud.
And plenteous funeral tears have washed
The red stains from each brow,
And the proud forms, by battle gashed,
Are free from anguish now.

The Neighing troop, the flashing blade,
The bugle's stirring blast,
The charge, the dreadful cannonade,
The din and shout, are past;
Nor war's wild note, nor glory's peal,
Shall thrill with fierce delight

From http://www.poetry-archive.com/o/the_bivouac_of_the_dead.html.

Those breasts that nevermore may feel
The rapture of the fight.

Like the fierce northern hurricane
That sweeps his great plateau,
Flushed with the triumph yet to gain,
Came down the serried foe.
Who heard the thunder of the fray
Break o'er the field beneath,
Knew well the watchword of that day
Was "Victory or Death."

Long had the doubtful conflict raged
O'er all that stricken plain,
For never fiercer fight had waged
The vengeful blood of Spain;
And still the storm of battle blew,
Still swelled the glory tide;
Not long, our stout old chieftain knew,
Such odds his strength could bide.

'T was in that hour his stern command
Called to a martyr's grave
The flower of his belovèd land,
The nation's flag to save.
By rivers of their fathers' gore
His first-born laurels grew,
And well he deemed the sons would pour
Their lives for glory too.

Full many a norther's breath has swept
O'er Angostura's plain,
And long the pitying sky has wept
Above its mouldered slain.
The raven's scream or eagle's flight,
Or shepherd's pensive lay,
Alone awakes each sullen height
That frowned o'er that dread fray.

Sons of the dark and bloody ground,
Ye must not slumber there,
Where stranger steps and tongues resound
Along the heedless air.
Your own proud land's heroic soil
Shall be your fitter grave;
She claims from war his richest spoil—
The ashes of her brave.

Thus 'neath their parent turf they rest,
Far from the glory field,
Borne to a Spartan mother's breast
On many a bloody shield;
The sunshine of their native sky
Smiles sadly on them here,
And kindred eyes and hearts watch by
The heroes' sepulcher.

Rest on, embalmed and sainted dead!
Dear as the blood ye gave;
No impious footstep here shall tread
The herbage of your grave;
Nor shall your story be forgot,
While Fame her record keeps,
Or Honor points the hallowed spot
Where Valor proudly sleeps.

Yon marble minstrel's voiceless stone
In deathless song shall tell,
When many a vanished age hath flown,
The story how ye fell;
Nor wreck, nor change, nor winter's blight,
Nor Time's remorseless doom,
Shall dim one ray of glory's light
That gilds your deathless tomb.

*Theodore O'Hara (1820–67)*

# Notes

| | |
|---|---|
| *FDS* | *Fredericksburg Daily Star* |
| *FFL* | *Fredericksburg Free Lance* |
| *FL* | *Fredericksburg Ledger* |
| *FLS* | *Fredericksburg Free Lance-Star* |
| *FN* | *Fredericksburg News* |
| FNC1 | Record Group 92: Records of the Office of the Quartermaster General, General Correspondence and Reports Relating to National and Post Cemeteries, 1865–ca. 1914, box 29, "Fredericksburg" packet 1, National Archives and Records Administration, Washington, D.C. |
| FNC2 | Record Group 92: Records of the Office of the Quartermaster General, General Correspondence and Reports Relating to National and Post Cemeteries, 1865–ca. 1914, box 29, "Fredericksburg" packet 2, National Archives and Records Administration, Washington, D.C. |
| FNC3 | Record Group 92: Records of the Office of the Quartermaster General, General Correspondence and Reports Relating to National and Post Cemeteries, 1865–ca. 1914, box 30, "Fredericksburg" packet 3, National Archives and Records Administration, Washington, D.C. |
| FNC4 | Record Group 92: Records of the Office of the Quartermaster General, General Correspondence and Reports Relating to National and Post Cemeteries, 1865–ca. 1914, box 30, "Fredericksburg" packet 4, National Archives and Records Administration, Washington, D.C. |
| FRSP | Fredericksburg and Spotsylvania County National Military Park |
| *FS* | *Fredericksburg Star* |
| Letters Received | Fredericksburg National Cemetery, Letters Received: January 1, 1921, to August 14, 1930, catalog #7703, Fredericksburg and Spotsylvania County National Military Park curatorial collection |

| Letters Sent | Fredericksburg National Cemetery, Letters Sent: December 1, 1913, to August 19, 1930, catalog #7704, Fredericksburg and Spotsylvania County National Military Park curatorial collection |
|---|---|
| LSW | Letter to/from the Secretary of War |
| NA | National Archives and Records Administration, Washington, D.C. |
| OR | U.S. War Department, *The War of the Rebellion: A Compilation of the Official Records of the Union and Confederate Armies*, 128 vols. (Washington, D.C.: U.S. Government Printing Office, 1880–1901). Unless otherwise noted, volumes belong to series 1. |
| QMGO | Quartermaster General's Office |
| RG | Record Group |
| *VS* | *Virginia Star* |
| *VH* | *Virginia Herald* |

## Introduction: The National Cemetery System

1. Hacker, "Census-Based Count of the Civil War Dead."
2. *OR*, series 3, 1:498.
3. Ibid., 2:2.
4. Sanger, *Statutes at Large . . . December 5, 1859, to March 3, 1863*, 12:596.
5. *Report of the Quartermaster General . . . for the Year Ending June 30, 1865*, 30; *Annual Reports of the Quartermaster-General*, 19.
6. Montgomery Meigs, QMGO, General Orders No. 65, dated October 30, 1865, copy in RG 92, entry 576, Box 29, NA.
7. Joint Resolution No. 21, 39th Congress, 1st sess., in Sanger, *Statutes at Large . . . December, 1865, to March, 1867*, 14:353 (see appendix 1).
8. "An Act to Establish and to Protect National Cemeteries," in ibid., 14:399–401 (see appendix 1).
9. *Annual Report of the Quartermaster General . . . for the Year 1870*, 68–71; *Annual Report of the Quartermaster-General . . . for the Fiscal Year Ending June 30, 1874*, 24.
10. Olsen, "Poplar Grove," 52–53, citing National Cemetery Regulations for September 15, 1947 (Washington, D.C.: Government Printing Office), 14; "History and Development of the National Cemetery Administration."
11. Phisterer, *Statistical Record*, 77–79.
12. "History and Development of the National Cemetery Administration"; "General History," National Cemetery Administration website. The eleven cemeteries transferred to the National Park Service in 1933 were Antietam,

Battleground, Chattanooga, Fort Donelson, Fredericksburg, Gettysburg, Poplar Grove, Shiloh, Stones River, Vicksburg, and Yorktown. Chattanooga returned to the army's jurisdiction in the 1940s due to the large number of continued interments there, but four others were added to the National Park Service: Andrew Johnson (1935), Chalmette (1939), Custer Battlefield/Little Bighorn (1946), and Andersonville (1971).

13. "History of Military Dog Tags"; "Lab Uses DNA Library to ID Troops."

### 1. Wartime Burials

1. *OR* 21:142.
2. O'Reilly, *Fredericksburg Campaign*, 445–46; James Watts letter, April 21, 1862, J. H. Scruggs Collection, Birmingham Public Library; Charles T. Furlow Journal, p. 30, Yale University Archives; William Slaughter letter, January 4, 1863, Slaughter Papers, Virginia Historical Society.
3. Cochran, "Brief Sketch of the Cochran Family," 34, FRSP.
4. Ibid.; Evan M. Woodward letter, December 16, 1862, Evan Woodward Papers, Huntington Library.
5. Post, *Regis de Trobriand*, 282–83.
6. O'Reilly, *Fredericksburg Campaign*, 446.
7. Teall, "Ringside Seat," 30–31; Joseph Taylor dispatch, December 16, 1862, FRSP; "From the 15th Regiment, C.V.," *Waterbury American*, January 23, 1863; Epstein, *Lincoln and Whitman*, 86–88; Sorrel, *Recollections*, 146–47. Writer Walt Whitman falsely claimed he accompanied the burial party across the river. See Whitman, "May 19, 1863, letter," 63.
8. *Fitchburg (Mass.) Sentinel*, January 2, 1863.
9. "From the 15th Regiment, C.V.," *Waterbury American*, January 23, 1863.
10. Ibid.
11. C. Cummings, "Battle of Fredericksburg," 358.
12. *OR* 21:261–62.
13. Mason, "Notes," 101.
14. Hiram Gerrish report, January 20, 1866, FNC1; "From the 15th Regiment, C.V.," *Waterbury American*, January 23, 1863.
15. Map in George C. Anderson Papers, copy at FRSP; Owen, *In Camp and Battle*, 196; Harrison, *Fredericksburg Civil War Sites*, 2:208–9; Gamma, *Gainesville (Fla.) Cotton States*, November 26, 1864; Landon, "Letters," 340. By contrast, Nathaniel C. Deane stated that one ditch held more than 240 bodies, and Heros von Borcke remembered seeing 300 corpses in one place. Shortly after the war, John T. Trowbridge visited the plain with a Southern guide. Although the fields were then planted in corn, the farmer had left a strip fifteen yards long and four yards wide unplanted because Northern troops were buried there. Trowbridge's guide insisted that the small trench

held 1,000 corpses. Washington Artillery adjutant William Miller Owen estimated that 1,500 Union soldiers were buried in the ditches. In 1866, Brevet Major Hiram Gerrish reported that at Fredericksburg "there are said to be 500 interred in one grave, and at another place 800 are buried in a trench none of them are marked." See *Fitchburg Sentinel*, January 2, 1863; Borcke, *Memoirs*, 2:148–49; Trowbridge, *South*, 112; Owen, *In Camp and Battle*, 196; and Hiram Gerrish report, January 20, 1866, FNC1.

16. Edward Heinichen memoir, typescript, Edward L. Heinichen Memoirs, Maryland Historical Society; Borton, *On the Parallels*, 232.

17. *Statement of the Disposition*, 26; Borcke, *Memoirs*, 2:148–49; Owen, *In Camp and Battle*, 196; Mason, "Notes," 101; Trowbridge, *South*, 112; Pepper, *Personal Recollections*, 448; *OR* 21:261–62; Gerrish, "List and Location of United States Soldiers Graves," FNC1. W. Roy Mason estimated that the icehouse held between four hundred and five hundred skeletons. John Trowbridge and Hiram Gerrish heard that five hundred men were buried there, while Heros von Borcke placed the figure as high as eight hundred. A captain in Major General William T. Sherman's army visited Fredericksburg Battlefield after the war and saw a "large hole" in which seven hundred Union soldiers reputedly were buried—an obvious reference to the icehouse pit. Howison Wallace owned "Federal Hill," a house that stood on Hanover Street, just east of the millrace. Those originally buried in this "hecatomb of skeletons" were later interred in Fredericksburg National Cemetery, division A, section B, graves #74–76, #89, #303–9, and #328–32. See Fredericksburg National Cemetery Register #7700, 131, 133–34.

18. Hiram Gerrish, "List and Location of United States Soldiers Graves," FNC1; Gamma, *Gainesville Cotton States*, November 26, 1864. For a published list of Fredericksburg-area gravesites and the number of bodies taken from each, see *Statement of the Disposition*, 23–30. For a more detailed account of Union burials in Fredericksburg, see Pfanz, "Reaping the Harvest of Death."

19. Francis B. Hall Journal, p. 12, State University of New York. 1 Corinthians 15:16–22 (KJV) reads:

> For if the dead rise not, then is not Christ raised: And if Christ be not raised, your faith is vain; ye are yet in your sins. Then they also which are fallen asleep in Christ are perished. If in this life only we have hope in Christ, we are of all men most miserable. But now is Christ risen from the dead, and become the firstfruits of them that slept. For since by man came death, by man came also the resurrection of the dead. For as in Adam all die, even so in Christ shall all be made alive.

20. Engle letter, June 3, 1863, found on the Civil War Letters of Charles Engle website.

21. Thompson, *Thirteenth Regiment of New Hampshire Volunteer Infantry*, 100.
22. Hiram Gerrish, "List and Location of United States Soldiers Graves," FNC1. A report submitted by the Quartermaster Department in January 1866 indicated that just 1,315 of 2,410 graves—54.5 percent—were marked.
23. Partridge letter, March 6, 1863, FRSP.
24. "History of the 107th Regiment New York Volunteers," *Canisteo Valley (N.Y.) Times*, December 4, 1869.
25. Paynton letter, February 16, 1863, FRSP.
26. *OR* 25:191.
27. Weygant, *History of the One Hundred and Twenty-Fourth Regiment*, 272–73.
28. Morhous, *Reminiscences of the 123d Regiment*, 186.
29. Hiram Gerrish report, January 20, 1866, FNC1. For accounts of Union burials at Chancellorsville, see Jones diary, May 16, 1865, FRSP; and Dority, "Civil War Diary," 26. After the war, William L. LeConte of the Second Georgia Battalion insisted that on May 1 Union soldiers padded their earthworks with the bodies of their dead comrades. In addition, he stated that he found the decomposing bodies of several hundred Union soldiers interred in the Chancellor family icehouse. I have found no evidence to corroborate LeConte's claims. See LeConte memoir, 13–14, FRSP.
30. *OR* 29 (1): 686.
31. Fredericksburg National Cemetery Register #7700, FRSP.
32. *OR* 36 (1): 12–13.
33. Lyman journal, April 15, 1866, Lyman Family Papers, Massachusetts Historical Society; Ward, "Amidst a Tempest," 2:401; Rhea, *Battles for Spotsylvania Court House*, 311; White letter, June 9, 1864, FRSP.
34. McVey letter, March 21, 1866, FRSP. The parenthetical names appear in the original letter.
35. Brown, *Diary of a Line Officer*, 40.
36. Holt letter, June 11, 1891, FRSP.
37. Michael F. Rinker letter, May 17, 1864, Rinker Papers, Virginia Military Institute; Gorman memoir, 2, FRSP; Tobie, *History of the First Maine Cavalry*, 289. A Twelfth Corps soldier who passed through the battlefield with Sherman's army in 1865 confirmed the large number of unburied Union dead. "The ground is covered with the remains of our soldiers who have never been buried," he wrote. "I saw hundreds of skeletons lying as they fell with clothes and accoutrements on. Nothing left but the white bones. A great many were buried but the earth was washed away and showed the bones of the dead." See McLean diary entry, May 15, 1865, FRSP.
38. Cronin, *Evolution of a Life*, 260–62.
39. Hiram Gerrish, "List and Location of United States Soldiers Graves," FNC1. Because Union troops had already constructed two cemeteries in

the Wilderness, Gerrish did not take the trouble to tabulate the number of known and unknown dead found there.

40. Harrison, *Fredericksburg Civil War Sites*, 2:209–10; Reed, *Heroic Story*, 22–23.
41. Gilbert, *Story of a Regiment*, 237, 291; Frassanito, *Grant and Lee*, 86; Pfanz, "Reaping the Harvest of Death," 22. Using Brady's photographs, historian Noel Harrison identified the location of Downs's burial trenches as being in the block now bounded by modern Prince Edward, Winchester, Lewis, and Amelia Streets. See Harrison, "Victims and Survivors."
42. Rhea, *To the North Anna River*, 319. Of the identified soldiers in Fredericksburg National Cemetery, thirty-four are known to have died at the North Anna.

## 2. Postwar Burials in the Wilderness and at Spotsylvania Court House

1. *OR* 51 (1): 1079, and series 3, 4:387, 892, 902; Heitman, *Historical Register*, 1:722. Moore's age comes from information in his compiled military service record at the National Archives.
2. *OR* 46 (3): 1263, and series 3, 5:318.
3. Report of Brevet Major James M. Moore, dated July 3, 1865, copy at FRSP (hereafter cited as Moore report). A copy of Moore's report, with minor alterations, appears in *Names of Officers and Soldiers*, 5–6; and in *Annual Reports of the Quartermaster-General*, 157–58, 162.
4. Heitman, *Historical Register*, 1:219.
5. Moore report; Landon, "'Prock's' Last Letters," 77, 79 (hereafter cited as Landon letter); James Riley to "Friend Belle," June 28, 1865, James Riley Papers, Indiana Historical Society.
6. Landon letter, 80.
7. Ibid.; James Riley to "Friend Belle."
8. Landon letter, 80; James Riley to "Friend Belle."
9. Landon letter, 77, 80–81; James Riley to "Friend Belle."
10. Untitled, *FL*, July 4, 1865.
11. Landon letter, 77; Colonel Charles Bird report, June 29, 1865, copy at FRSP (hereafter cited as Bird report); James Riley to "Friend Belle."
12. James Riley to "Friend Belle."
13. Bird report.
14. Ibid.; Phillis, "Death of Col. John Williams Patterson."
15. Bird report.
16. Moore report; Bird report; Landon letter, 77; FRSP Historical Photograph Collection, image #212.
17. Moore report; Bird report; Landon letter, 77; FRSP Historical Photograph Collection, image #212; James Riley to "Friend Belle." Moore may have meant to write "One hundred and eighty" but inadvertently left off the *y*.

18. Moore report; Bird report; Landon letter, 77; FRSP Historical Photograph Collection, image #244. Figures for the headboard's width and thickness are taken from actual measurements of Colonel John Patterson's headboard. The headboard was donated to the National Park Service by Patterson's great-grandson William A. Phillis. Headboards like the one placed over Patterson's grave foreshadowed those dictated for all army cemeteries in 1866. On February 13, the Office of the Quartermaster issued General Orders No. 13, which called for graves to be marked with "head-boards . . . about 4' long, 10" wide, and 1–3/8" thick; to stand 2 feet out of the ground. To be of wellseasoned wood; and to be painted with three coats of white paint; inscription in black letters 1" long." In actuality, headboards differed from place to place, and in some instances the army used wooden stakes.

19. James Riley to "Friend Belle."

20. Landon letter, 77. The field in question may have been the Cook farm, located on the east side of the Brock Road one-half mile south of its intersection with the Orange Plank Road.

21. Ibid., 78; FRSP Historical Photograph Collection, image #1953.

22. Landon letter, 77.

23. Ibid. Traveler John T. Trowbridge described the cemetery as being thirty yards square with seventy graves "each containing the remains of I know not how many dead." See Trowbridge, *South*, 126.

24. Moore report; Bird report; Landon letter, 77; James Riley to "Friend Belle."

25. Fredericksburg National Cemetery Register #7700, 77. These men are currently buried at Fredericksburg National Cemetery in graves #4533–37.

26. Landon letter, 81.

27. Ibid., 81–82; FRSP Historical Photograph Collection, image #2138.

28. James Riley to "Friend Belle."

29. Landon letter, 82; Bird report.

30. Landon letter, 82.

31. *OR* 36 (1): 448; Landon letter, 78.

32. Lyman journal, April 15, 1866, Lyman Family Papers, Massachusetts Historical Society.

33. James Riley to "Friend Belle." The *Roll of Honor* indicates that several hundred people were buried on the Sanford farm, which stood in the immediate vicinity of Spotsylvania Court House. A close examination of the names, however, reveals that they belonged almost exclusively to men of the Fifth and Sixth Corps. Those men did not die on Sanford's property, and it is unlikely that Sanford transported them there. Far more likely is that Major Hiram Gerrish, who compiled the list, assumed that the Spindle property belonged to Sanford. After all, the Spindle house had burned down in May 1864, and Sanford was on the property interring the dead. That might also

explain why the Union burial party made its camp behind the Bloody Angle rather than at Laurel Hill: Sanford had already buried the Laurel Hill dead.

34. Moore report; Bird report; James Riley to "Friend Belle." Of the unburied dead that he found at Spotsylvania, Bird wrote, "Those that were found were buried together in Coffins, and the graves numbered. There were but eighteen in all." It is uncertain from his description whether there were eighteen skeletons or eighteen coffins.

35. "Re-burying and Re-marking the Graves of the Union Soldiers Who Fell in the Wilderness," *Fredericksburg New Era*, July 4, 1865.

36. Moore report.

37. James Riley to "Friend Belle"; FRSP Historical Photograph Collection, image #2242.

38. James Riley to "Friend Belle."

39. Moore report; Landon letter, 77. Compare *Annual Reports of the Quartermaster-General*, 32–33, which states that Moore's party "marked" the graves of 1,500 Union soldiers. Making sense of the figures provided by Moore, Bird, Riley, and Landon is a daunting—perhaps impossible—task. When figures are mentioned, do they include the Wilderness, Spotsylvania, or both battlefields? Do the figures include Federal and Confederate graves or just Federal? Known dead, unknown dead, or both? Did graves hold one individual or several? Moreover, the evidence provided by the four men is often contradictory. For instance, Moore, Bird, and Landon each give different figures for the number of soldiers buried in the Wilderness national cemeteries, while the number of identified soldiers cited by Moore in his report (785) is greater than the number of names that appear on his tabulated list (722). Some figures may be in error, such as Moore citing 108 burials in Wilderness National Cemetery No. 1, when he may have meant 180. Other figures are omitted altogether, such as the number of unknown tablets that the burial party erected. Evidence taken from the various Fredericksburg National Cemetery registers only adds to the confusion. The registers themselves do not agree and are totally at odds with statements made by Moore, Bird, Riley, and Landon.

40. Moore report; Bird report.

41. Lyman journal, April 15, 1866, Lyman Family Papers, Massachusetts Historical Society.

42. Trowbridge, *South*, 126–27. "The woods were full of Rebel graves," wrote Trowbridge, "with here and there a heap of half-covered bones, where several of the dead had been hurriedly buried together."

43. *Names of Officers and Soldiers*, 7–20.

44. The names of Pennsylvania, New Jersey, Delaware, and Maryland soldiers, for example, appeared in the July 1, 1865, edition of the *Philadelphia Inquirer*. The quartermaster general's annual report for 1866 stated,

Lists of the dead in the various cemeteries are published in General Orders
for distribution to the principal newspapers in each congressional district, to
adjutant generals and agents of States, and to the principal public libraries
of the country. Six such lists have been published containing the names of
thirty-two thousand six hundred and sixty-six soldiers buried in cemeteries
in the District of Columbia, on the battle-fields of Virginia, at the prison
pen of Andersonville, Georgia, and in Texas. As these lists are completed,
it is proposed, with your approbation, to continue their publication. They
form an invaluable record for surviving friends and relatives.

See *Annual Reports of the Quartermaster-General*, 18–19.

45. I checked the accuracy of Moore's list against interments specifically mentioned
by William Landon. As Landon personally knew the men he mentioned, he
rendered the names accurately, a fact confirmed by regimental rosters. See
Landon letter, 78.

46. Mason, "Notes," 101. Although Mason refers to himself a major, he never rose
above the rank of lieutenant. He lived at the "Sentry Box," a house constructed
by Brigadier General George Weedon of Revolutionary War fame on lower
Caroline Street. During the Civil War, Mason served as aide-de-camp for
his brother-in-law, Major General Charles W. Field. See R. E. L. Krick,
*Staff Officers in Gray*, 217.

47. *Statement of the Disposition*, 26; Borcke, *Memoirs*, 148–49; Owen, *In Camp
and Battle*, 196; Mason, "Notes," 101; Trowbridge, *South*, 112; Pepper, *Personal
Recollections*, 448; Hiram Gerrish report, January 20, 1866, FNC1; Fredericksburg National Cemetery Register #7700.

### 3. A Call to Action

1. Joseph Williams & Co. to Edwin Stanton, September 2, 1865, FNC1.
2. Charles Kronenberger to Edwin Stanton, November 23, 1865, FNC1.
3. James Moore to Montgomery Meigs, December 2, 1865, FNC1. Moore
was appointed brevet major on March 13, 1865, for faithful and meritorious
service during the war and to lieutenant colonel on November 24, 1865, for
the same reason. He received full promotion to these ranks on June 13, 1867,
and on July 2, 1883, respectfully. He retired as a full colonel on October 26,
1901. See Heitman, *Historical Register*, 1:722.
4. George E. Chancellor to Edwin Stanton, December 1, 1865, FNC1.
5. James Moore to Daniel Rucker, December 20, 1865, FNC1.
6. Hiram Gerrish, "List and Location of United States Soldiers Graves," FNC1.
7. Ibid.
8. Ibid.; Hiram Gerrish to QMGO, January 20, 1866, FNC1; subscription list
for soldiers' monument, RG 92, entry 225, NA.

9. Hiram Gerrish to QMGO, January 20, 1866.

10. A. Watson to Chairman on Committee on Military Affairs, House of Representatives, February 20, 1866, FNC1.

11. Ibid. Although it may be a coincidence, T. Freaner & Company had opened a bone dust mill near Fredericksburg in August 1865. See "Bone Dust Mill in Operation," *FL*, August 17, 1865.

12. E. D. Townsend to Montgomery Meigs, April 2, 1866, FNC1; "The Agricultural Fair Grounds Seized by the United States," *FL*, April 13, 1866; James Moore to Montgomery Meigs, May 23, 1866, FNC1.

13. "Military Changes," *FL*, August 14, 1865; untitled, ibid., October 3, 1865.

14. "Military Changes," ibid., August 14, 1865; untitled, ibid., October 3, 1865; untitled, ibid., August 28, 1865; "Military Orders," ibid., January 9, 1866. The editor of the *Fredericksburg Ledger* wrote of General Carroll, "As far as is ascertained, General C. is polite and courteous in his manners, clear and reasonable in his decisions, and seems disposed to do all he can, within his authority to remove the difficulties which surround the present condition of affairs" (August 28, 1865).

15. Untitled, ibid., July 17 and August 28, 1865, and July 1, 1866; "A Federal Soldier Killed," ibid., July 20, 1865; "Another Change of Commanders," ibid., February 6, 1866; Happel, "History of the Fredericksburg and Spotsylvania County Battlefields Memorial National Military Park," 24

16. Untitled, *FL*, April 6, June 1, and October 30, 1866, April 2, 1869.

17. Happel, "History of the Fredericksburg and Spotsylvania County Battlefields Memorial National Military Park," 24; untitled, *FL*, September 11, 1865; "Sudden Death," *FL*, July 20, 1865.

18. "Things about Town," *FL*, September 29, 1868. For a list of cases brought before the provost marshal, District of Northeastern Virginia, see untitled, ibid., August 3 and 10, 1865.

19. "The Soldiers," ibid., November 16, 1866; "A Federal Soldier Killed," ibid., July 20, 1865; "Military Orders," ibid., January 9, 1866.

20. "Burying Federal Dead," ibid., May 29, 1866; untitled, ibid., May 22, June 1, June 12, 1866; "National Cemeteries," *Washington (D.C.) Chronicle*, n.d.

21. "Sudden Death," *FL*, February 21, 1868; James Moore to Montgomery Meigs, June 18, 1868, FNC2; Henry Hodges to Montgomery Meigs, November 29, 1870, FNC1; Timothy O. Howe to Edwin Stanton, July 27, 1867, FNC1.

22. The Coloured Teamsters to the War Department, January 1, 1867, RG 92, entry 225, box 289, NA.

23. The Laboring men at N. Cemetery to Andrew Johnson, May 29, 1868, FNC2; Richard Coran et al. to Ulysses Grant, June 25, 1868, FNC2; "A Rebel Falsehood Nailed," *Washington Chronicle*, November 12, 1866. There is no record of Richard Coran serving in the Union army.

24. James Moore to Montgomery Meigs, June 18, 1868. Cf. Fitzgerald, *Different Story*, 105.

25. Untitled, *FL*, August 7, 1866; "The Burial Corps," *Virginia Herald*, June 20, 1867.

26. Trowbridge, *Desolate South*, 138–39; Olsen, "Poplar Grove," 27.

27. Howison, "Childhood Memories," 2. Cf. Happel, "History of the Fredericksburg and Spotsylvania County Battlefields Memorial National Military Park," 24; and untitled, *FL*, April 2, 1869. An 1866 sketch shows the tents of the burial party just east of the Sunken Road. See Lossing, *Pictorial History*, 2:491.

28. Affidavit signed by L. C. Frost and D. C. Ellis, August 11, 1869, FNC2; Edward McMahon to J. G. Chandler, October 18, 1869, FNC2; James A. Bradley to [?], January 25, 1870, FNC2; Joseph Hall to Montgomery Meigs, February 16, 1870, FNC2; J. G. Chandler to Montgomery Meigs, February 3, 1870, FNC2; Alexander Perry to J. C. McFerron, January 13, 1870, FNC2. The Burial Corps appears to have completed its work by the fall of 1868. Occupation troops continued to occupy Hall's property until March 31, 1869, however.

29. Alexander Perry to J. C. McFerron, January 13, 1870, FNC2. Perry recommended that Hall receive $56.25 per acre of sod rather than $100.00 per acre, as the property owner requested. Perry based his recommendation on the amount paid for sod by the army to James H. Bradley of Fredericksburg in October 1868.

30. *Annual Reports of the Quartermaster-General*, 223; "A Rebel Falsehood Nailed," *Washington Chronicle*, November 12, 1866. Nationally, the average cost per body for transfer and reinterment to a national cemetery was $9.75, of which $4.00 was for the wooden coffin. In Virginia, the average cost was somewhat lower, about $8.00 per burial, of which $2.50 went toward the coffin and $1.25 toward the headboard. See *Annual Reports of the Quartermaster-General*, 18–19, 223, 239–40.

31. Trowbridge, *Desolate South*, 139–40; Trowbridge, *South*, 264, 266. If there were just one hundred men and each man examined the ground one-half yard on either side of him, the search party as a whole would have covered an area of just one hundred yards. Trowbridge likely meant to say each man examined two and one-half yards of ground on either side of him.

32. Olsen, "Poplar Grove," 28. At Fredericksburg, Mason described seeing coffins measuring six feet long by one foot wide made out of plain unpainted pine. Likewise, a correspondent who visited a Burial Corps camp at Lynchburg, Virginia, noticed a "great number of neat unpainted boxes" piled up at the camp. See Mason, "Notes," 101; and untitled, *Lynchburg Daily Virginian*, October 17, 1866.

33. Conwell, *Magnolia Journey*, 9; Thomas Elam to Hayes Walker, November 21, 1866, FRSP.
34. *Annual Report of the Quartermaster General . . . for the Year 1870*, 68–71.
35. *Revised Report*, 151. In 1867, a Union veteran named Thomas J. Franey accused the Burial Corps of knowingly interring hundreds of Confederates in Fredericksburg National Cemetery, but his charges appear to have been groundless. Later superintendents insisted that no Confederates were buried there. See Timothy Howe to Edwin Stanton, July 20, 1867, FNC1. The Compiled Service Records identify four men with the name of Thomas J. Franey. They served respectively in the Fourth Wisconsin, Nineteenth Wisconsin, Fifteenth New Jersey, and Eighty-Fourth Pennsylvania.
36. Letters Sent, p. 45.
37. *Revised Report*, 150. The identification process was much the same at Cold Harbor Battlefield, near Richmond. There, the Burial Corps identified soldiers by the names or markings on their uniforms, by medals or badges that they wore, and by inscriptions carved on headboards found over their graves. See United States Christian Commission, *Record of the Federal Dead*, 11–13. See also Steere, "Genesis," 154–55.
38. Frederick Mervine to Hayes Walker, May 15, 1863, FRSP; Thomas Elam to Hayes Walker, November 21, 1866, FRSP. Private Alexander J. Walker is buried in grave #2738. A soldier in the Third New Jersey, Walker was mortally wounded in the May 3, 1863, fighting at Salem Church and was taken back to Stafford County. He died nine days later and was buried at Chatham, a prominent estate in that county.
39. Charles Fitchett to Quartermaster Department, September 11, 1873, RG 92, entry 571, vol. 5, 79, 90, NA; Theodore Eckerson to Adjutant General of Ohio, February 13, 1874, FNC1. Letters to the adjutant generals of several others states appear in FNC1.
40. Fredericksburg National Cemetery Register #7701, 188, 190, 312, 314.
41. Letters Sent, pp. 63, 101, 129, 143, 147, 159, 201.
42. Anonymous, 1868 inspection report, found in Letter of the Secretary of War Communicating, in Obedience to Law, the Report of the Inspector of the National Cemeteries of the United States for 1869, 27–28 (hereafter cited as anonymous, 1868 inspection report, LSW). Although the inspection report states that 15,118 men were buried in the cemetery, a tabulation of the numbers used to reach that figure indicates that the total was actually 15,128.
43. Untitled, *FL*, April 2, 1869.

### 4. The Creation of Fredericksburg National Cemetery

1. James Moore to Montgomery Meigs, May 23, 1866, FNC1.
2. A. Watson to Montgomery Meigs, May 29, 1866, FNC1.

3. Untitled, *FL*, June 8, 1866; "'Willis Hill'—The Federal Cemetery," *VH*, June 7, 1866. "'Willis Hill' had been generally regarded as the desirable point for the Confederate soldiers who, so valiantly and successfully, defended it," wrote the editor of the *Virginia Herald*. "But we suppose we will have to hang our harps upon the willows. The Confederate dead were able while living, and their comrades after their fall, to prevent its occupation; but the living of to-day must confess their inability to do so—even though peace, 'so-called,' reigns; and pardons and amnesties have been granted professing to have restored us to our wonted position in the Federal Union, and to have re-invested us in the rights of property."

4. Abstract of Willis Hill ownership, FNC2; Mitchell, Willis Hill advertisement, *VH*, October 15, 1855.

5. "An Act to Establish and to Protect National Cemeteries," in Sanger, *Statutes at Large . . . December, 1865, to March, 1867*, 14:399–401; Douglas Gordon to Edwin Stanton, May 7, 1867, FNC2. See appendix 1.

6. G. Thomas to John Schofield, July 25, 1868, FNC2; "Descriptive Record of National Cemeteries, 1867–70," RG 92, entry 683, box 1, NA; deed to Fredericksburg National Cemetery, FNC2; description of land seized by the U.S. government from Douglas Gordon, FNC2; memoranda for national cemeteries, FNC2; Happel, "History of the Fredericksburg and Spotsylvania County Battlefields Memorial National Military Park," 24, which cites Fredericksburg Court Records, Deed Book V, 39–40; Theodore Eckerson to [?], June 13, 1874, RG 92, entry 571, 5:203, NA. The title papers were transmitted to the quartermaster general on February 2, 1869, and forwarded to the secretary of war on February 5. The papers and correspondence were transferred from the War Department to the judge advocate general on July 5, 1894. See "List of Plans of National Cemeteries," RG 92, entry 653, box 1, NA. Most of the correspondence between Gordon and the government are in FNC2. A handwritten copy of the deed appears at the back of Fredericksburg National Cemetery Register #7700, FRSP.

7. Untitled, *FL*, June 8, 1866.

8. Some of the angles are rather subtle and may not appear in figure 4.3.

9. Anonymous, 1868 inspection report, LSW; anonymous, 1871 inspection report in Letter of the Secretary of War, Communicating, in Obedience to Law, the Report of the Inspector of the National Cemeteries for the Years 1870 and 1871 (hereafter cited as anonymous, 1871 inspection report, LSW); *Annual Report of the Quartermaster General . . . for the Year 1870*, 68–71; William Gaw, July 1, 1875, inspection report, FNC3; James Reed, 1873 map, FNC4; M. M. Jefferys, 1909 questionnaire response, FNC4.

10. Richard Arnold, 1882 inspection report, FNC4.

11. Douglas Gordon to Edwin Stanton, FNC2; anonymous, 1868 inspection report, LSW; Oscar Mack, 1871 inspection report, FNC1; anonymous, 1874 inspection

report in Letter from the Secretary of War, Transmitting in Obedience to Law, the Report of the Inspector of the National Cemeteries for the Year 1874 (hereafter cited as anonymous, 1874 inspection report, LSW); M. M. Jefferys, 1909 questionnaire response, FNC4. The terraces were in existence by October 1868. The cemetery lodge was built on the lowest terrace, south of the entrance, while an access road to the maintenance area was subsequently constructed on the next lowest terrace.

12. Anonymous, 1868 inspection report, LSW; anonymous, 1874 inspection report, LSW; William Gaw, July 1, 1875, inspection report, FNC3.

13. Anonymous, 1868, 1871, and 1874 inspection reports, LSW; anonymous, 1882 inspection report, FNC3.

14. *Landscapes of Honor and Sacrifice.*

15. Memoranda for national cemeteries, FNC2; anonymous, 1868 inspection report, LSW; James Reed, 1873 map, FNC4. An inspector, viewing the cemetery in 1868, stated that the avenues divided the grounds into twenty irregular parcels known as sections; nineteen of these were used for burials, and the twentieth was set aside for the lodge.

16. Anonymous, 1868 and 1871 inspection reports, LSW; James Reed, 1873 map, FNC4.

17. Terrace #1 stood at the top of the hill; terraces #8 and #9 stood at the bottom.

18. Fredericksburg National Cemetery Register #7701

19. Letters Sent, pp. 83, 133. See handwritten notes on copy of 1892 map produced by the Office of the Quartermaster General (hereafter cited QMGO, 1892 map).

20. Anonymous, 1868 inspection report, LSW; James Reed, 1873 map, FNC4. Inspector William B. Gaw described the main carriageway as being twenty feet wide. See William Gaw, July 1, 1875, inspection report, FNC3.

21. Charles Fitchett to A. F. Rockwell, FNC1; W. H. Owen, 1886 inspection report, FNC1; Chenoweth 1873 inspection report, FNC2. It required 150 cartloads of gravel to fill the gullies.

22. James Gall, 1878 and 1883 inspection reports, FNC4; C. W. Foster, 1881 inspection report, FNC4; C. W. Foster, 1884 inspection report, FNC1; anonymous, 1882 inspection report, FNC3; Conwell, *Magnolia Journey*, 9.

23. James Gall, 1883 inspection report, FNC4.

24. C. W. Foster, 1884 inspection report, FNC1.

25. W. H. Owen, 1886 and 1888 inspection reports, FNC1; M. M. Jefferys, 1909 questionnaire response, FNC4.

## 5. Toward a More Permanent Cemetery

1. Memoranda for National Cemeteries, FNC2; anonymous, 1868 inspection report, LSW; Charles Fitchett to Theodore Eckerson, March 10, 1873, FNC1; Henry Hodges to Montgomery Meigs, May 13, 1871, FNC2. A cemetery

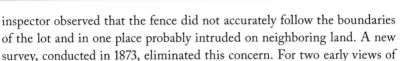

inspector observed that the fence did not accurately follow the boundaries of the lot and in one place probably intruded on neighboring land. A new survey, conducted in 1873, eliminated this concern. For two early views of the fence, see figures 5.2 and 7.4.

2. FRSP Historical Photograph Collection, image #2086. Fredericksburg was one of five cemeteries slated to receive such a gate. See *Annual Report of the Quartermaster General . . . for the Year 1870,* 68–71.

3. Fitchett to Eckerson, March 10, 1873, FNC1; Oscar Mack, 1873 inspection report, FNC1.

4. "National Cemetery," *FL,* May 30, 1873; "Contract Awarded," ibid., July 11, 1873. Wroten would later serve on the Fredericksburg City Council. See *FFL,* February 24, 1891.

5. Copy of contract in FNC2; A. J. McGonnigle to George Wroten, August 28, 1873, FNC1; "Contract Awarded," *FL,* July 11, 1873. An early Quartermaster Department report put the length of the national cemetery boundary at 2,831 feet, while an 1873 cemetery plat showed the wall to be 3,039 feet long. In 1889, Superintendent Andrew J. Birdsall measured the length of the wall at 3,025 feet and its height, above ground, at 5′8″. He was measuring the stone posts at the entrance. Twenty years later, Superintendent M. M. Jefferys put the height of the wall between the posts at just 4′8″. A sketch of the wall that accompanied the contract showed it to stand 4′10″ above the ground with a 2′4″ deep foundation. I measured the wall height at 4′9″ with the pillars standing 5′7″ tall. See James Reed, 1873 map, FNC4; Andrew Birdsall, 1889 questionnaire response, FNC1; M. M. Jefferys, 1909 questionnaire response, FNC4; and descriptive record, RG 92, entry 683, NA.

The number of bricks used by Wroten is unknown. Poplar Grove Cemetery, in Petersburg, Virginia, which has a shorter wall than Fredericksburg, utilized four hundred thousand bricks. Based on that figure, I estimate that Fredericksburg's wall contains more than half a million bricks. See Olsen, "Poplar Grove," 60.

6. G. D. Chenoweth to Judson Bingham, January 14, 1874, FNC2; G. D. Chenoweth to Montgomery Meigs, February 18, 1874, FNC3; G. D. Chenoweth to Montgomery Meigs, April 20, 1874, FNC2; "Work Condemned," *FL,* March 3, 1874.

7. George Wroten to Montgomery Meigs, May 8, 1874, FNC1; G. D. Chenoweth to Montgomery Meigs, March 28, 1874, FNC3.

8. G. D. Chenoweth to Montgomery Meigs, July 1, 1874, FNC3; G. D. Chenoweth to A. F. Rockwell, August 19, 1874, FNC3; Oscar Mack, 1874 inspection report, RG 92, entry 648, box 1, 2:105–9, NA.

9. A. F. Rockwell to George Wroten, September 2, 1874, FNC3. The granite gateposts were made by Westham Granite Company of Virginia.

10. FRSP Historical Photograph Collection, image #804; Letters Sent, pp. 109, 115. A sketch of the gates and gateposts that accompanied the contract appears in FNC2. A photograph of the gateway, taken in 1893, shows two granite blocks, like those used to mark the graves of unknown soldiers, standing in front of the two center columns. The blocks served one of two purposes: to stop the gates from opening too widely or to protect the gateposts from being struck by vehicles entering the cemetery. The granite posts are absent in a photograph taken in 1906, replaced by two dark objects, approximately one foot high—possibly large artillery shells. These objects appear in the 1893 image, to the left of the south pedestrian gate. A worn path leading to the south pedestrian gate in the 1893 photograph suggests that the gate was in active use at that time. See FRSP Historical Photograph Collection, images #2617 and #2676.

11. Letters Sent, p. 115; Letters Received, p. 31; Jefferys diary, May 6 and 9, 1912, FRSP. A 1906 photograph does not show the shields, but a colorized postcard produced shortly thereafter does. The shields also appear in a ca. 1950 image of the front gate. FRSP Historical Photograph Collection, images #2617 and #2729.

12. George Wroten to A. F. Rockwell, December 21, 1874, FNC3.

13. Ibid., May 4, 1875; William Gaw, July 1, 1875 inspection report, FNC3; G. D. Chenoweth to A. F. Rockwell, July 21, 1875, FNC4, G. D. Chenoweth to Montgomery Meigs, April 7, 1874, FNC3; George Wroten to A. F. Rockwell, May 24, 1875, FNC3.

14. G. D. Chenoweth to A. F. Rockwell, April 15, 1875, FNC3; Charles Fitchett to A. F. Rockwell, June 14, 1875, FNC4; James Gall, September 21, 1877 inspection report, FNC4; C. M. Clarke, 1879 inspection report, FNC4; James Gall, 1882 inspection report, FNC4; C. W. Foster, 1884 inspection report, FNC1; W. H. Owen, 1886 inspection report, FNC1.

15. W. H. Owen, 1886 and 1888 inspection reports, FNC1.

16. Letters Sent, pp. 95, 200; Letters Received, p. 150.

17. Anonymous, 1882 inspection report, FNC3.

18. James Gall, 1883 and October 8, 1877, inspection reports, FNC4. This contract was negotiated in early November 1882. See C. W. Foster to Quartermaster General, November 6, 1882, FNC4.

19. C. W. Foster to Quartermaster General, November 6, 1882, FNC4; M. M. Jefferys, 1909 questionnaire response, FNC4; Letters Sent, pp. 76, 155, 160; Letters Received, p. 94.

20. James Reed, 1873 map, FNC4; G. D. Chenoweth, 1873 inspection report, FNC2.

21. G. D. Chenoweth, 1873 inspection report, FNC2; G. D. Chenoweth to Judson Bingham, December 18, 1873, FNC1.

22. Theodore Eckerson to Montgomery Meigs, March 23, 1874, FNC2.

23. Oliver Cox, October 21, 1875, inspection report, FNC3; Oscar Mack, 1874 inspection report, RG 92, entry 648, box 1, 2:105–9, NA; G. D. Chenoweth, May 12, 1874, dispatch in RG 92, entry 571, 5:159, NA. Chenoweth's sketch of the steps appears in FNC1.

24. FRSP Historical Photograph Collection, images #2464 and #2466. Warrenton Roberts is buried in grave #3287. Ten days after Roberts's funeral, an elegy to his memory appeared in the *Fredericksburg Ledger*. Apparently written by a fellow soldier, the poem read:

> Our Brother's dead! he sleepeth now
> From care—his marble brow
> With death's cold damp is chill'd—
> The measure of his day's [*sic*] is filled.
>
> With patience his agonizing pain
> He bore—and with Christ to reign,
> Was all his prayer—his call
> On Him who died for all.
>
> No more his presence here—but we
> Must die!—hence let us flee
> To that refuge which will sustain,
> And bring us all with Christ to reign.

Fredericksburg National Cemetery roster; "Died," *FL*, March 26, 1867; "Inmemoriam [*sic*]," *FL*, April 5, 1867.

25. FRSP Historical Photograph Collection, image #2087.

26. Ibid., #2464.

27. The stone for the granite markers may have come from Proctor, Vermont. See Letters Received, p. 12.

28. *Annual Reports of the Quartermaster-General*, 234–35.

29. Oscar Mack, 1873 inspection report, FNC1.

30. "History of Government Furnished Headstones and Markers."

31. Ibid.; Olsen, "Poplar Grove," 56; Steere, "Evolution."

32. "Headstones for National Cemeteries," *FL*, September 12, 1873; "Headstones for National Cemeteries," *FL*, July 25, 1873.

33. *Congressional Globe*, 42nd Cong., 2nd sess. (1872), 805; Steere, "Evolution," 124-25.

34. "Headstones for Soldiers' Graves," *FL*, November 18, 1873. See also *Annual Report of the Quartermaster-General . . . for the Fiscal Year Ending June 30, 1874*, 23. Eight years earlier, as a lieutenant in the Sixteenth New York Cavalry,

Doherty led the detachment that tracked down and killed assassin John Wilkes Booth at the Garrett farm in Caroline County, Virginia.

35. Records of the Office of the Quartermaster General, Register of Letters Received, 1871–89, RG 92, entry 571, 4:185, 5:205, NA.

36. Ibid., 5:82, 169, 260.

37. Oscar Mack, 1874 inspection report, RG 92, entry 648, box 1, 2:105–9, NA.

38. E. P. Doherty to Quartermaster Department, August 1, 1874, RG 92, entry 571, 5:260, NA; ibid., August 22, 1874, 5:274.

39. Steere, "Evolution," 125. This was the standard for stones erected south of Washington, D.C. Those erected north of the city were forty-two inches long, thirty inches of which were to be below the ground surface.

40. "History of Government Furnished Headstones and Markers"; Steere, "Evolution," 125, indicates that six inches of stone were supposed to be above the ground surface. My field measurements reveal that stonemasons dressed the top four to five inches of the blocks.

41. Mollan, "Honoring Our War Dead"; "History of Government Furnished Headstones and Markers."

42. "History of Government Furnished Headstones and Markers"; Letters Sent, pp. 154, 170; Letters Received, p. 83. Ideally, Civil War–style and general-style headstones should stand twenty-four inches above the ground, but because of settling they are usually a few inches lower.

43. The Spanish-American War veterans who have general headstones are Rufus Brown (#4682C), Luther Miller (#6709), John Hoover (#6714), Thomas Weber (#6721), and John Ellington (#6727).

44. Most of the crosses are encompassed in a circle, but at least two are not.

45. Andrew Birdsall, 1889 questionnaire response, FNC1; Letters Sent, p. 167. The headstone appears in a very early image of the cemetery. It was not replaced and today is virtually illegible. See FRSP Historical Photograph Collection, image #2734.

46. *Roll of Honor*, 25:20, 24, 64–65, 122. Van Ness is listed as Peirce B. Van Ess in the first instance and as Pierre Van Ness in the second. In both entries he is listed as having been a private in Company F of the First Long Island. Collins was listed as being in Company D in one instance and in Company K in the other; however, no man by that name ever served in Company K.

### 6. The Superintendent's Lodge and Other Buildings

1. Montgomery Meigs to James Moore, July 16, 1866, FNC2; "Act to Establish and to Protect National Cemeteries," in Sanger, *Statutes at Large . . . December, 1865, to March, 1867*, 14:399–401.

2. Charles Fitchett to Henry Hodges, March 23, April 12, May 6, 1871, FNC3;

FRSP Historical Photograph Collection, image #2134; "Our National Cemeteries," *Harper's Weekly*, October 26, 1867.

3. Charles Fitchett to Henry Hodges, March 23, 1871, FNC3; Charles Fitchett to C. W. Foster, April 2, 1881, FNC4; anonymous, 1871 inspection report, LSW.

4. Charles Fitchett to Henry Hodges, May 6, 1871, FNC3; Judson Bingham to Henry Hodges, May 12, 1871, FNC1.

5. Bartlett, *Military Record of Louisiana*, 3; *History of the Thirty-Fifth Regiment*, 86; William Gaw, July 1, 1875, inspection report, FNC3; W. H. Owen, 1886 and 1888 inspection reports, FNC1; inscription on back of FRSP Historical Photograph Collection, image #3377. Compare Andrew Birdsall, 1889 questionnaire response, FNC1, in which Birdsall erroneously states that the house was made of granite.

6. "National Cemeteries with Meigs Lodges"; "National Cemetery Administration, Superintendent's Lodges, Washington, District of Columbia." The Fredericksburg lodge was one of twelve such structures built by the army in fiscal year 1871. Before it was through, the army would construct more than sixty-five lodges in national cemeteries throughout the country. Of that number, fewer than half remain.

7. Oscar Mack, 1873 inspection report, FNC1; anonymous, 1874 inspection report, LSW.

8. "National Cemeteries with Meigs Lodges"; FRSP Historical Photograph Collection, images #2134, #2617, and #2730; Letters Sent, p. 147; Letters Received, p. 77; Andrew Birdsall, 1889 questionnaire response, FNC1; anonymous, 1874 inspection report, LSW.

9. Anonymous, 1874 inspection report, LSW; A. J. McGonnigle to [?], July 9, 1870, FNC2.

10. Mansard roofs have four steeply sloping sides.

11. "National Cemeteries with Meigs Lodges"; FRSP Historical Photograph Collection, images #2134 and #2680. Later images of the lodge, however, taken early in the twentieth century clearly do show a lozenge design on the roof tiles. See FRSP Historical Photograph Collection, images #2615 and #2617.

12. W. H. Owen, 1886 inspection report, FNC1; Birdsall diary, October 6, 1891, FRSP; Charles Fitchett to C. W. Foster, April 2, 1881, April 1, 1882, FNC4.

13. M. M. Jefferys to [?], July 11, 1905, FRSP; Jefferys diary, July 25, November 14, 1905, April 23, 1907, FRSP; Letters Sent, pp. 28, 86, 128.

14. Letters Sent, pp. 86, 98, 125; M. M. Jefferys to [?], July 11, 1905, FRSP; Jefferys diary, September 8, October 24, 1905, FRSP; Letters Received, p. 11.

15. Letters Received, pp. 125–26, 135. For confirmation that the lodge had no cellar until the twentieth century, see M. M. Jefferys, 1909 questionnaire response, FNC4.
16. Letters Sent, pp. 176, 181, 184, 187. During excavation of the cellar, a seeping spring appeared on its western side.
17. Ibid., pp. 185–86, 189.
18. Fredericksburg National Cemetery Plan, FRSP. A corner of the porch appears in FRSP Historical Photograph Collection, image #2732.
19. Charles Fitchett to Henry Hodges, March 23, 1871, FNC3.
20. James Reed, 1873 map, FNC4. A photograph taken in the fall of 1874 shows a large building with vertical wooden timbers, directly north of the stone lodge. The wooden building had two distinct rooflines, suggesting that the army may indeed have joined the original lodge and toolhouse into a single edifice. In his 1874 inspection, Major Oscar Mack referred to the "old Lodge," which apparently was still standing behind the new lodge. See Oscar Mack, 1874 inspection report, RG 92, entry 648, box 1, 2:105–9, NA.
21. Oscar Mack, 1873 inspection report, FNC1; G. D. Chenoweth, 1873 inspection report, FNC2; anonymous, 1874 inspection report, LSW. Poplar Grove National Cemetery likewise moved its original wooden lodge and used it for storage. See August Miller letter, July 1, 1872, Petersburg National Battlefield.
22. Oliver Cox, August 28, 1875, inspection report, FNC3.
23. Ibid., October 21, 1875; C. M. Clarke, 1879 inspection report, FNC4; Charles Fitchett to C. W. Foster, April 2, 1881, FNC4.
24. James Gall to Benjamin Card, September 29, 1881, FNC4; C. W. Foster, 1881 inspection report, FNC4.
25. Charles Fitchett to C. W. Foster, April 1, 1882, FNC4; James Gall to Benjamin Card, April 15, 1882, FNC4; anonymous, 1882 inspection report, FNC3; W. H. Owen, 1888 inspection report, FNC1; Andrew Birdsall, 1889 questionnaire response, FNC1; Letters Received, pp. 11, 110, 128.
26. Charles Fitchett to C. W. Foster, April 1, 1882, FNC4.
27. James Gall to Benjamin Card, April 15, 1882, FNC4.
28. Richard Arnold, 1882 inspection report, FNC4.
29. W. H. Owen, 1888 inspection report, FNC1; Jefferys diary, January 14, 1905, FRSP.
30. W. H. Owen, 1888 inspection report, FNC1.
31. M. M. Jefferys, 1909 questionnaire response, FNC4.
32. Tommy Westbrook, telephone call to the author, April 10, 2006. Mr. Westbrook was then the buildings and grounds foreman at FRSP.
33. W. H. Owen, 1888 inspection report, FNC1; M. M. Jefferys, 1909 questionnaire response, FNC4; Letters Sent, p. 160; Letters Received, p. 89; QMGO, 1892 map.

34. Jefferys diary, May 25, October 25, 1897, October 7, 12, November 11, 16–23, 1909, FRSP.

35. Ibid., December 14, 1905, FRSP; M. M. Jefferys, 1909 questionnaire response, FNC4; QMGO, 1892 map.

36. Letters Sent, pp. 120–21, 132; Allen Kimbely, 1922 inspection report, in Letters Received, pp. 46–47. In his diaries, M. M. Jefferys mentions having a coal house at the cemetery. This seems to have been a separate structure from the woodshed, but whether it was a room in the brick maintenance building or a separate structure is hard to say. See Jefferys diary, April 19, 1907, FRSP.

37. W. II. Owen, 1888 inspection report, FNC1.

38. W. H. Owen, 1886 and 1888 inspection reports, FNC1; Fredericksburg National Cemetery register #7700, 473–74; QMGO, 1892 map (revised 1911). The graves removed to make way for the road were #231–65.

39. W. H. Owen, 1888 inspection report, FNC1; QMGO, 1892 map (revised 1911); Jefferys diary, November 4, 7, 17–18, 1905, FRSP; FRSP Historical Photograph Collection, image #2615. The work area ran in front of the various support structures attached to the lodge. A 1911 map shows it as being long and narrow in shape, extending from the back porch of the lodge to the cart shed adjacent to the north wall—the area today occupied by the asphalt driveway.

40. Letters Sent, p. 176.

41. FRSP Historical Photograph Collection, images #2134, #2730.

42. "National Cemeteries with Meigs Lodges"; FRSP Historical Photograph Collection, image #2314.

43. W. H. Owen, 1886 inspection report, FNC1. An early twentieth-century image of the lodge shows the living room chimney extending at five to ten feet above the roof and containing three flues, which extended another two to three feet above that. See FRSP Historical Photograph Collection, image #2250.

44. In the kitchen was a 1923 model U.S. Army Range made by Sexton and Company of Baltimore, which the government had installed when it added the kitchen in 1905. The range had a grate measuring fifteen inches by eight inches. Made by Fuller, Warren and Company of Troy, New York, the 1881 model "Splendid" Latrobe stove had a grate measuring twelve inches in diameter. Superintendents seem to have used the Latrobe stove only in the winter, storing it outside the lodge during other seasons of the year. See Letters Sent, pp. 126, 156, 181; and Jefferys diary, November 10, 1907, FRSP.

45. Letters Sent, pp. 118, 156; Letters Received, pp. 42–43. By 1928, the cemetery had acquired "miscellaneous stoves" and one airtight wood heater. When it obtained these stoves and where it employed them is unknown. Some of them may have been used in the upstairs bedrooms. See Letters Sent, p. 181.

46. Superintendent M. M. Jefferys purchased the wood from David Ennis. See Jefferys diary, July 23, 1908, FRSP; Letters Sent, pp. 152, 178; and Letters Received, pp. 44, 52, 62, 101, 117.

47. Letters Sent, p. 123.

48. Letters Sent, pp. 184, 190. The coal bin is no longer visible from outside the house, but it can be seen from inside the cellar.

49. Anonymous, 1868 and 1871 inspection reports, LSW; anonymous, 1882 inspection report, FNC3.

50. W. H. Owen, 1888 inspection report, FNC1; James Reed, 1873 map, FNC4; FRSP Historical Photograph Collection, image #2134. An anonymous inspection report submitted on March 10, 1882, stated that the well stood between the lodge and the brick maintenance building. This seems to contradict both the 1873 map and Owens's 1888 report.

51. W. H. Owen, 1888 inspection report, FNC1.

52. Anonymous, 1882 inspection report, FNC3; Richard Arnold, 1882 inspection report, FNC4; James Gall, 1882 and 1883 inspection reports, FNC4; W. H. Owen, 1888 inspection report, FNC1.

53. W. H. Owen, 1888 inspection report, FNC1; Samuel Holabird to G. B. Bandy, May 8, 1888, FNC1. A new pump was added in the spring of 1907. See Jefferys diary, April 10 and May 9, 1907, FRSP.

54. Letters Sent, pp. 104, 121; Letters Received, p. 18.

55. Anonymous, 1871 inspection report, LSW; James Reed, 1873 map, FNC4; Richard Arnold, 1882 inspection report, FNC4.

56. W. H. Owen, 1888 inspection report, FNC1; Andrew Birdsall, 1889 questionnaire response, FNC1; Meigs, "Specifications for Cisterns."

57. Jefferys diary, September 26, 28, 1905, FRSP.

58. QMGO, 1892 map (revised 1911); M. M. Jefferys, 1909 questionnaire response, FNC4; Letters Sent, p. 86. Responding to a questionnaire sent out by the Quartermaster Department, Superintendent Robinson in 1921 wrote that a lavatory and bathtub were connected to city water. See Letters Received, p. 10.

59. Letters Sent, pp. 143, 169, 171.

60. Anonymous, 1882 inspection report, FNC3.

61. M. M. Jefferys, 1909 questionnaire response, FNC4; QMGO, 1892 map (revised 1911). The hydrants were in place by 1906, when one appears in a photograph. See FRSP Historical Photograph Collection, image #2617.

62. Letters Sent, pp. 23, 42, 62, 171; Letters Received, p. 107. FRSP Historical Photograph Collection, image #2732, taken in 1937, shows a hose behind a short hedge at the carriageway fork, suggesting that a hydrant may still have been in operation at that late date.

63. Charles Fitchett to C. W. Foster, April 2, 1881, FNC4.

64. W. H. Owen, 1888 inspection report, FNC1.

65. Letters Sent, p. 86.
66. Ibid., p. 71.
67. M. M. Jefferys, 1909 questionnaire response, FNC4; Letters Sent, pp. 56, 71, 78–79, 98, 102. In June 1916, Robinson requested authority to employ four days' labor at $1.50 per day to dig a four-by-six-foot hole "to receive excreta from privy buckets" (Letters Sent, p. 56). From his descriptions it is clear that this pit was located on a narrow strip of land owned by the government, just outside the west wall.
68. M. M. Jefferys, 1909 questionnaire response, FNC4; Letters Sent, pp. 46, 63, 86, 129, 156, 169; Letters Received, p. 89.
69. Letters Received, pp. 10, 138; Letters Sent, pp. 28, 136.

## 7. Refinements

1. Anonymous, 1868 and 1871 inspection reports, LSW; FRSP Historical Photograph Collection, images #2086 and #2463; Oscar Mack, 187 and 1873 inspection reports, FNC1; G. D. Chenoweth to Montgomery Meigs, February 4, 1874, FNC3; Charles Fitchett to Theodore Eckerson, February 19, 1873, FNC2; "Our National Cemeteries," *Harper's Weekly*, October 26, 1867. The first flagstaff stood 117 feet above the mound, which was approximately eight feet tall.
2. Charles Fitchett to Theodore Eckerson, February 19, 1873, FNC2. The height of the mainmast (80 feet) plus the height of the topmast (40 feet) plus the height of the mound (7 feet), minus the subterranean portion of the mainmast (10 feet): total 117 feet.
3. FRSP Historical Photograph Collection, image #2734.
4. Charles Fitchett to Oscar Mack, November 16, 1873, FNC2.
5. G. D. Chenoweth to Montgomery Meigs, February 4, 1874, FNC3. Specifications for the flagstaff called for a slope of 1.5 feet to 1 foot. Following these guidelines, the base of the mound would have been 22 feet in diameter.
6. Jonathan Comfort to Montgomery Meigs, February 5, 1874, FNC3; Montgomery Meigs to Jonathan Comfort, February 11 and 15, 1874, FNC3; G. D. Chenoweth to Montgomery Meigs, February 18, 1874, FNC2.
7. R. Jones, 1878 inspection report, RG 92, entry 648, box 1, 1:229–30, NA; James Gall, September 21, 1877, inspection report, FNC4; Charles Fitchett to Oscar Mack, November 16, 1873, FNC2.
8. Andrew Birdsall, 1889 questionnaire response, FNC1; W. H. Owen, 1886 inspection report, FNC1; FRSP Historical Photograph Collection, images #629, #794, and #2238.
9. R. Jones, 1878 inspection report, RG 92, entry 648, box 1, 1:229–30, NA.
10. Wallace Stetson to A. F. Rockwell, August 30, 1878, FNC4; J. M. Marshall to Wallace Stetson, August 13, 1878, FNC4.

11. M. M. Jefferys, 1909 questionnaire response, FNC4; Jefferys 1905 diary entries for June 28, July 11, August 10, September 28, October 5–21, FRSP. The army painted the 1905 flagstaff white with gold leaf on the balls. Letters Sent, p. 90.

12. In 1908, three years after the flagpole was moved, cemetery officials erected the Humphreys Monument at the site of the earlier center mound. As Pennsylvania officials did not visit the cemetery until 1906, there appears to be no connection between the two events.

13. Daniel, "In an Old Virginia Town," 612. Superintendents kept two storm flags on hand: one for use and one as a backup. See Letters Received, p. 58.

14. Letters Sent, pp. 63, 73, 82, 87, 147, 164, 168, 171, 179, 182, 187.

15. August 28, 1868, circular order found in RG 92, entry 569, NA; anonymous, 1871 inspection report, LSW; Oscar Mack, 1871 inspection report, FNC1. A cannonball is wedged into the bore of each cannon to prevent water from getting inside the barrel.

16. A cast-iron brace held the plaque to the cannon; however, the first brace sent to the cemetery was too large. The Quartermaster Department sent a second brace, but when workers tried to install it, both the brace and the screws broke. Charles Fitchett to [?], December 11, 1873, RG 92, entry 571, 4:199, NA; Theodore Eckerson to [?], December 31, 1873, 5:1, ibid.; Charles Fitchett to [?], February 2, 1874, 5:48, ibid.

17. FRSP Historical Photograph Collection, image #2735; RG 92, box 3, entry 377, NA. The cannonball stands do not appear in the earliest view of the flagstaff mound, taken ca. 1871. See FRSP Historical Photograph Collection, image #2734.

18. FRSP Historical Photograph Collection, image #629.

19. Ibid., #815.

20. Ibid., #2617 and #2250. Superintendent Jefferys's crew built foundations for the cannonball stands at the Fifth Corps Monument on April 5, 1907, but the stands themselves were there earlier, for one of them appears in a 1906 photograph of the cemetery. See ibid., #2617.

21. Ibid., #766, #2463, #2734, #3452; C. W. Foster, 1884 inspection report, FNC1. There are actually five benches at Chatham, but one is slightly different from the others and was probably manufactured at a later date.

22. FRSP Historical Photograph Collection, images #2086 and #2134.

23. Ibid., #2091.

24. Ibid., #2465.

25. One placard bordered the grave of Corporal Francis J. Phelps (#3074); the other stood between graves #3078 and #3079, which respectively harbor twelve and eight unidentified soldiers.

26. FRSP Historical Photograph Collection, image #3451. The text and

information about Ingram's poem are at the following website: http://www.
iol.ie/~fagann/1798/songs3.htm.

27. FRSP Historical Photograph Collection, image #3451.

28. Ibid., #2734 and #3451.

29. O'Sullivan, "Theodore O'Hara"; Albert Brackett, "Colonel Theodore O'Hara";
"Theodore O'Hara," 202.

30. As evidence of the poem's early popularity, the burial party sent to Spotsylvania Battlefield in June 1865 painted a stanza of the poem on a board and
nailed it to a tree at the Bloody Angle.

31. Leach, "Theodore O'Hara's 'Bivouac of the Dead.'" For the full text of this
poem, see appendix 2.

32. FRSP Historical Photograph Collection, images #766 and #892; M. M.
Jefferys, 1909 questionnaire response, FNC4; Letters Sent, p. 85.

33. M. M. Jefferys, 1909 questionnaire response, FNC4; Letters Sent, p. 85.
Jefferys's questionnaire response included sizes for each tablet and the texts
for each of the "Bivouac of the Dead" stanzas.

34. FRSP Historical Photograph Collection, image #2617.

35. Ibid.; M. M. Jefferys, 1909 questionnaire response, FNC4;

36. Jefferys diary, December 16–17, 1909, April 24, 1911, FRSP; FRSP Historical
Photograph Collection, image #2730.

37. Untitled, *FL*, September 22, 1865. The preliminary meeting was held on
September 16, 1865.

38. Ibid., October 17, 1865.

39. Ibid.; subscription list, RG 92, entry 225, NA.

40. Anonymous, 1882 inspection report, FNC3; James Reed, 1873 map, FNC4.

41. Hussey, *History of the Ninth Regiment*, 327, 654; Pfanz, "History through Eyes
of Stone," 57–59; "Dedication," *VS*, September 27, 1890; W. A. H., "Recovery
of a Long-Lost Soldier's Body," *FFL*, January 26, 1892; FRSP Historical
Photograph Collection, image #2741.

42. FRSP Historical Photograph Collection, image #2086; Pfanz, "History
through Eyes of Stone," 65–73; Society of the Army of the Potomac, *Report*,
50.

43. Pfanz, "History through Eyes of Stone," 74–78.

44. Ibid., 79–85.

45. Ibid., 102–5.

46. The soldiers' monument mound was removed prior to 1882. In that year, an
inspector reported "a circular plat" at the location where the mound had
been. Anonymous, 1882 inspection report, FNC3.

47. W. H. Owen, 1888 inspection report, FNC1; Letters Received, p. 8; Birdsall
diary, April 22, May 6, August 13, 1890, FRSP; QMGO, 1892 map (revised
1911); Jefferys diary, October 7, 25–28, 1909, FRSP; Letters Sent, p. 168.

48. FRSP Historical Photograph Collection, images #2617, #2729, #2730, and #2250; Jefferys diary, May 2, 14, 1907, FRSP.
49. FRSP Historical Photograph Collection, image #2617; Jefferys diary, May 20, 1907, FRSP. Strangely, the hitching posts appear in a photograph dated 1906. See image #2617.
50. Anonymous, 1868 inspection report, LSW.
51. Olsen, "Poplar Grove," 57. James G. Reed's plat, drawn in May 1873, shows a large tree in the center of the grassy triangle formed by the carriageway fork as well as several other large trees on the lowest terrace, just south of the main gate, in the area now occupied by the Fifth Corps Monument. Photographs taken at that same time show no large trees in the grassy triangle, suggesting that Reed's trees may have simply been graphic embellishments. See James Reed, 1873 map, FNC4; FRSP Historical Photograph Collection, images #2086 and #2462.
52. Anonymous, 1874 inspection report, LSW; James Gall to A. F. Rockwell, March 6, 1876, FNC4; James Gall, 1878 inspection report, FNC4; C. M. Clarke, 1879 inspection report, FNC4.
53. James Gall, 1878 inspection report, FNC4; C. W. Foster to the Quartermaster General, July 4, 1881, FNC2; Richard Arnold, 1882 inspection report, FNC4; W. H. Owen, 1888 inspection report, FNC1; Letters Sent, pp. 23, 31, 67, 72–73, 90, 196–97; C. W. Foster, 1881 inspection report, FNC4; C. W. Foster, 1884 inspection report, FNC1; James Gall, 1882 and 1883 inspection reports, FNC4; Birdsall diary, July 17–19, 1890, June 15–16, July 3, 6, 1891, FRSP. Compare W. H. Owen, 1886 and inspection reports, FNC1.
54. QMGO, 1892 map (revised 1911). At Poplar Grove National Cemetery, the Quartermaster Department planted twelve hundred cedar trees alone. See Olsen, "Poplar Grove," 39.
55. QMGO, 1892 map (revised 1911).
56. Letters Sent, pp. 23, 67, 72–73, 107, 184, 199, 202; Tree Key Sketch, FRSP.
57. Oscar Mack, 1871 inspection report, FNC1; anonymous, 1871 inspection report, LSW. An Osage orange hedge likewise enclosed Poplar Grove National Cemetery. Planted in 1870–71, the hedge consisted of no fewer than four thousand plants! See Olsen, "Poplar Grove," 58; and August Miller letter, March 7, 1871, Petersburg National Battlefield.
58. Oscar Mack, 1874 inspection report, RG 92, entry 648, box 1, 2:105–9, NA; anonymous, 1874 inspection report, LSW; Andrew Birdsall, 1889 questionnaire response, FNC1. The hedge is visible in FRSP Historical Photograph Collection, image #2675.
59. W. H. Owen, 1886 and 1888 inspection reports, FNC1; FRSP Historical Photograph Collection, image #2732. Both the Osage orange and arbor vitae hedges appear in image #2728.

60. James Gall, 1883 inspection report, FNC4; anonymous, 1882 inspection report, FNC3; W. H. Owen, 1886 and 1888 inspection reports, FNC1; Jefferys diary, November 12, 1907, FRSP; Andrew Birdsall, 1889 questionnaire response, FNC1.

61. FRSP Historical Photograph Collection, images #2617 and #2729.

62. C. W. Foster to the Quartermaster General, July 4, 1881, FNC2; Birdsall diary, April 22, May 6, 1890, FRSP; Jefferys diary, April 24, 1912, FRSP. Jefferys planted castor beans around the walls.

63. FRSP Historical Photograph Collection, images #629, #651, and #2086; Jefferys diary, April 30, 1912, FRSP.

64. Jefferys diary, October 2, 1908, FRSP; Birdsall diary, April 24–25, May 10, August 25–26, 1890, March 26, 30, April 28–29, June 17–18, October 1–6, 1891, FRSP; FRSP Historical Photograph Collection, image #2615; Letters Sent, p. 196.

65. Birdsall diary, May 3, 5, 10, 1890, FRSP; Letters Sent, pp. 14, 88, 123, 151, 174; Letters Received, pp. 9, 148. The department appears to have suspended shipments of flowers in the early 1900s, prompting Superintendent Jefferys to purchase flowers locally from a man named Covey. See Jefferys diary, May 25, 1907, FRSP.

66. Letters Sent, pp. 88, 99, 197; Charles Fitchett to [?], February 13, 1874, RG 92, entry 571, 5:58, NA; Jefferys diary, April 24, May 1, 21, May 23–24, June 6, November 20, 1907, April 16, 1909, FRSP.

67. James Reed, 1873 map, FNC4; Fredericksburg National Cemetery Register #7700, 477.

68. Birdsall diary, December 1, 1891, FRSP; Jefferys diary, October 29, 31, 1904, FRSP; Letters Sent, p. 123.

69. George Wroten to Judson Bingham, October 14, 1873, FNC1; G. D. Chenoweth to A. J. McGonnigle, November 21, 1873, FNC1.

70. George Wroten to Theodore Eckerson, August 6, 1873, FNC2. Wroten proposed that the brick walls be just two feet above the ground, but an 1873 photograph of the structure indicates that they were nearly twice that high.

71. RG 92, entry 571, p. 19, NA; George Wroten to Theodore Eckerson, August 6, 1873, FNC2; Charles Fitchett to G. D. Chenoweth, October 8, 1873, FNC2.

72. George Wroten to Judson Bingham, October 14, 1873, FNC1; G. D. Chenoweth to A. J. McGonnigle, November 21, 1873, FNC1. It was later found that the building had defective drainage. See Charles Fitchett to [?], RG 92, entry 571, 5:58, NA; and G. D. Chenoweth to [?], RG 92, entry 571, 5:144, NA.

73. FRSP Historical Photograph Collection, image #2134; anonymous, 1874 inspection report, LSW; Oscar Mack, 1874 inspection report, RG 92, entry 648, box 1, 2:105–9, NA; R. Jones, 1878 inspection report, RG 92, entry 648, box 1, 1:229–30, NA.

74. Sketch of Fredericksburg National Cemetery Lodge, FNC2; QMGO, 1892 map (revised 1911).

75. Jefferys diary, April 18, 1912. Jefferys referred to the hotbed as "the pit."

76. Letters Sent, p. 65. Superintendent Jefferys spoke of removing an "old pit" in 1905 and using its bricks for a walk. This may refer to a second hotbed. Apparently he did not do so, for he mentions putting geraniums in "the pit" in November 1907. Jefferys diary, November 15–16, 1905, November 18, 1907, FRSP.

## 8. Cemetery Employees

1. See Letters Received, p. 68.

2. *Landscapes of Honor and Sacrifice; Congressional Globe*, 42nd Cong., 2nd sess. (1872), 730.

3. Anonymous, 1874 inspection report, LSW; Military Posts and Reservations, pages from an unidentified book, published ca. 1904, in the files of the NA (copy sent to author by Sara Leach, senior historian, National Cemetery Administration), 593; Jefferys diary, September 8, 1904, FRSP. By 1920, the superintendents' salary increased to $95 per month, and by 1928 it jumped to $105. See Letters Sent, pp. 90, 122; and Letters Received, p. 111.

4. *Congressional Globe*, 42nd Cong., 2nd sess. (1872), 730; Letters Sent, pp. 90, 151. From the superintendents' salaries the U.S. government deducted 3.5 percent for the Civil Service Retirement Fund. The deductions were based not only on the superintendents' salaries alone but also on the value of their quarters and allowances. In 1926, Superintendent James McCall's salary was $95 per month, and the value of his quarters and allowances were estimated at $64 a month. Consequently, his deduction in pay was calculated at 3.5 percent of $159—or $5.57 a month. The superintendents complained, but the Quartermaster Department was powerless to reduce the 3.5 percent rate. Instead, it circumvented the law by reducing the estimated value of the superintendents' allowances from $735 a year to just $120 a year. See Letters Received, pp. 86, 91.

5. Letters Sent, pp. 40, 101, 122, 133; Letters Received, 50, 57, 63, 103, 117, 132, 137.

6. "Act to Establish and to Protect National Cemeteries," in Sanger, *Statutes at Large . . . December, 1865, to March, 1867*, 14:399–401. For the full text of this legislation, see appendix 1.

7. Letters Received, pp. 60–61, 74. In 1930, the Quartermaster Department formalized this practice, creating a file that showed the cemeteries to which superintendents desired to transfer. See ibid., p. 146.

8. Of Fredericksburg's fourteen superintendents, five transferred to other cemeteries (Fitchett, Birdsall, Dillon, Jefferys, and McCall), two resigned

from the service (McMahon and Magoon), and five either expired in office or died within weeks after submitting their resignations (McAlpine, Hill, Robinson, Wagner, and Nelson). Of the two remaining superintendents, William K. Sump probably transferred to another cemetery and Emmet H. Sacrey remained in Fredericksburg.

9. "Transfer of Cemetery Superintendents," *FN*, November 24, 1883; Letters Received, p. 146.

10. F. W. Dillon briefly served as superintendent when his father, William Dillon, transferred to a cemetery in Arkansas.

11. "Major Birdsall Transferred," *FFL*, July 26, 1892.

12. W. H. Owen, 1886 inspection report, FNC1.

13. Edward H. McMahon compiled service record, NA; Phisterer, *New York*, 2,872.

14. Bates, *History of Pennsylvania Volunteers*, 6:914; RG 92, entry 605, p. 48, NA; anonymous, 1882 inspection report, FNC3; "Pensioners," *VS*, January 19, 1884.

15. W. H. Owen, 1888 inspection report, FNC1; FRSP images #6212, #6213, #6214, and #6216.

16. Quint, *Second Massachusetts Infantry*, 307.

17. Richard Hill tombstone inscription, grave #6670, Fredericksburg National Cemetery; *Official Roster of the Soldiers of the State of Ohio*, 10:347; "Richard B. Hill," *FFL*, March 9, 1920; RG 92, entry 642, 2:39, NA.

18. Ayling, *Revised Register*, 46.

19. This information on Magoon's military service comes directly from his compiled service records on file at the National Archives. Compare contradictory information about his service in Andrews, *Minnesota in the Civil and Indian Wars*, 1:71.

20. RG 92, entry 607, n.p., NA; ibid., entry 610, p. 38; Major J. B. Bellinger orders, July 13, 1904, in possession of Mrs. Sarah Thayer, Grafton, W.V.; Letters Sent, pp. 10–12; Sarah Thayer to Donald Pfanz, personal e-mail, April 6, 2004; "Death of Maj. M. M. Jefferys," *FFL*, February 28, 1920; Melker J. M. Jefferys compiled service record, NA.

21. Thomas B. Robinson compiled service record, NA; Letters Sent, p. 88; Thomas Robinson tombstone inscription, grave #6666, Fredericksburg National Cemetery. There is some confusion about the identity of Robinson's original regiment. Slips in his compiled service record at the National Archives indicate that he served for three years in Company A, Thirty-Sixth Illinois Cavalry. By contrast, the National Park Service's computerized "Soldiers and Sailors" index and the inscription on Robinson's own headstone indicate that he served in Company I, Fifteenth Illinois Cavalry, a unit that also appears on his headstone inscription.

22. Letters Sent, p. 114; Fredericksburg National Cemetery roster, FRSP; "Frederick E. Wagner," *FFL*, May 23, 1925; "Col. F. Wagner," *FDS*, February 9, 1922; Allen Kimbely, 1922 inspection report, in Letters Received, p. 47.

23. Letters Sent, p. 190.

24. Typed list of superintendents found in Fredericksburg National Cemetery Register #7699. Sump's dates of service are derived from interment records located in FRSP's cemetery research binders.

25. Fredericksburg National Cemetery Register #7699; Fredericksburg City Directory for 1938; "Nelson Succumbs to Heart Attack," *FLS*, March 18, 1940; George Nelson tombstone inscription, Officers Row, grave #6. Nelson's dates of service are derived from interment records located in FRSP's cemetery research binders. The Fredericksburg City Directory listed Nelson's wife's name as Violet.

26. Dennis Sacrey to John Hennessy, e-mail, June 16, 2004, FRSP; "Sacrey Is Appointed to Be Supt. of National Cemetery," *FLS*, November 25, 1940. Sacrey's dates of service are derived from interment records located in FRSP's cemetery research binders.

27. "Death of Major McAlpine," *FDS*, October 8, 1895; "Local and Current Comments," *FFL*, October 11, 1985; RG 92, entry 642, p. 222, NA. Buried next to Thomas Robinson is Thomas H. Mahama, who was the cemetery's acting superintendent for several weeks prior to his sudden death on November 26, 1870. See Henry Hodges to Montgomery Meigs, November 29, 1870, FNC1.

28. See Birdsall diary, May 4, 11, November 19–25, 1890, FRSP; and Letters Received, p. 88. In 1927, the president of the United States decreed that four hours' labor constituted a full day of work on Saturdays. Reacting to this, the Quartermaster Department instructed superintendents to avoid employing part-time workers on Saturdays and to employ full-time workers on that day only when they had worked the previous Monday through Friday. See Letters Received, p. 102.

29. Jefferys diary, September 14, 28, October 1, 5, December 20, 1904, January 6, 14, March 22, 1905, FRSP. For workers' daily chores, see throughout Jefferys's diaries and Birdsall's diaries.

30. "Mr. Wm. Hogan Dead," *FFL*, April 14, 1921; "Old Confederate Soldier Dead," ibid., April 16, 1921; "Col. T. F. Proctor, War Vet, Dead," *FLS*, October 10, 1933; "Last Veteran of Local Battle Dies," *FLS*, September 17, 1934; R. K. Krick, *30th Virginia Infantry*, 104, 120; Holland, *24th Virginia Cavalry*, 176.

31. Letters Received, pp. 79, 124–25.

32. Theodore Eckerson to Charles Fitchett, April 28, 1874, RG 92, entry 571, 5:140, NA; James Gall, 1883 inspection report, FNC4.

33. M. M. Jefferys, 1909 questionnaire response, FNC4; Jefferys diary, April 22, 1912, February 18, 1914, FRSP; Letters Sent, pp. 18–21, 79, 85, 87, 96, 99, 106, 120, 125, 172, 183; Letters Received, pp. 26, 65. The cemetery used "Philadelphia" brand mowers, Style A.

34. Happel, "History of the Fredericksburg and Spotsylvania County Battlefields Memorial National Military Park," 24.

35. Map of land surveyed by Jno. S. Caldwell and others, June 1856, Deed Book S, Fredericksburg City Circuit Court, Va.; Cowles, *Official Military Atlas*, plates 32-2, 33-1, and 41-1; FRSP image #1499; John S. Caldwell plat of Mercer Square, in Deed Book S, Fredericksburg City Circuit Court.

36. Carter M. Braxton, 1867 plan, on University of Mary Washington College website: http://departments.umw.edu/hipr/www/Fredericksburg/plats/htm. A photograph taken from Marye's Heights ca. 1881–82 clearly shows the road. See FRSP Historical Photograph Collection, image #2675.

37. "Roadway to National Cemetery," *FFL*, April 24, 1891.

38. Alvey, *Streets of Fredericksburg*, 49–50; Letters Sent, p. 43; Happel, "History of the Fredericksburg and Spotsylvania County Battlefields Memorial National Military Park," 24. People called National Boulevard by several names in the early twentieth century. Superintendent M. M. Jefferys called it the National Cemetery Roadway or simply "the Boulevard." Jefferys's successor, Thomas B. Robinson, referred to it as "the national road or the "Government roadway." See Jefferys diary, August 24, 1907, October 3, 27, 30, 1908, FRSP; Letters Sent, pp. 47, 72, 77, 91.

39. M. M. Jefferys, 1909 questionnaire response, FNC4.

40. Birdsall diary, November 10, 1891, FRSP; Jefferys diary, October 26, 30, 1908, FRSP.

41. Jefferys diary, May 14, 1914, FRSP. The maple trees may have been planted along a parking strip that bordered the road. See ibid., May 13, 1914. The 425-yard stretch of the Court House Road north of National Boulevard was also called the Sunken Road, the name that it bears today.

42. "The National Boulevard Contract Awarded," *FFL*, May 2, 1896; M. M. Jefferys, 1909 questionnaire response, FNC4; Letters Sent, pp. 43, 47, 55, 72, 77.

43. Letters Sent, pp. 91, 111, 131.

44. Ibid., pp. 51, 91, 118, 131.

45. Letters Received, p. 83; Letters Sent, p. 153; Alvey, *Streets of Fredericksburg*, 49–50.

46. The arbor appears in FRSP Historical Photograph Collection, image #2134.

47. Birdsall diary, August 23, October 29, 1890, FRSP; W. H. Owen, 1886 and 1888 inspection reports, FNC1. The horse mower appears in FRSP Historical Photograph Collection, image #629.

48. Birdsall diary, July 9, 16, 1890, August 11, 1891, FRSP.

49. Ibid., November 19 to December 12, 1890, FRSP; C. W. Foster, 1884 inspection report, FNC1. Foster reported that soil for filling the depressions was purchased from the lot adjoining the cemetery.

50. Birdsall diary, April 7, 1891, FRSP.

51. Ibid., April 30, May 12, October 6, 1890, March 31, April 30, May 31, August 12, 1891; Kerbey, *On the War Path*, p. 164.

52. "Whose Business That?" *FL*, June 22, 1887; "Local and Current Comments," *FFL*, May 12, 1891; Birdsall diary, August 20, 1891, FRSP.

53. M. E. Andrews to sister, October 2, 1892, FRSP.

54. Benson, *"Yank" and "Reb,"* 50.

55. Jefferys diary, August 18, 1905, August 2, 4, September 24, 30, November 2, December 31, 1908, FRSP.

56. For examples of Jefferys's contacts with other superintendents, see his diary entries for August 12, 20, 25, 27, 30, September 6, 24, 1904, February 13, 15–16, 20, March 16, 21–23, July 16, 1905, August 7, 8, December 15, 1908.

57. Letters Sent, pp. 15, 18.

58. Ibid., pp. 21, 30–31. While serving as a private in Company A, Ninety-First Pennsylvania, Kiger attacked Fredericksburg's stone wall near Hanover Street. During his residence in Fredericksburg, he lived on Willis Street with the Bratton family, one of whom described him as having a beard like Santa Claus. After leaving Fredericksburg, Kiger supposedly served as superintendent at Culpeper, Staunton, and one of the national cemeteries near Richmond. He died after being struck by a truck. See Ellis Batton interview.

59. Letters Sent, p. 16.

60. Ibid., pp. 18–19.

61. Ibid., p. 22.

62. Ibid., pp. 38–39.

63. Ibid., p. 64. Clara Robinson died on August 4, 1917.

### 9. Interments

1. Fredericksburg National Cemetery Register #7701, FRSP. In response to a 1909 questionnaire sent out by the Quartermaster Department, Superintendent Jefferys calculated that 2,288 remains had come from Fredericksburg Battlefield, 73 from Salem Church, 1,150 from Chancellorsville, 3,637 from the Wilderness Battlefield, and 428 from Spotsylvania Court House and vicinity. See M. M. Jefferys, 1909 questionnaire response, FNC4.

2. Charles Fitchett to Theodore Eckerson, October 16, 1873, FNC2.

3. Anonymous, 1868 inspection report, LSW; Mollan, "Honoring Our War Dead."

4. *Roll of Honor*; Charles Fitchett to A. J. McGonnigle, July 20, 1871, FNC3.

5. Conwell, *Magnolia Journey*, 9; Thomas Elam to Hayes Walker, November 21, 1866, FRSP.

6. Theodore Eckerson, various letters written to the adjutant generals of Northern states between February and May 1874 regarding soldiers buried at Fredericksburg National Cemetery, FNC1; list of Maine soldiers, FNC1; list of New Hampshire soldiers, FNC1; list of unidentified soldiers buried in Fredericksburg National Cemetery, FNC2; RG 92, entry 571, 4:79, 5:90, NA.

7. Robert K. Krick to Michael Elliott, August 9, 1994, FRSP.

8. *National Cemetery Operations Guideline*, chap. 10, p. 1.

9. Conwell, *Magnolia Journey*, 10; "Memoranda for National Cemeteries," FNC2.

10. Fredericksburg National Cemetery Register #7701. The remains from Wilderness National Cemetery No. 2 were buried in division B, section C, graves #473–77, #487–512, and #522.

11. Graves #2199, #2429, #3039, #3127, #4084, #4653, and #5515.

12. Graves #1164, #1174, and #2915.

13. "Admol L. Jett, War Veteran, Is Dead," *FLS*, November 27, 1940; "Cpl. Jett's Body Is Being Returned," ibid., May 17, 1949; "Cpl. Jett Rites Will Be Sunday," ibid., May 20, 1949; Fredericksburg National Cemetery Register #7699, 83. A plaque bearing Admol G. Jett's name and those of sixteen others who died in World War II stands in front of James Monroe High School. Jett was the last soldier *buried* in Fredericksburg National Cemetery; however, in 1986 relatives scattered the ashes of Corporal Roy G. Butler over the grave of his father, Sergeant Jack Butler.

14. Happel, "History of the Fredericksburg and Spotsylvania County Battlefields Memorial National Military Park," 58.

15. Just four known Civil War soldiers were buried in Fredericksburg National Cemetery between 1871 and 1900: Wilbur F. Morris (#6620), James Best (#6623), Charles C. Cockerill (#6627), and Charles J. Bolander (#6630). Morris, Cockerill, and Bolander died in the 1890s. Best died in 1863, but apparently he was not buried in the cemetery until the 1890s. A modified version of the slab-style headstone marks the grave of each of these men.

16. Anonymous, 1868 inspection report, LSW; *Roll of Honor*.

17. *Annual Reports of the Quartermaster-General*, 222–23. The depot of Washington administered six national cemeteries in the District of Columbia as well as Virginia cemeteries that were more than thirty-five miles from Washington, D.C.

18. Phillis, "Death of Col. John Williams Patterson"; J. Cummings, "'Your Husband's Noble Self-Sacrifice.'" Wiebecke was interred in division B, section A, grave #63 (grave #3289 in the current numbering system) until May 1870, when his remains were transferred to Fairmount Cemetery in Newark,

N.J. See *Roll of Honor*, 125. An old cemetery roster indicates that Collins occupied grave #1118 but that his remains were removed. In 1870, cemetery officials buried Thomas Mahama in the plot that Collins had occupied. See Fredericksburg National Cemetery Register #7700, 178.

19. Charles Fitchett, classified statement of interments (June 30, 1875), FNC4. Lyons occupied grave #6738. See Fredericksburg National Cemetery: Open Reservations file, FRSP.
20. Merritt appears in the *Roll of Honor*, 27, as Private E. D. Merritt.
21. "Burial of Col. Hill," *FDS*, January 9, 1900.
22. Fredericksburg National Cemetery Register #7700, 478.
23. "A Heroic Colored Physician," *FFL*, April 6, 1917; "Killed on Battlefield," *FFL*, November 5, 1918; "Widow's Burial Here Ends Chapter in City's History," *FLS*, October 29, 1986.
24. Fredericksburg City Directory for 1938; "Nelson Succumbs to Heart Attack," *FLS*, March 18, 1940.
25. M. M. Jefferys, 1909 questionnaire response, FNC4.
26. Letters Sent, pp. 83, 133.
27. Fredericksburg National Cemetery roster.
28. The women in question were Mrs. Charles Bowie (#6756), Mrs. George C. Baker (#6745), Mrs. Clarence D. Summers (#6747), Mrs. William A. Thompson (#6748), and Mrs. Ernest Franks (#6749). Each of the women was to be buried in the same grave as her husband, except for Mrs. Bowie, who had reserved a separate plot beside her spouse. She was buried at Waller's Church instead. Larry James, August 5, 1991, note, and notes scribbled on October 12, 1953, Quartermaster Corps letter, Fredericksburg National Cemetery: Open Reservations file, FRSP.

## 10. Special Populations

1. The exception is Officers Row, a twentieth-century creation. See chapter 9.
2. Bates, *History of Pennsylvania Volunteers*, 6:981. First Lieutenant Francis Cassidy described Crowther's death in a letter to the colonel's wife dated May 18, 1863, copy at FRSP.
3. Francis Cassidy to Mrs. James Crowther, May 18, 1863, FRSP; Mertz, "No Turning Back," 9.
4. Hussey, *History of the Ninth Regiment*, 327.
5. Ibid., 325, 327, 334; Jaques, *Three Years' Campaign of the Ninth, N.Y.S.M.*, 187–88.
6. Pfanz, "History through Eyes of Stone"; Hussey, *History of the Ninth Regiment*, 654.
7. Pfanz, "History through Eyes of Stone."
8. Fredericksburg National Cemetery roster.

9. Mulholland, *Military Order*, 417–20; *Medal of Honor*, 160. For an account of Hill's burial, see "Burial of Col. Hill," *FDS*, January 9, 1900.
10. *Medal of Honor*, 155. The flag captured by Jones must have belonged to another, as yet unidentified, regiment.
11. *Landscapes of Honor and Sacrifice.*
12. Fredericksburg National Cemetery Register #7701, 158–59.
13. *Roll of Honor*, 40. The "Soldiers and Sailors" database is a website managed by the National Park Service.
14. "Former Slave Dead," *FLS*, February 2, 1926.
15. Anonymous, 1868 inspection report, LSW; anonymous, 1871 inspection report, LSW; anonymous, 1874 inspection report, LSW; Richard Arnold, 1882 inspection report, FNC4; Charles Fitchett, classified statement of interments, FNC4. The reference to the unknown soldier comes from Fredericksburg National Cemetery Register #7700, 471. Page 154 lists two unidentified men found buried at the Freedman's Hospital who were re-interred in graves #238–39 of section AA. As the men were identified as soldiers, it is unlikely that they were black, however. Fredericksburg National Cemetery Register #7700, 471, lists an unidentified soldier being buried in grave #455 of section AB. Next to the name is the notation "Said to be a Colored Soldier." As the soldier undoubtedly died fighting at Fredericksburg and no black regiments existed at that time, the man was probably white.
16. Fredericksburg National Cemetery Register #7700, 476.
17. "Will Be Buried in National Cemetery," *FN*, November 11, 1922; Fredericksburg National Cemetery Register #7700.
18. "Widow's Burial Here Ends Chapter in City History," *FLS*, October 29, 1986; "Dr. Urbane F. Bass," FRSP.
19. "A Heroic Colored Physician," *FFL*, April 6, 1917; "Killed on Battlefield," ibid., November 5, 1918; "Widow's Burial Here Ends Chapter in City History," *FLS*, October 29, 1986.
20. The Quartermaster Department sent Superintendent Thomas Robinson detailed instructions regarding Bass's interment. A copy of those instructions appears in Letters Received, pp. 14–16. Bass's citation reads: "The Distinguished Service Cross is presented to Urbane F. Bass, First Lieutenant (Medical Corps), U.S. Army, for extraordinary heroism in action near Monthois, France, October 1–6, 1918. During the attack on Monthois Lieutenant Bass administered first aid in the open under prolonged and intense shell fire until he was severely wounded and carried from the field."
21. "Dr. Urbane F. Bass," FRSP.
22. "Widow's Burial Here Ends Chapter in City History," *FLS*, October 29, 1986. The other two African American women buried at Fredericksburg are Annie King (#4674C) and Josephine Washington (#4689B).

23. Mink, "Native Americans," 4, FRSP; *Roll of Honor*, 13; Bates, *History of Pennsylvania Volunteers*, 10:1343.
24. Annie Florence Lockhart military service records, NA; "Miss Lockhart Dies at Hospital," *FLS*, January 1, 1935; "Remembering Two Who Served," *FLS*, May 27, 2006.
25. Letters Sent, p. 193; "World War I Era Yeomen"; Veterans Cemeteries, 1800–2004 Record, and U.S. census records for the years 1920 and 1930, Ancestry.com, http://www.ancestry.com; "French-Rose," *FDS*, February 21, 1917; "Mr. Powhatan Rose Dead," *FLS*, April 5, 1919; "Death of Miss Edith B. Rose," *FLS*, November 19, 1929; "Miss Edith Rose Buried in National Cemetery," *FLS*, November 22, 1929.
26. Richard Arnold, 1882 inspection report, FNC4; anonymous, 1882 inspection report, FNC3.
27. Charles Fitchett to C. W. Foster, April 1, 1882, FNC4; "Died," *VS*, August 25, 1877.
28. Mary Ann Hill and Arthur Hill tombstone inscriptions, grave #6636, Fredericksburg National Cemetery; M. M. Jefferys, 1909 questionnaire response, FNC4; Fredericksburg National Cemetery Register #7700, 476; "Death of Mrs. R. B. Hill," *FDS*, January, 9, 1900.
29. Rebecca Capobianco to John Hennessy, e-mail, February 27, 2014, FRSP.
30. Rokus, "Veterans Day Salute," *FLS*, November 11, 1906; Jack Butler military service record, copy at FRSP.
31. Ibid.
32. Ibid.
33. Ibid.; Fredericksburg National Cemetery Register #7699, 78; "Funeral Servic[e]s for Jack Butler," *FLS*, November 3, 1930.
34. Mrs. Doris Butler Van Swaringen (Roy Butler's sister), telephone conversation with the author, August 7, 2006. The family scattered the ashes without the knowledge of the National Park Service.

## 11. Stories

1. Hopkins, Seventh Regiment Rhode Island Volunteers, 174, 407, 408.
2. Ibid., 408.
3. John Warner pension file, NA.
4. Brainard, Campaigns of the 146th Regiment, 575.
5. Lang, "Rescued from Obscurity," 36–40; Peter D. Froeligh pension file, NA.
6. Hewitt, *Roster of Union Soldiers*, 4:271; Bates, *History of Pennsylvania Volunteers*, 5:404.
7. See the Wynning History website: https://wynninghistory.com/2017/05/12 /workman-brothers/.

8. Henry Kaiser diary, May 13, 1864, Harrisburg Civil War Round Table Collection, United States Army Military History Institute.
9. Wynning History website.
10. Fredericksburg National Cemetery roster, FRSP.
11. 1865 Burial Roster, FRSP.
12. Wynning History website.
13. Fredericksburg National Cemetery Register #7700, 475; "Killed by the Train," *FLS*, August 8, 1898.
14. Bennett, *Sons of Old Monroe*, 404.
15. Welch, "Mrs. Allison's Ultimate Sacrifice," FRSP.
16. Charles Fitchett to Theodore Eckerson, October 16, 1873, FNC2.
17. *Record of Service of Michigan Volunteers*, 26, 122; Bertara and Crawford, *Fourth Michigan Infantry*, 119.
18. "The Fourth Regiment," *Adrian (Mich.) Watchtower*, January 5, 1863.
19. Bennett, *Sons of Old Monroe*, 382, 391.
20. Crowninshield, *Massachusetts Cavalry Volunteers*, 83, 184, 329.
21. Bates, *History of Pennsylvania Volunteers*, 2:903; Stevens family genealogical chart, FRSP.
22. F. Stevens, "Sketches by Frank D. Stevens," FRSP; E. Stevens, unpublished history of the Stevens family, FRSP.
23. F. Stevens, "Sketches by Frank D. Stevens," FRSP.
24. Ibid.; Muffly, *Story of Our Regiment*, 219.
25. F. Stevens, "Civil War Reminiscence of Franklyn Dyson Stevens," FRSP. The final quote comes from the song "The Vacant Chair."
26. Richard Jacoby, e-mails to Kathleen Logothetis, May 17 and 30–31, 2012, FRSP; William J. Reichard to his father, February 20, 1863, FRSP; William Reichard to "Sister Sallie," February 23, 1863, FRSP.
27. Thompson, *Thirteenth Regiment of New Hampshire Volunteer Infantry*, 100.
28. Ibid.
29. Rhea, *Battle of the Wilderness*, 145–50.
30. Bennett, *Sons of Old Monroe*, p. 365.
31. From my conversation with Susan Bennett of Wyandotte, Michigan, great-great-grandchild of Liberty Richards.
32. Gaff and Gaff, *Our Boys*, 82.
33. Chapman, *Roster of Wisconsin Volunteers*, 566; Gaff and Gaff, *Our Boys*, 81–83.
34. Silliker, *Rebel Yell and Yankee Hurrah*, 157.
35. Maurus Oestreich Journal, p. 48, United States Army Military History Institute.
36. Pfanz, "History through Eyes of Stone," FRSP.
37. Bilby, *Three Rousing Cheers*, 136.

38. Ibid., 135–36.
39. Ibid., 138; Mulholland, *Story of the 116th Regiment*, 252.
40. Gavin, *Campaigning with the Roundheads*, 367–68, 421, 708–9.
41. "Cemetery Suicide Remains a Mystery," *FLS*, October 16, 2004; "Fatal Justice," ibid., March 12, 2005.
42. "One Rose Will Mark Union Soldier's Grave," ibid., May 30, 1931.
43. Hurt, "Home of the Brave," 69–73.

### 12. Memorial Day Commemorations

1. Elizabeth C. French diary, May 3, 1866, Virginia Historical Society.
2. Taylor, *Memorial Addresses*, 203.
3. "Colored Excursion," *FL*, September 11, 1868; "Colored Excursionists—Rowdy Proceedings," *VH*, June 15, 1871; Charles Fitchett to Henry Hodges, June 14, 1871, FNC1.
4. "Colored Excursion," *FL*, September 11, 1868; "Colored Excursionists—Rowdy Proceedings," *VH*, June 15, 1871; Charles Fitchett to Henry Hodges, June 14, 1871, FNC1.
5. Charles Fitchett to Henry Hodges, June 14, 1871, FNC1; Judson Bingham to Charles Fitchett, June 23, 1871, FNC1.
6. "The Federal Cemetery," *VH*, May 18, 1871.
7. Mussey was colonel of the 100th U.S. Colored Troops during the war, and from April to November 1865 he served as private secretary to President Andrew Johnson. Truex served as colonel of the Fourteenth New Jersey prior to his appointment as brevet brigadier general. At the end of the war, he commanded a brigade in the Sixth Corps.
8. "The Federal Cemetery," *VH*, May 18, 1871; "Soldiers' Memorial Day," *FL*, June 2, 1871; "Correction," *FL*, June 6, 1871.
9. Quoted in "Honoring the Dead," *FL*, June 2, 1871.
10. "Memorial Day," ibid., June 4, 1872.
11. "Decoration Day," ibid., May 26, 1874; "Address of Mr. Ives," ibid., June 5, 1874.
12. "Decoration Day—The Lesson of the Flowers upon the Soldiers' Graves," ibid., June 3, 1873; "National Decoration Day," *VS*, June 1, 1878; "Decoration of Federal Soldiers' Graves," *VS*, June 2, 1880.
13. Quoted in *National Memorial Day Services*, 23. The original article, called "Now and Then," appeared in the May 30, 1893, edition of the *Fredericksburg Free Lance*.
14. "Memorial Day," *FL*, June 4, 1872. Both Griffith and Beckley had received federal appointments because of their strong Unionist sympathies.
15. "National Decoration Day," *FS*, June 4, 1884.
16. Ibid.; "Memorial Day Is Spoiled by Rain," *FLS*, May 31, 1933; "In Memory: Area Black Residents Once Decorated Union Graves for Memorial Day,"

*FLS*, May 24, 1997; *National Memorial Day Services*, 23. Shiloh Cemetery stands at the corner of Littlepage Street and Monument Avenue.

17. "Memorial Day," *FS*, June 6, 1885.
18. Kerbey, *On the War Path*, 160.
19. Ibid., 161; "The Fredericksburg National Cemetery," *FFL*, August 17, 1888.
20. "The Blue and the Gray," *FS*, May 30, 1888; "The Dead Heroes," ibid., June 2, 1888; Kerbey, *On the War Path*, 160–65.
21. Kerbey, *On the War Path*, 165.
22. Ibid., 165–66; "Federal Decoration Day," *VS*, June 1, 1889.
23. "National Decoration Day," *FS*, June 4, 1890; "Federal Decoration Day," *VS*, May 30, 1891; "National Memorial Day," *VS*, June 1, 1892; "National Decoration Day," *FDS*, May 31, 1894; "National Decoration Day," *FDS*, May 30, 1895. For excellent descriptions of programs from this period, see *National Memorial Day Services* and "Strewn with Flowers," *FS*, June 3, 1891.
24. "National Decoration Day," *VS*, May 30, 1896; "Their Graves Decorated," ibid., May 29, 1897; "The Union Dead," *FDS*, May 30, 1898; "Union Decoration," *FDS*, May 30, 1899; "Memorial Day," *FN*, May 30, 1900.
25. "Decoration Day," *FDS*, May 30, 1903.
26. "National Decoration Day," ibid., May 30, 1895.
27. "Decorated Graves of Dead Comrades," ibid., May 31, 1910.
28. Jefferys diary, May 30, 1905, FRSP; "Decoration Day," *FDS*, May 31, 1909. The Spanish-American veterans also decorated the grave of an unknown soldier. They conducted a similar ceremony on Marye's Heights in 1916. See "Honored Deceased Members," *FFL*, June 1, 1916.
29. "National Memorial Day," *FDS*, May 26, 1917.
30. Ibid.
31. "Memorial Exercises," *FFL*, June 1, 1918.
32. Ibid.
33. See, for example, "Memorial Day," *FFL*, June 2, 1923; "Decoration Day," ibid., June 3, 1924; "Services Here Honor War Dead," *FLS*, May 31, 1932; and "Honor Memory of Nation's Soldiers," *FLS*, May 31, 1929.
34. "Decoration Day Exercises Here," *FLS*, May 31, 1930; "Gets Memorials Mixed but Does Splendidly," ibid., May 31, 1930.

### Epilogue: Fredericksburg National Cemetery under the National Park Service

1. Olsen, "Poplar Grove," 44; Harriet Wright, e-mail to the author, November 30, 2004.
2. Olsen, "Poplar Grove," 45–46.
3. Happel, "History of the Fredericksburg and Spotsylvania County Battlefields Memorial National Military Park," 62, 65.

4. The 2003 luminaria was canceled due to rain.
5. Partridge letter, March 6, 1863, copy at FRSP.

### Appendix 1: Key Orders and Legislation in Establishing National Cemeteries

1. *OR*, series 3, 2:2.
2. Thirty-Seventh Cong., sess. 2, chapter 200, in Sanger, *Statutes at Large . . . December 5, 1859, to March 3, 1863*, 12:596.
3. Thirty-Ninth Cong., sess. 1, Resolution No. 21, in Sanger, *Statutes at Large . . . December, 1865, to March, 1867*, 14:353.
4. Thirty-Ninth Cong., sess. 2, chapter 61, in ibid., 399–401.

# Bibliography

*This listing includes sections for Fredericksburg and Spotsylvania County National Military Park, government publications, manuscripts, the National Archives and Records Administration, newspapers, published works, and other sources.*

### Fredericksburg and Spotsylvania County National Military Park

1865 Burial Roster.

Anderson, George C. Burial trench map. Ms. #00630.

Andrews, M. E. Letter, October 2, 1892. Ms. #06042.

Batton, Ellis. Oral history interview, May 19, 1979. Ms. #07082.

Bird, Charles P. Report, June 29, 1865. Ms. #06307.

Birdsall, Andrew J. Diaries, 1890–91. Ms. #02412.

Capobianco, Rebecca. E-mail to John Hennessy, February 27, 2014.

Cassidy, Francis. Letter, May 18, 1863. Ms. #06049.

Cochran, George W. "A Brief Sketch of the Cochran Family." Ms. #06611.

"Development of the National Cemetery System." Undated paper.

"Dr. Urbane F. Bass." Unpublished monograph.

Elam, Thomas J. Letter, November 21, 1866. Ms. #02593.

Fredericksburg and Spotsylvania County National Military Park Historical Photograph Collection.

Fredericksburg National Cemetery, Letters Received: January 1, 1921, to August 14, 1930. Catalog #7703. Curatorial collection.

Fredericksburg National Cemetery, Letters Sent: December 1, 1913, to August 19, 1930. Catalog #7704. Curatorial collection.

Fredericksburg National Cemetery: Open Reservations file.

Fredericksburg National Cemetery Plan, 1940.

Fredericksburg National Cemetery Registers. Undated. Catalogs #7699, #7700, and #7701. Curatorial collection.

Fredericksburg National Cemetery roster.

Gorman, John C. Memoir. Ms. #05192.

Happel, Ralph. "A History of the Fredericksburg and Spotsylvania County Battlefields Memorial National Military Park," 1955.

Holt, Lewis G. Letter, June 11, 1891. Ms. #07397.

Howison, Mary. "Childhood Memories of Braehead and the Battlefield Park." Ms. #05921.

Jefferys, Melker Jefferson Martin. Diaries, 1904–14. Mss. #06213–06221.

———. Letter, August 15, 1903. Ms. #06224.

———. Letter, November 23, 1904. Ms. #06224.

———. Letter, June 28, 1907. Ms. #06046.

Jones, George W. Diary, 1865. Ms. #05479.

Kimbely, Allen. 1922 inspection report. Fredericksburg National Cemetery Letter Book, 1921–30. Ms. #06309.

Krick, Robert K. Letter, August 9, 1994.

LeConte, William L. Memoir. Ms. #05149.

McLean, William C. Diary entry, May 15, 1865. Ms. #07407.

McVey, William. Letter, March 21, 1866. Ms. #05429.

Meigs, Montgomery C. "Specifications for Cisterns at U.S. National Cemeteries." Ms. #06038.

Mervine, Frederick. Letter, May 15, 1863. Ms. #02593.

Mink, Eric J. Memorandum, September 29, 2003. Copy in "Fredericksburg National Cemetery" file in Cultural Resources Office.

———. "Native Americans in the Battles of the Wilderness and Spotsylvania." Ms. #02709.

———. Sketch of Wilderness Military Cemetery No. 2, 1997. Copy in "Fredericksburg National Cemetery" file.

Moore, James M. July 3, 1865, report of expedition to bury Union dead on the Wilderness and Spotsylvania Court House battlefields. (See also in National Archives and Records Administration section.)

Office of the Quartermaster General, U.S. Army. 1892 map; revised in 1911. Ms. #06201.

Partridge, Samuel S. Letter, March 6, 1863. Ms. #02409.

Paynton, William. Letter, February 16, 1863. Ms. #06606.

Pfanz, Donald C. "History through Eyes of Stone: The Story of the Monuments in Fredericksburg National Military Park," 2006.

Reichard, William J. Letters, February 20 and 23, 1863. Ms. #06240.

Robinson, Thomas B. Letter to E. L. Landram, July 30, 1915. Ms. #06122.

Stevens, Emory. Unpublished history of the Stevens family. Ms. #06315.

Stevens, Franklyn D. "Civil War Reminiscence of Franklyn Dyson Stevens." Unpublished manuscript, 1914. Ms. #06315.

———."Sketches by Frank D. Stevens." Unidentified newspaper article. Ms. #06315.

Stevens family genealogical chart. Ms. #06315.

Taylor, Joseph H. Dispatch, December 16, 1862. Ms. #04438.

Tree Key Sketch, Fredericksburg National Cemetery. August 17, 1934.

U.S. Department of the Interior, National Park Service. Fredericksburg National Cemetery Development Plan, 1940.

Ward, David A. "Amidst a Tempest of Shot and Shell: A History of the Ninety-Sixth Pennsylvania Volunteers." Unpublished manuscript. Ms. #05434.

Welch, Barbara B. "Mrs. Allison's Ultimate Sacrifice." Booklet. Ms. #06439.

White, James L. Letter, June 9, 1864. Ms. #05841.

### Government Publications

*Annual Report of the Quartermaster General Made to the Secretary of War for the Year 1870.* Washington, D.C.: Government Printing Office, 1870.

*Annual Report of the Quartermaster General to the Secretary of War, for the Fiscal Year Ending June 30, 1871.* Washington, D.C.: Government Printing Office, 1871.

*Annual Report of the Quartermaster-General to the Secretary of War for the Fiscal Year Ending June 30, 1874.* Washington, D.C.: Government Printing Office, 1874.

*Annual Reports of the Quartermaster-General for 1861 to 1866.* Washington, D.C.: Government Printing Office, 1880.

*Congressional Globe*, 42nd Cong., 2nd sess. (May 18, 1872).

"History of Government Furnished Headstones and Markers." Article on Veterans Administration website: http://www.cem.va.gov/hmhist.htm. FRSP Ms. #06180.

Letter from the Secretary of War, Transmitting in Obedience to Law, the Report of the Inspector of the National Cemeteries for the Year 1874. Senate Executive Document 28, 43rd Cong., 2nd sess., pp. 36–38. Published in *The Executive Documents Printed by Order of the Senate of the United States for the Second Session of the Forty-Third Congress, 1874–'75, and the Special Session of the Senate in March, 1875.* Washington, D.C.: Government Printing Office, 1875.

Letter of the Secretary of War Communicating, in Obedience to Law, the Report of the Inspector of the National Cemeteries of the United States for 1869. Senate Executive Document 62, 41st Cong., 2nd sess., pp. 27–28. Published in *Index to the Senate Executive Documents for the Second Session of the Forty-First Congress of the United States of America, 1869–'70.* Washington, D.C.: Government Printing Office, 1870.

Letter of the Secretary of War, Communicating, in Obedience to Law, the Report of the Inspector of the National Cemeteries for the Years 1870 and 1871. Senate Executive Document 79, 42nd Cong., 2nd sess., pp. 32–33. Published in *The Executive Documents Printed by Order of the Senate of the United States for the Second Session of the Forty-Second Congress, 1871–'72.* Washington, D.C.: Government Printing Office, 1872.

Mollan, Mark C. "Honoring Our War Dead: The Evolution of the Government Policy on Headstones for Fallen Soldiers and Sailors." In *Prologue*, an electronic publication of the U.S. National Archives and Records Administration, 35, no. 1 (Spring 2003). Found at the NARA website: http://www.archives.gov/publications/prologue. (Also FRSP Ms. #05978.)

"National Cemeteries with Meigs Lodges." Article on Veterans Administration website: http://www.va.gov/facmgt.historic/Meigs.asp. (Also FRSP Ms. #06044.)

"National Cemetery Administration, Superintendent's Lodges, Washington, District of Columbia, DC." Article on Library of Congress website: https://www.loc.gov/item/dc1156/.

*Report of the Quartermaster General of the United States Army to the Secretary of War, for the Year Ending June 30, 1865.* Washington: Government Printing Office, 1865.

Sanger, George P., ed. *The Public Statues at Large of the United States of America.* 18 vols. Boston: Little, Brown, 1845–78.

U.S. War Department. *The War of the Rebellion: A Compilation of the Official Records of the Union and Confederate Armies.* 128 vols. Washington, D.C.: Government Printing Office, 1880–1901.

### Manuscripts

Birmingham Public Library, Birmingham, Ala.
  J. H. Scruggs Collection
Civil War Library and Museum, Philadelphia, Pa.
  Mulholland Papers
Huntington Library, San Marino, Calif.
  Evan Woodward Papers
Indiana Historical Society, Indianapolis
  James Riley Papers
Maryland Historical Society, Baltimore
  Edward L. Heinichen Memoirs
Massachusetts Historical Society, Boston
  Lyman Family Papers
State University of New York at Plattsburgh
  Francis B. Hall Journal
U.S. Army Military History Institute, Carlisle Barracks, Pa.
  Henry Kaiser Diary
  Maurus Oestreich Journal
Virginia Historical Society, Richmond
  Elizabeth C. French Diary
  Slaughter Papers
Virginia Military Institute, Lexington
  Rinker Papers
Yale University Archives, New Haven, Conn.
  Charles T. Furlow Journal

## National Archives and Records Administration

Moore, James M. July 3, 1865, report to Major General Winfield S. Hancock, commanding the Middle Military Division, regarding burials on the Wilderness and Spotsylvania Court House battlefields, M1335, 1865, enclosure 4.

Record Group 92: Records of the Office of the Quartermaster General.

Record Group 92.17: Still Pictures (General), 1860–1938.

## Newspapers

*Adrian (Mich.) Watchtower*

*Beaver Dam (Wisc.) Argus*

*Boston Transcript*

*Canisteo Valley (N.Y.) Times*

*Dodge County (Wisc.) Citizen*

*Fitchburg (Mass.) Sentinel*

*Fredericksburg Daily Star* (includes *Fredericksburg Daily Evening Star*)

*Fredericksburg Free Lance*

*Fredericksburg Free Lance-Star*

*Fredericksburg Ledger*

*Fredericksburg New Era*

*Fredericksburg News*

*Fredericksburg Star*

*Fredericksburg Star Advertiser*

*Gainesville (Fla.) Cotton States*

*Harper's Weekly*

*Juneau (Wisc.) Independent*

*Lynchburg Daily Virginian*

*Philadelphia Inquirer*

*Philadelphia Weekly Times*

*Virginia Herald* (Fredericksburg)

*Virginia Star* (Fredericksburg)

*Washington (D.C.) Chronicle*

*Waterbury (Conn.) American*

## Published Works

Adjutant General of the State of New York. *Second New York Heavy Artillery.* 2 vols. Albany: Wynkoop, Hallenbeck, and Crawford, 1897.

Alvey, Edward, Jr. *The Streets of Fredericksburg.* Fredericksburg: Mary Washington College Foundation, 1978.

Andrews, C. C., ed. *Minnesota in the Civil and Indian Wars, 1861–1865.* 2 vols. St. Paul: Pioneer Press, 1891.

Ayling, Augustus D. *Revised Register of the Soldiers and Sailors of New Hampshire in the War of the Rebellion, 1861–1866.* Concord: Ira C. Evans, 1895.

Bartlett, Napier. *Military Record of Louisiana, Including Biographical and Historical Papers Relating to the Military Organizations of the State.* Baton Rouge: Louisiana State University Press, n.d.

Bates, Samuel P. *History of Pennsylvania Volunteers, 1861–5.* 10 vols. Harrisburg: B. Singerly, 1871.

Baxter, Nancy N. *The Gallant Fourteenth: The Story of an Indiana Civil War Regiment.* Indianapolis: Guild Press of Indiana, 1991.

Bennett, Brian A. *Sons of Old Monroe: A Regimental History of Patrick O'Rorke's 140th New York Volunteer Infantry.* Dayton, Ohio: Morningside, 1992.

Benson, C. H. *"Yank" and "Reb": A History of a Fraternal Visit Paid by Lincoln Post, No. 11, GAR of Newark, NJ.* Newark: M. H. Neuhut, 1884.

Bertara, Martin N., and Kim Crawford. *The Fourth Michigan Infantry in the Civil War.* East Lansing: Michigan State University Press, 2010.

Bilby, Joseph G. *Three Rousing Cheers: A History of the Fifteenth New Jersey from Fleming to Appomattox.* Hightstown, N.J.: Longstreet House, 1993.

Borcke, Heros von. *Memoirs of the Confederate War for Independence.* 3 vols. Edinburgh, Scotland: William Blackwood and Sons, 1866.

Borton, Benjamin. *On the Parallels.* Woodstown, N.J.: Monitor-Register, 1903.

Brackett, Albert G. "Colonel Theodore O'Hara." In *Southern Historical Society Papers* 19 (1891): 275–81.

Brainard, Mary G. *Campaigns of the 146th Regiment New York State Volunteers Also Known as Halleck's Infantry, the Fifth Oneida, and Garrard's Tigers.* Daleville, Va.: Schroeder, 2000.

Brewer, Abraham T. *History of the Sixty-First Regiment Pennsylvania Volunteers, 1861–1865.* Pittsburgh: Art Engraving and Printing Company, 1911.

Brown, Augustus C. *The Diary of a Line Officer.* N.p., 1906.

Chapman, Chandler P. *Roster of Wisconsin Volunteers, War of the Rebellion, 1861–1865.* 2 vols. Madison: Democrat Printing Company, 1886.

Coffin, Howard. *Full Duty: Vermonters in the Civil War.* Woodstock, Vt.: The Countryman Press, 1995.

Conwell, Russell H. *Magnolia Journey: A Union Veteran Revisits the Former Confederate States.* Edited by Joseph C. Carter. University: University of Alabama Press, n.d.

Cowles, Calvin D. *The Official Military Atlas of the Civil War.* New York: Fairfax Press, 1978.

Cronin, David E. *The Evolution of a Life Described in the Memoirs of Major Seth Eyland, Late of the Mounted Rifles.* New York: S. W. Green & Son, 1884.

Crowninshield, Benjamin W. *A History of the First Regiment of Massachusetts Cavalry Volunteers.* Boston: Houghton, Mifflin, 1891.

Cummings, C. C. "The Battle of Fredericksburg." *Confederate Veteran* 23 (August 1915): 358.

Cummings, John F., III. "'Your Husband's Noble Self-Sacrifice': Life and Death on Myer's Hill." *North and South* 7, no. 4 (June 2004): 75–79.

Daniel, Frederick. "In an Old Virginia Town." *Harper's New Monthly Magazine*, March 1885, 601–12.

Dority, Orin G. "The Civil War Diary of Orin G. Dority." *Northwest Ohio Quarterly* 37, no. 1 (Winter 1964–65): 7–26.

Epstein, Daniel M. *Lincoln and Whitman: Parallel Lives in Civil War Washington.* New York: Random House, 2005.

Fitzgerald, Ruth Coder. *A Different Story: A Black History of Fredericksburg, Stafford, and Spotsylvania, Virginia.* N.p.: Unicorn, 1979.

Frassanito, William A. *Grant and Lee: The Virginia Campaigns, 1864–1865.* New York: Charles Scribner's Sons, 1983.

Gaff, Alan, and Maureen Gaff. *Our Boys: A Civil War Photograph Album.* Mt. Vernon, Ind.: Windmill Publications, 1996.

Gavin, William G. *Campaigning with the Roundheads: The History of the Hundredth Pennsylvania Veteran Volunteer Infantry Regiment in the American Civil War, 1861–1865.* Dayton, Ohio: Morningside, 1989.

Gilbert, Frederick. *The Story of a Regiment, Being a Record of the Military Services of the Fifty-Seventh New York Volunteer Infantry.* Chicago: C. H. Morgan, 1895.

Hacker, J. David. "A Census-Based Count of the Civil War Dead." *Civil War History* 54, no. 4 (December 2011): 306–47.

Harrison, Noel G. *Fredericksburg Civil War Sites, December 1862–April 1865.* 2 vols. Lynchburg, Va.: H. E. Howard, 1995.

———. "Victims and Survivors." *Military Images* 20, no. 3 (November–December 1998): 11–19.

Heitman, Francis B. *Historical Register and Dictionary of the United States Army.* 2 vols. Washington, D.C.: Government Printing Office, 1903.

Hewitt, Janet B., ed. *The Roster of Union Soldiers, 1861–1865.* 33 vols. Wilmington, N.C.: Broadfoot, 1998.

Hileman, Robert, Jr. *The Crowther Letters: Families, Companies, and Rebels.* Tarentum, Pa.: Hileman House, 2003.

*History of the Thirty-Fifth Regiment Massachusetts Volunteers, 1862–1865.* Boston: Mills, Knight, & Co., 1884.

Holland, Darryl. *24th Virginia Cavalry.* Lynchburg, Va.: H. E. Howard, 1997.

Hopkins, William P. *The Seventh Regiment Rhode Island Volunteers in the Civil War, 1862–1865.* Providence: Providence Press, 1903.

Hurt, Henry. "Home of the Brave." *Reader's Digest,* May 1994, 69–73.

Hussey, George A. *History of the Ninth Regiment N.Y.S.M.—N.G.S.N.Y. (Eighty-Third N.Y. Volunteers), 1845–1888.* New York: Veterans of the Regiment, 1889.

Jaques, John W. *Three Years' Campaign of the Ninth, N.Y.S.M., during the Southern Rebellion.* New York: Hilton, 1865.

Johnson, Robert U., and Clarence C. Buel, eds. *Battles and Leaders of the Civil War.* 4 vols. New York: Century, 1888.

Kerbey, J. O. *On the War Path: A Journey over the Historic Grounds of the Late Civil War.* Chicago: Donohue, Henneberry, 1890.

Krick, Robert E. L. *Staff Officers in Gray: A Biographical Register of the Staff Officers in the Army of Northern Virginia.* Chapel Hill: University of North Carolina Press, 2003.

Krick, Robert K. *30th Virginia Infantry.* Lynchburg, Va.: H. E. Howard, 1983.

Landon, William. "Letters to the Vincennes Western Sun." *Indiana Magazine of History,* September 1937, 334–48.

———. "'Prock's' Last Letters to the Vincennes Western Sun." *Indiana Magazine of History,* March 1939, 76–82.

Lang, Wendell W. "Rescued from Obscurity." *North South Trader's Civil War Magazine,* May–June 1995, 36–40.

Lossing, Benson J. *Pictorial History of the Civil War of the United States of America.* 2 vols. Hartford, Conn.: T. Belknap, 1868.

Marbaker, Thomas D. *History of the Eleventh New Jersey Volunteers from Its Organization to Appomattox to Which Is Added Experiences of Prison Life and Sketches of Individual Members.* Trenton, N.J.: MacCrellish and Quigley, 1898.

Mason, W. Roy. "Notes of a Confederate Staff-Officer." In *Battles and Leaders of the Civil War,* ed. Robert U. Johnson and Clarence C. Buel, 3:100–101. New York: Century, 1888.

*The Medal of Honor of the United States Army.* Washington, D.C.: Government Printing Office, 1948.

Mertz, Gregory A. "No Turning Back: The Battle of the Wilderness." *Blue and Gray Magazine,* April 1995, 8–23, 53–63.

Morhous, Henry C. *Reminiscences of the 123d Regiment, N.Y.S.V.* Greenwich, N.Y.: People's Journal Book and Job Office, 1879.

Muffly, J. W., ed. *The Story of Our Regiment: A History of the 148th Pennsylvania Vols.* Des Moines: Kenyon Printing, 1904.

Mulholland, St. Clair A. *Military Order: Congress Medal of Honor Legion of the United States.* Philadelphia: n.p., 1905.

———. *The Story of the 116th Regiment, Pennsylvania Volunteers in the War of the Rebellion.* Philadelphia: F. McManus Jr., 1903.

*Names of Officers and Soldiers Found on the Battle-fields of the Wilderness and of Spotsylvania Court House, Va.* Washington, D.C.: Government Printing Office, 1865.

*National Memorial Day Services, under the Auspices of Phil Kearny Post, No. 10, G.A.R. Department of Virginia and N.C. at Fredericksburg National Cemetery, Fredericksburg, Va.* Richmond: Patrick Keenan, 1893.

Norman, J. Gary. "Kenmore's Last Soldier." *Fredericksburg Times*, April 1992, 31–37.

*Official Roster of the Soldiers of the State of Ohio in the War of the Rebellion, 1861–1866*. 12 vols. Cincinnati: Ohio Valley Company, 1889.

O'Reilly, Francis A. *The Fredericksburg Campaign: Winter War on the Rappahannock*. Baton Rouge: Louisiana State University Press, 2003.

O'Sullivan, Daniel E. "Theodore O'Hara." *Southern Bivouac* 2, no. 8 (January 1887): 489–94. Reprinted in *Southern Bivouac*, 6:489–94. Wilmington, N.C.: Broadfoot, 1992–93.

Owen, William M. *In Camp and Battle with the Washington Artillery of New Orleans*. Boston: Ticknor, 1885.

Pepper, George W. *Personal Recollections of Sherman's Campaigns, in Georgia and the Carolinas*. Zanesville, Ohio: Hugh Dunne, 1866.

Pfanz, Donald C. "Reaping the Harvest of Death: The Burial of Union Soldiers at Marye's Heights in December 1862 and May 1864." *Fredericksburg History and Biography* 12 (2013): 8–30.

Phillis, William A. "The Death of Col. John Williams Patterson in the Wilderness." *Wilderness Dispatch* 8, no. 2 (Summer 2003): 1–2.

Phisterer, Frederick. *New York in the War of the Rebellion, 1861 to 1865*. Albany: J. B. Lyon, 1912.

———. *Statistical Record of the Armies of the United States*. New York: Charles Scribner's Sons, 1907.

Post, Marie Caroline, ed. *The Life and Memoirs of Comte Regis de Trobriand*. New York: E. P. Dutton, 1910. Translation of December 16, 1862, letter by Robert Roser.

Quint, Alonzo H. *The Record of the Second Massachusetts Infantry, 1861–65*. Boston: James P. Walker, 1867.

*Record of Service of Michigan Volunteers in the Civil War, 1861–1865*. Detroit: Detroit Book Press, n.d.

Reed, William H. *The Heroic Story of the United States Sanitary Commission, 1861–1865*. Boston: Geo. H. Ellis, 1910.

*Revised Report of the Select Committee Relative to the Soldiers' National Cemetery, Together with the Accompanying Documents, as Reported to the House of Representatives of the Commonwealth of Pennsylvania*. Harrisburg: Singerly and Myers, 1865.

Rhea, Gordon C. *The Battle of the Wilderness, May 5–6, 1864*. Baton Rouge: Louisiana University Press, 1994.

———. *The Battles for Spotsylvania Court House and the Road to Yellow Tavern, May 7–12, 1864*. Baton Rouge: Louisiana State University Press, 1997.

———. *To the North Anna River: Grant and Lee, May 13–25, 1864*. Baton Rouge: Louisiana University Press, 2000.

Robertson, Robert S. "Diary of the War, by Robt. S. Robertson." Edited by Charles N. and Rosemary Walker. In *Old Fort News* 28, no. 4 (October–December 1965).

*Roll of Honor (No. XXV). Names of Soldiers Who Died in Defense of the Union, Interred in the National Cemeteries at Fredericksburg, Virginia; Mobile, Alabama; and Fort Gibson, Indian Territory; and Names Not Heretofore Published of Union Soldiers Interred in the National Cemeteries at Hampton, Virginia; Barrancas, Florida; and Alexandria, Louisiana.* Washington, D.C.: Government Printing Office, 1870.

Silliker, Ruth L., ed. *The Rebel Yell and Yankee Hurrah: The Civil War Journal of a Maine Volunteer.* Camden, Maine: Down East Books, 1985.

The Society of the Army of the Potomac. *Report of the Thirty-First Annual Reunion at Fredericksburg, Va., May 25th and 26th, 1900.* New York: MacGowan and Slipper, 1900.

Sorrel, Gilbert Moxley. *Recollections of a Confederate Staff Officer.* New York: Neale, 1917.

*Statement of the Disposition of Some of the Bodies of Deceased Union Soldiers and Prisoners of War Whose Remains Have Been Removed to National Cemeteries in the Southern and Western States.* Vol. 4. Washington, D.C.: Government Printing Office, 1869.

Steere, Edward. "Early Growth of the National Cemetery System." *Quartermaster Review,* March–April 1953, 20–22, 121–26.

———. "Evolution of the National Cemetery System, 1865–1880." *Quartermaster Review,* May–June 1953, 22–24, 120–26.

———. "Expansion of the National Cemetery System, 1880–1900." *Quartermaster Review,* September–October 1953, 20–21, 131–37.

———. "Genesis of American Graves Registration, 1861–1870." *Military Affairs* 12, no. 3 (Fall 1948): 149–61.

Taylor, W. B., ed. *Memorial Addresses on the Life and Character of John Alexander Logan, (A Senator from Illinois), Delivered in the Senate and House of Representatives, February 9 and 19, 1887, with the Funeral Services at Washington, D.C., Friday, December 31, 1886.* Washington: Government Printing Office, 1887.

Teall, William. "Ringside Seat at Fredericksburg." *Civil War Times Illustrated* 4, no. 2 (May 1965): 17–34.

"Theodore O'Hara." *Confederate Veteran* 7, no. 5 (May 1899): 202.

Thompson, S. Millett. *Thirteenth Regiment of New Hampshire Volunteer Infantry in the War of the Rebellion, 1861–1865.* Boston: Houghton, Mifflin, 1888.

Tobie, Edward P. *History of the First Maine Cavalry.* Boston: Press of Emery and Hughes, 1887.

Trowbridge, John T. *The Desolate South, 1865–1868: A Picture of the Battlefields and of the Devastated Confederacy.* Edited by Gordon Carroll. New York: Duell, Sloan and Pearce, 1956.

———. *The South: A Tour of Its Battle-fields and Ruined Cities, a Journey through the Desolated States, and Talks with the People* . . . Hartford, Conn.: L. Stebbins, 1866.

United States Christian Commission. *Record of the Federal Dead Buried from Libby, Belle Isle, Danville & Camp Lawton Prisons, and at City Point, and in the Field before Petersburg and Richmond.* Philadelphia: Jas. B. Rogers, 1865.

Vance, J. W. *Report of the Adjutant General of the State of Illinois.* 8 vols. Springfield: H. W. Rokker, 1886.

Weygant, Charles H. *History of the One Hundred and Twenty-Fourth Regiment, N.Y.S.V.* Newburgh, N.Y.: Journal Printing House, 1877.

Whitman, Walt. "May 19, 1863, letter to Nat and Fred Gray." *American Heritage* 8, no. 6 (October 1957): 63.

## Other Sources

"About VA." U.S. Department of Veterans Affairs website: https://www.va.gov /about_va/vahistory.asp.

Engle, Charles. June 3, 1863, letter found on the Civil War Letters of Charles Engle website: http://www.sugarfoottales.org/1 -630603/.

Fredericksburg City Directory for 1921. At the University of Mary Washington website: http://departments.umw.edu/hipr/www/fredericksburg/1921directory .htm.

Fredericksburg City Directory for 1938. At the University of Mary Washington website: http://departments.umw.edu/hipr/www/fredericksburg/1938directory .htm.

General Orders No. 11. From the U.S. Memorial Day website: http://www. usmemorialday.org/order11.html.

Gray, O. W., & Son 1878 map. On University of Mary Washington College website: http://departments.umw.edu/hipr/www/Fredericksburg/plats /graysmap1878.jpg.

"History and Development of the National Cemetery Administration." Information provided by the National Cemetery Administration, Department of Veterans Affairs, http://www.cem.va.gov/ncahistfact.htm. Updated in January 2004.

"History of Military Dog Tags." An article on the Armed Forces History Museum website: http://armedforcesmuseum.com/history-of-military-dog -tags/.

"Lab Uses DNA Library to ID Troops." Article on the Military.com website: http://www.military.com/NewContent/0,13190,FL_dna_041503,00.html.

*Landscapes of Honor and Sacrifice: The History of the National Cemeteries,* a video-tape produced by the Department of Veterans Affairs, National Cemetery Administration, Communications Management Service, History Program, in September 2003.

Leach, Sara A. "Theodore O'Hara's 'Bivouac of the Dead.'" Unpublished article on the National Cemetery Administration found at http://www.cem.va.gov /bivouac.htm.

Miller, August. Letters, 1869–72. Petersburg National Battlefield, Va.

Mink, Eric J. "Indians at Brompton." From the Mysteries and Conundrums website: http://npsfrsp.wordpress.com/2012/06/14/indians-at-brompton/.

*National Cemetery Operations Guideline*, NPS-61, Release No. 1, November 1985.

Olsen, Herbert. "Poplar Grove National Cemetery History." Unpublished report completed in 1954. Copy available on Petersburg National Battlefield at the following website: http://www.cr.nps.gov/history/online_books/pete /PoplarGrove.pdf.

"World War I Era Yeomen (F)—Overview and Special Image Selection." Article on Department of the Navy website: http://www.history.navy.mil/photos /prs-tpic/females/yeomen-f.htm.

# Index

*Italicized page numbers indicate illustrations.*

Ricketts, Maj. Gen. James B., 39
Riley, Pvt. James, 23–24, 26–27, 31–32
Ritter, Pvt. Morris, 151
Roberts, Lt. Warrenton G., 62–63, *63*, 209n24
Robinson, Clara, 119, 138, 224n63
Robinson, Cpl. Reuben, 71
Robinson, Thomas B., 82–85, 104, 108–9, 127; conflicts with superior, 117–19; death, 119; Memorial Day exercises, 175–76; military service, 221n21; National Boulevard, 112
Rock Island Arsenal, 93–94
Roe, Chaplain Alfred C., 130
Rolfe, Maj. Frank A., 131
*Roll of Honor*, 71, 120, 125, 132–33, 135
Root, Elihu, 95
Rostrum, 99, 102, 113, 172
Rowe, George, 11
Rucker, Bvt. Maj. Gen. Daniel H., 37
Ryan, Col. George, 151, 155
Ryan, Lt. Henry, 94
Ryerson, Col. Henry O., 125

Sacrey, Emmet H., 109, 220n8
Salem Church, battle of, 149, 204n38
Salem Church Battlefield, 224n1
Sanford, Joseph, 30
Sanford farm, 122, 157, 199n33
Schofield, John, 49
Sedgwick, Maj. Gen. John, 14, 152–53
sewage, 73, 84
Sherman, Maj. Gen. William T., 30
shields, 59
Shiloh Baptist Church (New Site), 133, 135
Sickles, Maj. Gen. Daniel, 95
Sieger, Sgt. Joseph M., 155–56
signs, 91–94; Act to Establish and to Protect National Cemeteries (1867), 91, 93; General Orders No. 80, 91, 93; poetry, 91–93; welcome, 93–94
Society of the Army of the Potomac, 95, 131

Soldiers' monument, 39, *53*, 94–95
Special Orders No. 75 (September 11, 1861), 1
Special populations: African Americans, 132–33, *134*, 134–35; children, 138–39; Confederate soldiers, 139; field-grand officers, 129–31; foreign soldiers, 140, *141*, 142; Medal of Honor recipients, 131–132, *132*; Native Americans, 135; Women, 136, *137*, 138
Spotsylvania Court House, battle of, 5, 9, 16–17, 21, 131, 143, 147; deaths at, 125, 131–32, 139, 143, 148–49, 151–52, 157, 159, 162. *See also* individual actions
Spotsylvania Court House Battlefield, xviii, 36, 122, 125; estimated burials, 38; interments, 224n1; June 1865 burial expedition, 28–31, 33; proposed cemetery, 37–38; unburied dead, *xviii*, 32, 33, 197n37; wartime burials, 17–19. *See also* Alsop farm; Bloody Angle; Harris farm
Spotsylvania Court House Road, 50, 59, 61, 112. *See also* Sunken Road
Sprow, Pvt. Charles H., 133
Stafford County, 32, 154–56; Cunningham house, 144; desolation, 22–23; estimated burials, 38; wartime burials, 11–14; winter encampment, 11–14, 154
Stanton, Edwin M., 2, 36–37, 39, 64–65, 94; selects Willis Hill as site for cemetery, 47–48
Stephens, Edward, 11
Stetson, Wallace, 88–89
Stevens, Sgt. David W., 152, *153*
Stevens, Lt. Frank D., 152–53
Stevens, Chaplain William, 152–53
Stratton house, 9, 38
"Stripes and the Stars, The" (Meitike), 91–92
structures, 56, 72–77, 211n6; plats *53*, *78*. *See also individual structures*
Sumner, Maj. Gen. Edwin V., Sr., 7

Donald C. Pfanz was born in Gettysburg, Pennsylvania, and is a graduate of the College of William and Mary. In his thirty-two-year career with the National Park Service, he worked at three parks: Fredericksburg and Spotsylvania County National Military Park, Petersburg National Battlefield, and Fort Sumter National Monument. He is a founding member of the Association for the Preservation of Civil War Sites (now the Civil War Trust) and has written five books about the Civil War, including *Richard S. Ewell: A Soldier's Life* and *War So Terrible: A Popular History of the Battle of Fredericksburg.*

# ENGAGING
### —the—
# CIVIL WAR

Engaging the Civil War, a series founded by the historians at the blog Emerging Civil War (www.emergingcivilwar.com), adopts the sensibility and accessibility of public history while adhering to the standards of academic scholarship. To engage readers and bring them to a new understanding of America's great story, series authors draw on insights they gained while working with the public—walking the ground where history happened at battlefields and historic sites, talking with visitors in museums, and educating students in classrooms. With fresh perspectives, field-tested ideas, and in-depth research, volumes in the series connect readers with the story of the Civil War in ways that make history meaningful to them while underscoring the continued relevance of the war, its causes, and its effects. All Americans can claim the Civil War as part of their history. This series helps them engage with it.

*Chris Mackowski and Brian Matthew Jordan, Series Editors*

Queries and submissions
emergingcivilwar@gmail.com